T0305884

FINANCE IN
DEVELOPING COUNTRIES

Finance
in
Developing
Countries

Edited by
P. C. I. AYRE

Routledge
Taylor & Francis Group

LONDON AND NEW YORK

Contents

Introduction

by P. C. I. Ayre*

This issue of the Journal is devoted to papers dealing with various features of the financial process in developing countries. Although the field of finance has tended to be a neglected branch of development studies, there has recently been an upsurge of interest in this area stimulated, in large part, by the publication in 1973 of the influential books by McKinnon and Shaw. This interest is reflected in the increased number of papers concerned with finance which have been received by the Journal since 1973. Some of these papers, as well as some specially solicited, are presented here to provide an indication of the wide range of work currently in progress.

While the majority of papers included deal with various aspects of the domestic financial system, a paper is included which lies in the field of international finance and there are two papers within the field of public finance as conventionally defined. It will be seen, therefore, that the concept of finance has been broadly interpreted. The justification for this lies in the fact that it is often very misleading to treat money, taxation and international finance in separate compartments for, as both McKinnon and Shaw stress, the workings of domestic banking and financial systems, tax policy and international financial aspects of development are very closely interrelated, with policy choices in one area having implications for feasible choices in other areas.

This interrelation is perhaps nowhere more clearly demonstrated than in the analysis of the effects of inflation. It has long been realised that inflation acts as a particular kind of tax, with money balances serving as the tax base. At the margin, therefore, monetary expansion can be considered a substitute for other forms of taxation and there is no *a priori* reason for believing that it is necessarily more inefficient or distributionally objectionable to tax money balances than to tax commodities, land or labour.

Newlyn, in the first paper, subjects the concept of the inflation tax to a searching analysis, one result of this analysis being to call into question the widespread practice in earlier studies [e.g. *Mundell, 1965*] of deriving quantitative predictions of the effects of moderate rates of inflation from equations derived from hyper-inflation conditions, usually using Cagan's [*1956*] model. Newlyn goes on to show on the basis of an empirical analysis of a large sample of less-developed countries that the use of inflation as a source of revenue is feasible in many cases. Nevertheless,

* Lecturer in Economics, School of Oriental and African Studies, University of London. I am grateful to Michael Lipton for helpful comments. Remaining errors are mine.

he ends by cautioning against the general adoption of inflationary policies because of the adverse side effects on resource allocation which follow in a situation where some prices, notably interest rates and foreign exchange rates, are pegged. It is still possible, however, that at moderate rates of inflation the resource mobilisation effect could exceed the efficiency effect, giving a net benefit from inflation. A full assessment would require one to compare the costs involved with the costs associated with distortions introduced by other taxes which would be needed to replace the revenue lost from the inflation tax.[1]

Newlyn's paper is followed by two case studies dealing with the relationship between monetary expansion, inflation and the balance of payments in Sri Lanka and Indonesia. The impact of a given rate of expansion of central bank assets depends critically on the precise nature of the demand function for money and on the extent to which real supply can be augmented by increasing imports. De Silva shows that up till the mid-1960s this latter factor meant that there was little inflation in Sri Lanka despite fairly rapid rates of monetary expansion, whereas from about 1966 the rate of inflation is much more closely related to the rate of expansion of the money supply.

The willingness of, indeed necessity for, people to accumulate real balances as income rises, which forms a crucial element in the analysis of the impact of inflation, is an important source of real savings in an economy. Aghevli, in an econometric analysis of the monetary process in Indonesia between 1968 and 1973, shows how significant the growth in demand for real balances has been for Indonesia and how knowledge of the relationships involved is crucial to satisfactory integration of financial, fiscal and balance of payments planning.

It may be noted that the demand for money equations fitted by de Silva and Aghevli imply quantitatively very different behaviour, with the income elasticity of demand for real balances being much greater in the Indonesian case. As Aghevli points out, the Indonesian case is rather special and the specific quantitative results could not be applied to other countries, or even to Indonesia in later periods, since the rapid rate of growth in demand for real balances was almost certainly associated on the one hand with the restoration of confidence following the stabilisation measures of the late 1960s which succeeded in reducing the inflation rate from around 600 per cent in 1965–66 to single figures by the early 1970s and, on the other hand, with a growth in monetisation of the economy, itself at least in part a response to the ending of the inflationary excesses of the last years of the Sukarno era.[2]

Especially in the short term, there is great variety between countries in the relationship between increases in real income and increases in the demand for real balances, in the extent to which it is possible for Governments to permit an import surplus to absorb some of the consequences of monetary expansion and in the way in which the demand for money responds to changes in the inflation rate (a point brought out in Newlyn's discussion of the inflation tax). There is, therefore, no substitute for a detailed analysis of each country's circumstances as a basis for financial planning (one crucial aspect of which is to try to ensure that the target rate of inflation is achieved) although cross section studies such as Adekunle's [*1968*] can be helpful in suggesting broad empirical regularities. Aghevli's study illustrates how the tools of econometric analysis can contribute to the development of a framework for financial planning which uses money demand and supply analysis as its basis.

The fourth paper, by Vicente Galbis, addresses itself to the implications of interest rate controls on financial institutions for the efficiency with which investment resources are allocated. This is one of the main themes discussed by McKinnon and Shaw and their arguments are reviewed and extended by Galbis in the context of a two sector model. Galbis agrees with Shaw and McKinnon that the structure of the financial sector of an economy does have an important impact on the pace and pattern of economic development and argues that financial reforms can make a significant contribution to development. This view, while not unchallenged,[3] is being echoed in policy-oriented documents such as the recently published International Labour Office report on the Philippines, which devotes a good deal of space to recommending changes in financial policy to assist in the achievement of more rapid and equitable growth [*I.L.O., 1974, Chapter 7*].

Significant distortions of real rates of return between sectors and between financial assets of various types are frequently, at least in part, a consequence of inflation and must be counted as perhaps the major cost to be set against any benefits which result from the mobilisation of investment resources and the expansion of favoured sectors through inflation. This is because inflation typically occurs in an institutional environment in which nominal rates of interest paid on deposits and charged on loans are pegged with the consequence that real rates of interest are depressed, leading to a state which can be called financial repression [*McKinnon, 1973, Ch. 7; Shaw, 1973, Ch. 4*], one important feature of which may be a reduction of investment in indivisible capital assets which is a consequence of the deterrent effect of inflation on the willingness and ability of individuals to accumulate real balances over time—a process which is a prerequisite to purchasing these assets by firms which find loans difficult to obtain [*McKinnon, 1973: 57–61*]. At the same time, the limited flow of real savings through financial intermediaries associated with a repressed financial system can be argued to encourage resort to inflationary policies by the authorities as a means of obtaining command over investible resources either for themselves or for favoured elements in the private sector.[4] The cumulative resort to inflationary finance is strengthened to the extent that inflation reduces the real revenue from other taxes (as occurred in the case of the land tax in nineteenth-century Japan, discussed by Bird in a paper in this volume).

Galbis' paper is followed by three papers which deal with institutional features of the capital market. Drake examines the extent to which promotion of a securities market can be expected to be beneficial to the development process. He argues persuasively that the resource costs of securities markets are relatively low and that constraints on their development, notably the shortage of local sources of funds for equity investment, have been exaggerated by other writers. The large capital *outflows* which have taken place from many developing countries despite exchange controls is indicative of the existence of potentially investible funds. Provision of a variety of local securities may be a potent way of reversing this outflow and reducing the dependence of developing countries on borrowing from abroad. It should be emphasised that the supply of local securities by private firms is crucially affected by the terms of access of firms to bank credit. Increases in loan interest rates could be expected to encourage the issue of securities. This is another illustration of the interdependence of financial market policies.

Khatkhate's paper is a case study of the way in which policies aimed at the promotion of Government bond sales may turn out to hamper the growth of a genuine market in bonds. Khatkhate is concerned with the implications of this for the evolution of open market operations as a tool of monetary policy, but his paper clearly has implications for policies aimed at the general development of capital markets. Government paper can provide a nucleus around which capital market skills can develop (as occurred, for example, in eighteenth- and nineteenth-century Britain), but only to the extent that the paper is genuinely tradable.

The third contribution in this group, by Subrata Ghatak, develops and extends some of his earlier work on the Indian rural money market. Around the theme of attempting to explain inter-state variations in rural interest rates, Ghatak is able to highlight some of the structural character-istics of the demand and supply sides of the rural money market and is able to draw some tentative conclusions about how this structure changed over a decade under the impact of differential growth rates of the co-operative movement and of real income in the Indian states.

As the author would be the first to admit, the findings are inevitably tentative and suffer from the inadequacies of data which plague studies of the unorganised financial sector. There is a great need for the collection of detailed data at village and district level to provide a basis for further analysis of this crucial part of the financial system. Nevertheless, Ghatak shows that quite a lot can be achieved by an imaginative use of data which are already available.

The paper by Crockett and Nsouli examines the criteria which should govern the choice of exchange regime by a developing country. While they give attention to the classic choice between fixed and flexible exchange rates they also bring out the fact that the meaning of a fixed rate is complex today in view of the movement of exchange rates between the major world currencies. This gives rise to the very important problem of what currency or currencies a particular country should use as a basis for pegging its exchange rate.

The choice is seen to lie broadly between pegging to a single currency such as the US dollar, to a basket of currencies or to the S.D.R. The former choice may only be suitable for developing countries which have very close economic ties with the country to whose currency they are pegged. This follows from the fact that, if the currency concerned fluctuates against other major currencies, the developing country will experience changes in its effective exchange rate with the rest of the world which may have little economic rationale. As part of their analysis of these matters, the authors present some valuable empirical data on the magnitude of exchange rate fluctuations implied for various developing countries according to the alternative feasible pegs which could be adopted.

In their analysis of the implications of opting for a fully flexible exchange rate system, Crockett and Nsouli make the point that if such a system is to give reasonable stability of the exchange rate in the short run there needs to be a well developed exchange market dealing in both spot and forward positions. Many less developed countries clearly do not yet have the necessary institutional framework and a dilemma presents itself that if the Government smooths out exchange rate fluctuations the incentives for the long term development of private exchange market institutions are blunted.[5]

A further point is that the adoption of a fully flexible rate means that the Government cannot use the exchange rate as a tool of resource allocation and distribution policy. This is an important consideration for many developing countries as is the fact that uncontrolled dealing in spot and forward exchange runs counter to the prevailing ethos of suspicion concerning the efficacy of free market forces.[6] In these circumstances, freely fluctuating exchange rates may not be optimal for developing countries.

The argument against flexible rates is strengthened in the case of small, open economies where considerations associated with the concept of optimum currency areas become especially important.[7] Wide fluctuations in the exchange rate greatly reduce the liquidity of domestic money in such economies since a high proportion of expenditure is on tradable goods. Indeed, in such circumstances, Gresham's Law properly interpreted[8] implies that foreign money will tend to replace domestic money as the dominant medium of exchange therefore depriving the Government of the revenue advantages of money issue[9] in a situation where the demand for real balances is growing.

The final two papers in this collection address themselves to problems in the field of public finance. Rosenberg analyses the incidence of payroll taxes in the Philippines and shows that in situations where there are large wage differentials between the sectors effectively covered by the taxes and the rest of the economy the implications of these taxes are somewhat different to those which might be expected. Since the incidence is argued to fall on the relatively highly paid workers the tax is progressive. Backward shifting also implies that the efficiency effects on the choice of factor proportions may not be as serious as often believed.

It may be mentioned in passing that there is frequently an important institutional link between payroll taxes and financial intermediation since, as in the case of the Philippines, payroll taxation is linked to insurance schemes which are administered by special financial institutions which frequently play an important role in the workings of the capital market, not only buying Government paper but also lending to the private sector.[10]

In the final paper Richard Bird surveys the evidence relating to the role of the land tax in the Japanese fiscal system of the late nineteenth century, and reaches the conclusion that the reforms in the land tax were much less important for the raising of revenue than has often been thought. Another important point to emerge from his discussion is the way in which land tax revenue in real terms was affected by inflation and deflation, bringing out again the close interdependence between monetary management policies and the impact of fiscal arrangements. It would certainly not have been sensible in Japanese circumstances to have treated the land tax and the inflation tax as additive.

NOTES

1. Elimination of inflation is argued by McKinnon [*1973*] and Shaw [*1973*] to result in a rise in voluntary savings so that loss of inflation tax revenue might not require replacement by other taxes. However, as Taylor [*1974: 83*] points out, there is no guarantee that the increase in voluntary savings will be equal to or greater than the loss of inflation tax revenue. Another important dimension of inflation and other alternative taxes which would require investigation is the distributional impact. Even in the case of fully anticipated inflation one could not expect a neutral impact between groups since access to alternative assets and the extent to which cash balances can be economised will vary between income groups and industries.

2. Sundrum [*1973: 81*] argues that from 1970 increasing monetisation of the economy was more important in increasing the demand for real balances than the pure price expectations effect.

3. See, for example, Taylor [*1974*], Reubens [*1974*].

4. The precise distribution of the gains from financial repression depends on such factors as the way in which the central bank expands high powered money and the reserve ratio of the commercial banks together with their lending practices—which may well, of course, be affected by regulations appertaining, for example, to the eligibility of various types of paper for rediscounting at the central bank.

5. It might be argued that foreign-owned banks could provide these facilities. However, the limited number of these banks in most less developed countries raises the possibility of monopolistic/oligopolistic manipulation of rates.

6. Sohmen [*1971*] has stressed the importance of removing all controls from the operation of spot and forward markets if speculation is to be stabilising under flexible rates. It should also be emphasised that where the Central Bank intervenes to stabilise exchange rates private dealings may well result in gains which are transferred abroad if the spot rate is overvalued.

7. See Tower and Willett [*1976*] for an up-to-date review of the issues.

8. Gresham's Law properly interpreted implies that stable monies drive out variable monies with otherwise similar characteristics [*Melitz, 1974: 146 and 159; and Brunner and Meltzer, 1971: 803*].

9. Harberger [*1972*] and Maynard [*1970*] have argued that in the case of small, open economies there is little case for an independent currency.

10. This point is noted by Drake (p. 82 below).

REFERENCES

Adekunle, J. O., 1968, 'The Demand for Money: Evidence from Developed and Less Developed Countries', *I.M.F.: Staff Papers*, November.

Brunner, K. and A. Meltzer, 1971, 'The Uses of Money: Money in the Theory of an Exchange Economy', *American Economic Review*, December.

Cagan, P., 1956, 'The Monetary Dynamics of Hyper-Inflation', in M. Friedman, ed., *Studies in the Quantity Theory of Money*, Chicago.

Harberger, Arnold C., 1972, 'Reflections on the Monetary System of Panama', in D. Wall, ed., *Chicago Essays in Economic Development*, Chicago: University of Chicago Press.

International Labour Office, 1974, *Sharing in Development*, Geneva: International Labour Office.

McKinnon, R. I., 1973, *Money and Capital in Economic Development*, Washington D.C.: The Brookings Institution.

Maynard, J., 1970, 'The Economic Irrelevance of Monetary Independence: the Case of Liberia', *Journal of Development Studies*, January.

Melitz, J., 1974, *Primitive and Modern Money*, Reading, Mass.: Addison-Wesley Publishing Co.

Mundell, R. A., 1965, 'Growth, Stability and Inflationary Finance', *Journal of Political Economy*, April.

Reubens, Edwin R., 1974, Review of McKinnon (1973), *Journal of Economic Literature*, June, pp. 500–1.

Shaw, E. S., *Financial Deepening in Economic Development*, New York: Oxford University Press.

Sohmen, E., 1971, 'Currency Areas and Monetary Systems', in Bhagwati, J., *et al.*, *Trade, Balance of Payments and Growth*, Amsterdam.

Sundrum, R. M., 1973, 'Money Supply and Prices: A Re-interpretation', *Bulletin of Indonesian Economic Studies*, November.

Taylor, L., 1974, Review of McKinnon (1973) and Shaw (1973), *Journal of Development Economics*, June, pp. 81–84.

Tower, E., and Thomas D. Willett, 1976, *The Theory of Optimum Currency Areas and Exchange-Rate Flexibility*, Princeton: Special Papers in International Economics, No. 11, May,

The Inflation Tax in Developing Countries[1]

by W. T. Newlyn*

The concept of the inflation tax is best described initially by the following quotation from Harry Johnson:

> In order to maintain its real balances constant in the face of inflation, the public must accumulate money balances at a rate equal to the inflation; this accumulation of money balances in order to preserve real balances is achieved at the cost of sacrificing the consumption of current real income in order to maintain real balances intact, the release of current real income constituting the equivalent of a 'tax' on the holders of real balances; the tax on real balances, in turn, accrues as revenue to the beneficiaries of the inflationary increase in the money supply. [*Johnson, 1967, Ch. III.*]

A qualification must be made as to how the 'tax revenue accrues to the beneficiaries'. The use of the term 'tax' does not imply that the beneficiary is necessarily the government; it may be a private institution which is enabled to appropriate the real resources given up by money holders. In this respect there is a strong similarity between the forced saving resulting from inflation and what the present writer has called the 'involuntary saving' resulting from the need to accumulate transactions balances associated with real growth [*Newlyn 1962: 162*]. The distinction is that in the latter case real balances increase whereas in the case of the inflation tax nominal balances have to be accumulated in order to maintain a given level of real balances. But in both cases the revenue accrues as a result of borrowing from the financial intermediary which issues the money (thereby obtaining a share of the benefit in the form of interest) and in this respect differs from ordinary tax revenue.

In the case of government borrowing from the central bank the term 'monetary authorities' removes the interface and the interest payment is nominal; in the case of government and private borrowing from private banks the tax concept can be retained by regarding the interest payment as a cost of tax collection since the *incidence* is on the money holders in all cases. Moreover it is the total incremental finance resulting from inflation which is relevant to increases in potential investment resulting from forced saving and the estimates in this study are therefore based on total domestic monetary credit expansion (DCE) assuming that external payments are kept in balance so that DCE is identical with the change in the money stock. This assumption, though implicit, has not been stated in other studies. Money stock (M2) includes time and savings deposits excluded from M1.

---

* Professor of Economics, University of Leeds.

All the studies of the inflation tax have, in fact, been concerned with it as an instrument to raise government revenue and have confined their estimates of its effects to government borrowing from the central bank. Hence a necessary parameter has been the ratio of the government deficit so financed to the total inflationary increase in the money supply for which the currency/money ratio (C/M) has been used as a proxy.

This exclusion of governments from borrowing any of the commercial banks' additional credit resulting from the expansion of the reserve base was not unreasonable as an assumption twenty years ago but it is no longer tenable. It is still true that the governments of many developing countries have made surprisingly little use of commercial bank credit but they will certainly wish to see a substantial proportion of commercial banks' assets in the form of government securities if this is not already the case. For this reason the appropriate measure is the marginal share of government in total domestic credit expansion. The extent to which governments had borrowed from the commercial banks up to 1976 is indicated by the ratio of government securities to their total deposit liabilities of which the median value for sixty-eight developing countries was 0·22, the quartile range being 0·11 to 0·31.[2] If it is assumed that the maximum would be 0·5 in predominantly capitalist economies it is clear that there is considerable scope for expansion. Moreover, so long as this is the case, there is no limit to the marginal share; the observed ratio only acts as a constraint on the marginal share if it has reached its maximum. Indeed, the Uganda Government actually acquired 0·98 of the total annual increment in monetary credit in 1972 but this was in a political climate which hardly favoured expansion in the private sector. Nevertheless it shows that a government bent on increasing its expenditure would not find it technically difficult, through controls by its central bank, to appropriate the whole of the increase of monetary credit over a short period; but unless it paid high rates of interest it could not persist in this policy for long if the banks were to remain in the private sector.

Thus the magnitude of the government's share in total domestic monetary credit expansion will be determined by the marginal C/M2 ratio and the share in commercial bank credit expansion. Assuming the latter to be 0·5, and using the median value of C/M2 of the same set of sixty-eight countries (0·46) as a proxy for the marginal ratio, the government share in total domestic monetary expansion would be 0·66.

The empirical literature of the effects of the inflation tax is dominated by a succession of articles in the *Journal of Political Economy* starting with that by Martin J. Bailey [*Bailey, 1956*] whose object was to estimate the welfare costs associated with the government's share of national income pre-empted by the inflation tax. It is assumed that the government announces its intention to induce a constant rate of inflation. The impact effect is assumed to raise all prices immediately to the point at which the reduction in the real value of existing balances is checked by the rise in the nominal rate of interest as determined by the elasticity of the demand curve. Thereafter the annual increase in prices is offset by the annual increase in nominal balances, thus perpetuating the initial loss as an annual tax equal to the rate of inflation. The welfare cost is identified as the reduction in the area below the demand curve which measures the 'excess costs' of the inflation tax.

The range of results is very large, as is illustrated by comparing the figures for two extreme examples: Austria and Hungary. The excess burden, as a percentage of the budget deficit associated with pre-emption of 2 per cent of national income, is 20 per cent for Austria and only 3 per cent for Hungary. But this is due entirely to the difference in the observed values of the currency/money ratio (c) which are 0·3 for Austria and 0·9 for Hungary. If a value of unity is given to c for both countries the cost for Austria falls from 20 per cent to 3 per cent while that for Hungary is only fractionally reduced below 3 per cent. On the other hand, assuming a value of unity for all seven examples still leaves a very wide range of costs from below 1 per cent to 8 per cent, at the 2 per cent level of pre-emption.

The empirical basis for these estimates of welfare loss is the study of P. Cagan [Cagan, 1956] of hyper-inflation in seven European countries in the inter-war years. Bailey's description of the costs show that they relate to conditions in which the flight from money has already rendered it incapable of continuing for long to function as a means of payment let alone as an asset. Bailey's study is important however in establishing Cagan's work as the basis for successive empirical estimates of the yield of the inflation tax. Before proceeding to the empirical analysis Bailey concedes a key point in the following passage:

> Although no very precise conclusions can be drawn from the available evidence about real cash balances that people would desire to hold at fully anticipated but relatively *low* rates of inflation, a great deal of precise and useful information about desired cash balances at very high rates of inflation is given in Cagan's study of seven European hyper-inflations.
>
> (Emphasis added by the writer)

Bailey observes that 'his results very convincingly suggest the hypothesis that this form of demand equation for real cash balances is generally representative of the form of such demand equations for most or all economically interesting countries'. He then proceeds to project Cagan's relationship down to a zero rate of inflation to obtain his estimates and this methodology and its results have become part of the 'received wisdom' of the subject.

Bailey's object was to examine the welfare cost of inflation in relation to the cost of collection of other forms of taxation and, for this purpose, the benefits from government expenditure were not relevant. In order to relate costs to benefits we must examine the effectiveness of the inflation tax in accelerating the rate of growth of real income. For this purpose we turn to the work of Robert Mundell [Mundell, 1965], the results of which are in terms of the relationship between the rate of inflation and the rate of growth resulting from the increase in government investment financed by inflationary deficit finance.

Mundell's manipulation of the relevant relationships gives the following expression relating the rate of inflation to the rate of growth which it finances, assuming that government uses its share of the proceeds to finance capital formation

$$\pi = \frac{V_0 - r\Phi}{r\Phi - \eta\lambda}\lambda$$

where π is the rate of inflation; V_0 is velocity at zero inflation; r is the government's share of credit expansion (equal to C/M in our terms); Φ is the inverse of capital output ratio; η is the coefficient relating V to the rate of inflation; λ is the real rate of growth.

The most significant variable in this expression is η. If it is zero there is no limit to the rate of inflation which will increase growth. Mundell illustrates this special case with values of $V_0 = 3$ and $\Phi = 0\cdot5$ and $r = 0\cdot3$. In this case the inflation rate would be nineteen times the credit-induced growth rate. Mundell dismisses this result because inflation must change the value of v. When η is given a positive value, this puts an upper limit to the rate of growth which can be financed by inflation. For the same values of the other variables as above, Mundell assumes that velocity doubles as the rate of inflation increases from zero to 30 per cent per annum making η equal to ten, gives a maximum rate of growth of 1·5 per cent, but this is associated with *infinite inflation*. The substitution of a velocity function derived from Cagan's hyper-inflation study gives a maximum rate of growth of only 0·008 per cent, but this is based on the same dubious assumption as that made by Bailey that the Cagan relationships can be projected to zero inflation.

Clearly these estimates are highly sensitive to the behaviour of velocity during inflation but it seems quite extraordinary that the validity of projecting the experience of hyper-inflation (which Cagan defines as exceeding 50 per cent per month) into the universe of discourse of the use of inflationary finance as a policy instrument should have remained untested so long. A more recent article by Robert J. Barro [*Barro, 1972*] makes further elaborations on the same theme and concludes that the revenue maximising rate of inflation is 140 per cent *per month* giving revenue equal to 15 per cent of national income! Abstractions of this kind have no relation whatever to the order of magnitude that the most foolhardy government would entertain as an instrument of policy. Moreover, the basis for believing that the same relationship between expected price change and the demand for real money balances observed in hyper-inflation is applicable at low rates of inflation appears to be based solely on an inference by Bailey in respect of Cagan's demand function extrapolated to zero rate of inflation. He states that 'since the intercept of the demand curve on the cash balances axis is at a smaller value than the observed cash balances in a non-inflationary year, it may be inferred that the actual demand for real cash balances at low rates of inflation must be much more elastic than is implied by extrapolating the demand curve observed at high rates of inflation' [*Bailey, 1956: 98*]. Milton Friedman, in commenting on the empirical values of the elasticity of demand for real balances states that 'Bailey has shown [*sic*] that the slope is almost surely much higher at low rates of inflation than at rates that prevailed during hyper-inflation' [*Friedman, 1971*].

This inference is not consistent with common experience or with *a priori* reasoning about the process of inflation. Moreover it is clear from the

evidence which has been provided by A. J. Brown [*Brown, 1955*] and
others that there is a significant region of insensitivity to inflation.
Consistent with this evidence is the hypothesis which follows from the
distinction between the asset demand and the transactions demand for
money. This hypothesis is that there is a sensitivity threshold below which
very low rates of inflation will be 'tolerated' without significant effect
on velocity, but that some higher rate, if sustained, will cause a reduction
in demand for money by the more sophisticated holders who have access
to close substitutes for money as an asset. But since money balances of
these holders are never very great because of the availability of alternatives,
this effect will be small. At higher rates of inflation this asset substitution
effect will spread more widely through the economy until checked at the
point at which money balances have been reduced to the minimum required
for transactions within *the existing institutional payments complex.* At
much higher rates of inflation the elasticity of expectation of increases in
prices will become greater than one and the institutional factors determining the time-lag in the circular flow of income will be significantly modified
causing an acceleration in the increase in velocity up to the point at which
the physical limit to the rate of transfer of money is approached. Alternatively, the effect of a steady sustained inflation on velocity may taper off
to zero before this hyper-inflation stage is reached if expectations and all
contracts are fully adjusted to the steady rate of price increase.

Figure 1 shows these hypothetical relationships between the velocity of
circulation of money and the rate of increase of prices, V_0 being velocity
at zero inflation and T being the postulated threshold of sensitivity. The
expected shape of the function reflecting our hypothesis is shown together
with two linear functions one of which (AA) represents Cagan's demand
relationship expressed in terms of the velocity effect and BB represents a
linear function which might reflect the relationships between modest rates
of inflation and velocity. This shows that Bailey may well be right in his
inference that the relationship observed by Cagan implies a steeper slope
at lower rates of inflation than those observed at hyper-inflation but the
projection of this relationship to zero inflation (the broken line in the
diagram) is clearly not valid. It seemed appropriate therefore to test the
effect of inflation at more modest rates in respect of developing countries
in which the combination of small tax bases (particularly for direct taxation) and ambitious development plans, might justify the use of the inflation
tax. Rich countries have no such excuse for the inflation which, subsequent
to the period of this study, they have been exporting to the third world.

As a preliminary test of this hypothesis, pooled data for ten to fifteen
years for the forty developing countries for which consistent price series
were available was used in a series of regressions of absolute velocity and
the rate of change of velocity on the rate of change of prices, using M1
and M2 in each case, with and without time lags but the correlation and
regression coefficients were very low indeed. A further test for such a
correlation was carried out by using the Spearman rank correlation
procedure on the highest V value ranked against two measures of inflation.
The correlation coefficients were: 0·19 for $V1$ on the average of the three
highest successive values of $\dot{P}$ and 0·15 for $V2$ on the overall average

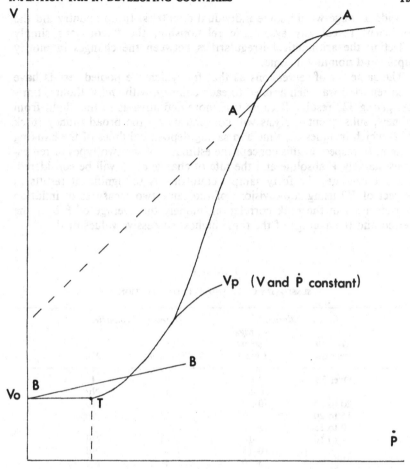

Figure 1   HYPOTHETICAL VELOCITY BEHAVIOUR

value of $\dot{P}$. The positive value is not significantly different from zero in either case. Clearly other factors determining the M/Y relationship *between* countries are more powerful than the effect of inflation. The next step was to analyse the time-series relationship in each of the forty countries.

The first test applied was a calculation of the A. J. Brown coefficient of sensitivity [*Brown, 1955*] which when applied to discrete periods is expressed as:

$$\frac{\Delta \log V}{\Delta \log (P_t/P_{t-1})}$$

This is an approximation to the elasticity of change in velocity to change in the rate of increase of prices over a period t. In this case it was calculated for M1 and M2 on an annual basis to reflect the year to year sensitivity as distinct from the medium term (2 decades) tested by regressions. The set of coefficients ranged between -63 and $+76$ for all countries, with nearly as wide a range within some individual countries. In no country did the coefficient reveal any systematic relationship, the fluctuations simply reflecting the arithmetical irregularities between the changes in money supply and nominal income.

The same set of regressions as that for which the pooled results have been reported was then applied to each country, with and without a time-lag, giving 320 results. Because it is more definitive as to the 'flight from money', subsequent analysis will concentrate on the broad money stock (M2) which includes the time and saving deposit liabilities of the banking system. In respect of this concept the estimates of the two types of regressions, namely V absolute and the rate of change of V, will be considered. Table 1 classifies the forty sample countries as to significant results in respect of $V2$ using sub-divisions of the same two measures of inflation as were used in the rank correlation, namely the average of $\dot{P}$ over the period and the average of the three highest successive values of $\dot{P}$.

TABLE 1

SENSITIVITY OF V2 AND RATE OF INFLATION

Rate of inflation %		Number of countries	
Overall average	Average highest 3 years	Significant	Not
Over 30	50+	9	1
	30–50	1	Nil
20 to 30	40+	1	Nil
15 to 20	20–30	1	1
10 to 15	15–20	1	1
5 to 10	5–10	Nil	Nil
Under 5 {	10–15	4	Nil
	5–10	4	Nil
	0–5	5	11
Total	37*	21	16

* Three of the forty countries were significant only in respect of $V1$.

The table shows very little relationship between $\dot{P}$ and sensitivity; for three countries having relatively high inflations the sensitivity of velocity to $\dot{P}$ is not significant which is consistent with full adjustment. On the other hand it is clear that a substantial proportion of countries having very low rates of inflation show some evidence of sensitivity of $V2$ to $\dot{P}$: in the lowest bracket 5 out of 16 and, in the under 5 per cent bracket as a whole, thirteen out of twenty-four. Disregarding the actual values of the coefficients and relying only on the fact that they are significantly different from zero, it is evident that it is not possible to identify a sensitivity threshold as assumed in Figure 1.

Table 2 shows, for the twenty-one 'sensitive' countries, the gradient coefficients for the V regressions and the intercept and gradient for the V

regressions; the two final columns give the two measures of the rate of inflation calculated from the data.

Of the twenty-six sensitive results shown in the table, three are in respect of. $V1$ only. In these cases the velocity of the *total* money stock remains unaffected by $\dot{P}$ but the currency plus demand deposits component is sensitive. This implies a shift into interest-bearing savings and time deposits either in an effort to get some compensation for inflation or in response to increased nominal or real rates of interest on these deposits. These responses are consistent with the hypothesis of moderate asset substitution in mild inflation in the absence of easily available claims to real assets (equities).

In general it would seem from this evidence that sensitivity to the rate of change in prices is a highly unpredictable relationship, being determined by factors which are peculiar to each country, based on differences in past experience of inflation (a factor which A. J. Brown identified in his global study of the period 1939 to 1951) [*Brown, 1955*] and on institutional, structural and psychological differences. In the context of this general conclusion, attention is now directed to the particular values of the coefficients.

TABLE 2

VELOCITY AND RATE OF INFLATION
(21 'sensitive' countries)

Country	$\dot{V}$	Absolute V		$\dot{P}$	
	Gradient	Intercept	Gradient	Average	Average highest 3 successive values
	(1)	(2)	(3)	(4)	(5)
Argentina	—	3·062	0·029	20·6	27·2
Bolivia	1·148	6·567	0·234	5·2	8·8
Chile	0·374	—	—	25·8	40·4
Colombia	0·739	—	—	10·3	15·5
Dominican Republic	—	5·802	0·071	2·4	11·9
Ecuador	0·744	—	—	3·9	4·9
Ghana	1·063	—	—	7·6	14·3
Greece	—	2·336	0·353	2·5	3·2
Ireland	—	1·528	0·015	3·8	5·9
Korea	1·627	3·432	0·199	15·4	26·0
Libya	—	4·694	0·081	4·6	10·3
Mexico	1·187	—	—	3·9	3·5
Morocco	1·636	3·011	0·037	4·1	5·5
Pakistan	0·963	—	—	4·5	7·4
Paraguay	0·939	6·998	0·343	4·7	10·8
Philippines	0·835	—	—	5·6	8·5
Taiwan	—	3·115	0·142	4·1	8·3
Thailand	0·310	—	—	1·87	4·2
Tunisia	1·188	—	—	2·8	4·2
Uruguay	0·894	3·058	0·012	51·5	96·6
Venezuela	0·373	—	—	2·2	4·2

It will be convenient to look first at the relationship between the rate
of change of velocity as shown in the coefficients in column 1. If $\dot{V}$ is
rising this would be reflected in Figure 1 as a movement of velocity from
its value at zero rate of inflation (V_0) either: (i) to a fully adjusted higher
value of velocity (V_p) consistent with a stable positive rate of inflation;
or (ii) towards hyper-inflation. In either case the necessary (though not
sufficient) condition for incremental finance to be increased by inflation
is that the coefficient should be less than unity.

The values in column 1 show that this necessary condition is not satisfied
in six out of the fifteen significant cases (six out of forty in respect of the
whole sample). Moreover only in two cases, Bolivia and Korea, is a coefficient greater than unity combined with a significant coefficient in respect
of the absolute value of V. These are therefore the only two cases in which
it is possible that the amount of incremental finance attainable at constant
prices might be reduced by inflation. Whether this is the case will depend
on whether or not the inflation has a greater proportional effect on
velocity than on nominal income which reflects real growth as well as
inflation. Inspection of the data shows that this is not the case in either
country. It can be concluded that there are no cases in the sample in which
inflation reduces incremental finance attainable at constant prices.

Turning to the relationship between the absolute level of V and $\dot{P}$,
which corresponds with Mundell's linear formulation, two elements can
be distinguished: that associated with the intercept and that associated
with the coefficient. The intercept is an estimate of the magnitude of
velocity at zero inflation (V_0) and this will reflect institutional and
structural factors determining the normal demand for money at a currently
stable price level. But it may also reflect the effect of inflation *prior* to the
period under examination if the economies in money use induced by inflation have permanently altered the psychological institutional and structural
determinants of the demand for money. Where this is so the low money/
income ratio will of course imply a low potential for incremental finance
at any $\dot{P}$ including zero. On the other hand, the intercept coefficient measures
the relationship between velocity and inflation during the period covered
by the regression analysis, but a non-significant or very low coefficient
may mean full adjustment.

Any further analysis of the characteristics of inflation would require
much more sophisticated techniques than those used here which are
intended solely to establish the order of magnitude of incremental finance
at moderate rates of inflation. It has been argued that the subject has been
dominated by the incorrect analogy with hyper-inflation and that the
feasibility of modest rates of inflationary taxation or forced saving has
been neglected. In a discussion of Mundell's estimates, Harry Johnson
cites the maximum increase in the growth rate of 1·5 per cent to which
reference has been made above, and says: 'Contrary to Mundell's own
judgement, these are not negligible figures, when compared with the savings
ratios and growth rates characteristic of under-developed countries. But
they are extreme estimates and likely to exceed substantially the contribution that inflation could make even under the most favourable circumstances' [*Johnson, 1967: 289*]. Johnson is certainly correct in saying that

an additional 1·5 per cent growth rate is not negligible, it may be crucial; he fails however to observe that Mundell's estimate involves an infinite rate of inflation and is in error in regarding that order of magnitude as an extreme estimate of what is feasible.

TABLE 3

INFLATIONARY FINANCE

	$\Delta M/Y$ per cent				
	$\dot P = 10\%$	$\dot P = 20\%$	$\dot P = 30\%$	$\dot P = 40\%$	$\dot P = 50\%$
Argentina	3·0	5·5	7·6	9·4	11·0
Bolivia	1·2	1·8	2·2	2·5	2·8
Dominican Rep.	1·5	2·8	3·8	4·6	5·5
Greece	1·7	2·2	2·4	2·5	2·5
Ireland	5·9	11·0	15·9	19·2	22·1
Korea	1·8	2·6	3·3	3·6	3·8
Libya	1·8	3·2	4·3	5·1	6·8
Morocco	3·0	5·3	7·4	8·9	10·3
Paraguay	1·0	1·4	1·7	1·9	2·1
Taiwan	2·2	3·4	4·1	4·6	4·9
Uruguay	3·2	6·0	8·8	11·2	13·8

The eleven V coefficients reported in column 3 of Table 2 imply the relationship between $\dot P$ and $\Delta M/Y$ per cent shown for each country in Table 3. For comparison of these results with Mundell's maximum estimate, *at infinite inflation*, his 1·5 per cent additional growth has to be multiplied by his capital output ratio of 2 which gives 3·0 per cent of income. But Mundell assumed only one-third of ΔM (the government's share) would be invested, so the equivalent total incremental finance to that associated by Mundell with infinite inflation is 9 per cent of income. Four of the thirteen sensitive countries attain this level at or below 40 per cent instead of infinity, and the median percentage of income at 30 per cent inflation is 4 per cent for the *sensitive* countries; for the non-sensitive countries there is no diminution in the magnitude of incremental finance as the rate of inflation increases so long as the insensitivity lasts.

In the subsequent estimates based on the V coefficient (b) and using various combinations of the other determinants, the inflationary element is superimposed on the real growth element to show the extent of the inflationary gain; an aspect of the matter not considered in the literature cited. The range of feasible values can be derived from the combination of the maximum value of b (0·353) for Greece and the median value of b (0·081) for Libya, combined with the median and minimum values of V_0 and with the median and maximum values of $Y(R)$ for the countries covered by the study. The results are shown in Table 4 for rates of inflation equal to 0, 5, 10 and 30 per cent, this being the maximum range of deliberate policy.

The only case in which inflation reduces incremental finance is 1(i) in which the proportional increase in velocity exceeds the proportional increase in nominal income. Taking $\dot P = 10$ per cent as the example, the proportional increase in V is $5·78/2·25$ which is $2·57$ and that of nominal income is $0·19/0·085$ which is $2·37$. In all other cases inflation increases $\Delta M/Y$, at a decreasing rate.

TABLE 4

INCREMENTAL FINANCE

	V_0	$\dot{Y}r$	b	$\dot{P} = 0$	$\dot{P} = 5\%$	$\dot{P} = 10\%$	$\dot{P} = 30\%$
				\multicolumn{4}{c}{$\Delta M/Y\%$}
1 (i)	2·25	0·085	0·353	3·78	3·47	3·35	3·19
(ii)	2·25	0·085	0·081	3·78	5·24	6·32	8·77
(iii)	2·25	0·051	0·353	2·27	2·58	2·70	2·85
(iv)	2·25	0·051	0·081	2·27	3·90	5·10	7·82
2 (i)	4·34	0·085	0·353	1·96	2·28	2·46	2·75
(ii)	4·34	0·085	0·081	1·96	2·93	3·76	6·06
(iii)	4·34	0·051	0·353	1·17	1·63	1·98	2·45
(iv)	4·34	0·051	0·081	1·17	2·18	3·03	5·41

The magnitudes of equivalent rows in Sections 1 and 2 of the table differ by an inverse scale factor reflecting the relative values of V_0 hence the values of $\Delta M/Y$ for higher values of V_0 can be obtained by simply scaling down the reported values. Thus the values for $V_0 = 8·68$ are half those for $V_0 = 4·34$ namely: $0·83$, $1·14$, $1·23$ and $1·32$.

So far it has been assumed that V is affected only by inflation, but this leaves out an important element, namely the rate of increase of the money/income ratio (k) resulting from the expansion of the money economy which is associated with growth in real income (Yr). Values for k were obtained from the set of forty developing countries comprising the sample, by regression of time series of the form

$$k = a + bYr + cP$$

designed to separate the two effects. From those results which were significant the median and maximum values of $0·02$ and $0·05$ have been applied to the values of $\Delta M/Y$ already calculated. The complete set of combinations is very large and Table 5 reproduces only those relating to the median values of V_0 ($4·34$) and $\dot{Y}r$ ($0·051$). This procedure naturally underestimates the range which in the complete set of combinations is between $1·6$ and $17·8$ per cent of GNP at 30 per cent inflation: the corresponding maximum at zero inflation being $7·7$ per cent.

Even with median values for V_0 and $\dot{Y}$ it is clear that the effect of an annual increment in the money/income ratio is substantial in those countries to which it applies. It cannot, however, be regarded as a general characteristic and the general conclusions of this analysis are based on the estimates in Table 4.

TABLE 5

INCREMENTAL FINANCE

Adjusted for rate of growth of k

			$\Delta \dfrac{M'}{Y}\%$			
$V = 4{\cdot}34$				$Yr = 0{\cdot}051$		
$\dot{k}$	b	$\dot{P} = 0$	$\dot{P} = 5\%$	$\dot{P} = 10\%$	$\dot{P} = 30\%$
1 (i) 0·02	0·353	1·652	2·386	2·796	3·459
(ii)	0·081		3·078	4·278	7·939
2 (i) 0·05	0·353	2·399	3·466	4·061	5·025
(ii)	0·081		4·471	4·278	11·096

Note: $\dfrac{\Delta M'}{Y} = \left(1 + \dot{k} + \dfrac{\dot{k}}{Yr}\right) \dfrac{\Delta M}{Y}$

These conclusions can now be summarised. It has been shown that a substantial number of countries in the sample fail to reveal sensitivity to inflation. On the other hand sensitivity is significant at low levels of price increase. The study has failed therefore to confirm the hypothesis that there is a threshold below which sensitivity is zero as represented in Figure 1. It has, however, been shown that it is inappropriate for the experience of hyper-inflation to be projected into the area in which the rate of price increase is bounded by the upper limit of 30 per cent which should more than cover the most extreme case of inflation deliberately used as a policy instrument.

Within that limit it has been shown that for countries having median parameters it is feasible to finance growth rates which have hitherto been associated with infinite inflation, but that the actual amount of inflationary finance varies greatly with the degree of sensitivity to inflation and the values of the parameters. Only with extremely unsatisfactory combinations of parameters does inflation decrease incremental finance; in general it increases it at a diminishing rate. It has also been shown that for some countries V is so sensitive to $\dot{P}$ that $\Delta M/Y$ decreases so rapidly as to make the ratio of inflation to real growth untenable.

Although these conclusions show that the attainment of substantial benefits from modest inflation is feasible, it does not follow that any government can conclude that it would be safe and wise deliberately to aim at inflation at 30 per cent. There are substantial costs which must be weighed against the benefits.

In pure theory it is possible to have an equilibrium situation at zero inflation or at 30 per cent inflation. In neither case is equilibrium achieved in practice but the possibility of approximating to the rigorous conditions necessary to attain full adjustment in the inflationary situation is very remote. This is because the necessary adjustments to relative prices, particularly rates of interest and exchange rates, are strongly resisted. The former tend to be constrained within narrow limits by the traditional institutions in developing countries thus giving rise to large divergencies in rates prevailing in unconventional financial markets, the inefficiency of which is starkly revealed in a recent volume by Edward Shaw [*Shaw, 1973*] powerfully criticising 'shallow' finance as distinct from the free operation of financial markets in developing countries. Devaluation is politically hazardous; a strong tendency for the responsible minister or government to fall as a result has been demonstrated by R. N. Cooper [*Cooper, 1971*]. Without elaborate fiscal arrangements and full financial market rate adjustments, efficiency and equity are greatly distorted by inflation.

These defects in financial policy are by no means confined to developing countries any more than is inflation, but in the least developed countries the chronic difficulty of achieving the rate of growth of exports necessary for development is greatly increased by erratically fluctuating rates of inflation and over-valued currencies. These are the real costs of inflationary finance rather than the welfare loss associated with theoretical specification of an area under the demand curve for real balances and, though they cannot be quantified, they are undoubtedly substantial.

On the other hand it can be argued that in the least developed countries the preservation of equilibrium in a non-optimal structural context is less important than costs of enforcing the saving necessary for transforming the structure in view of the small tax base and absence of a substantial corporate sector. This is not the place for a discussion of the structuralist approach to inflation, but it is surely true, and not inconsistent with either a Keynesian or monetarist approach, that in economies in which the objective is transformation of the structure rather than the preservation of equilibrium there is bound to be inflation because of the ratchet and spread effects of price increases necessary for the initial mobilisation or shifting of resources. There can be no dispute about it being highly relevant to credit policy that the binding constraints should be identified in order that finance may be allocated so as to direct resources to these critical areas; indeed, the allocation of inflationary finance is a substantial factor determining how inflationary it will prove to be. Without deliberately resorting to inflation, however, a significant influence can be exerted by the optimal allocation of the necessary amounts of incremental credit expansion associated with real growth, which has been shown by the foregoing analysis to be substantial in general and in particularly favourable conditions to amount to 7·7 per cent of GNP.

In addition to this, there is bound to be some undesigned inflation even with a guide line to contain DCE to real growth requirements and developing countries would do well to consider very carefully their potential for increased 'tax effort' for increasing investment or government capacity-creating expenditure, before risking the deliberate use of inflation for this purpose. There is now substantial evidence that increasing tax rates *does* succeed in increasing the aggregate savings rate without adverse effect on private investment with which government expenditure on infra-structure is complementary [*Newlyn, forthcoming, Chs. 3 and 5*].

Finally, we are brought back to the vulnerability of developing economies in their external relationships, the effect of the inflation tax on imports having been entirely neglected in the literature, in spite of the implications of the concept of DCE and of the Polak model [*Polak and Argy, 1971*]. As argued elsewhere [*Newlyn, 1969*], the constraint on inflation in developing countries is more likely to be the need to maintain external balance in the context of fixed exchange rates, rather than the need to contain domestic inflation. Unfortunately, however, the pressure on external reserves tends to lead to import restrictions which then redirect the inflationary pressures into the domestic economy. Although import restrictions may be highly desirable in a country in which imports include substantial quantities of luxury consumer goods, they can be very damaging if they have to be applied to producers' goods. If inflationary finance leads to this constraint on development, in addition to its adverse effects on export growth, the costs are almost certain to exceed the benefits.

NOTES
1. By kind permission of Oxford University Press, this article draws upon W. T. Newlyn, *Financing Economic Development*, Chapter 2, 'Intermediation and Credit Creation', forthcoming.
2. Appendix to [*Newlyn, forthcoming*] which is based on IMF *International Financial Statistics*.

REFERENCES
Bailey, M. J., 1956, 'The Welfare Cost of Inflationary Finance', *Journal of Political Economy*, April.
Barro, R. J., 1972, 'Inflationary Finance and the Welfare Cost of Inflation', *Journal of Political Economy*, September/October.
Brown, A. J., 1955, *The Great Inflation*, London.
Cagan, P., 1956, 'The Monetary Dynamics of Hyper-inflation', in M. Friedman, ed., *Studies in the Quantity Theory of Money*, Chicago.
Cooper, R. N., 1971, 'Currency Devaluation in Developing Countries', in G. Ranis, ed., *Government and Economic Development*, New Haven and London.
Friedman, M., 1971, 'Government Revenue from Inflation', *Journal of Political Economy*, July/August.
Johnson, H. G., 1967, *Essays in Monetary Economics*, London: Allen and Unwin.
Mundell, R. A., 1965, 'Growth, Stability and Inflationary Finance', *Journal of Political Economy*, April.
Newlyn, W. T., 1962, *Theory of Money* (2nd edition), Oxford.
Newlyn, W. T., 1969, 'Monetary Analysis and Policy in Financially Dependent Economies', in I. G. Stewart, ed., *Economic Development and Structural Change*, Edinburgh.
Newlyn, W. T., forthcoming, *Financing Economic Development*, Oxford.
Polak, J. J., and V. Argy, 1971, 'Credit Policy and the Balance of Payments', *International Monetary Fund Staff Papers*, March.
Shaw, E. S., 1973, *Financial Deepening in Economic Development*, New York: Oxford University Press.

Money Supply, Inflation and the
Balance of Payments in Sri Lanka (1959-74)

by K. E. A. de Silva*

This study estimates the influence of monetary expansion on inflation in Sri Lanka during the period, 1959-74. After a brief discussion of the historical background, a theoretical model is presented to show the link between money supply, inflation, and balance of payments deficits. The rest of the paper is devoted to the statistical testing of the model. One of the findings of this study is that, for the entire period, 1959-74, money supply has not exerted a statistically significant influence on domestic inflation. But for the more recent period, 1967-74, the impact of money supply on inflation appears to be statistically significant. It is also found that domestic inflation has not been strong enough to have an adverse effect on exports, although further research is obviously necessary to shed more light on this question.

I. THE MONETARIST INTERPRETATION OF INFLATION

Developing countries which embark on development programmes often experience inflation and balance of payments difficulties. Johnson [*1964*] has argued that the particular method of financing economic development is sometimes responsible for these problems. Specifically, Johnson's hypothesis is that monetary expansion associated with government borrowing from the banking system is a key factor contributing to inflation and balance of payments deficits. This hypothesis is often referred to in the literature as the monetarist interpretation of inflation.[1]

The present paper is an attempt to examine the relevance of the monetarist interpretation to Sri Lanka's experience during the period 1959-74. Between 1959 and 1966 Sri Lanka enjoyed a period of relative price stability, as the Consumer Price Index[2] increased, on the average, at a mere 1 per cent annually (Table 1); but since 1967 the Consumer Price Index has shown a more rapid increase (between June 1967 and June 1974 the average annual increase has been approximately 7 per cent).

Section II provides a broad outline of the main economic developments in Sri Lanka during the period under examination. In section III we present the basic model to be tested and discuss its important features. Section IV deals with the limitations of data and the statistical analysis. The main conclusions are summarised in section V.

* Economist, Department of Consumer and Corporate Affairs, Ottawa. The author wishes to thank J. A. Galbraith, J. Handa, A. Vicas, and the anonymous referees of this Journal for their helpful comments and suggestions. Needless to say, any remaining errors are the author's sole responsibility. Computer assistance provided by R. Parent is also gratefully acknowledged.

TABLE 1

THE COLOMBO CONSUMER PRICE INDEX

		(1952 = 100)
1959		105·2
1960		103·5
1961		104·8
1962		106·3
1963		108·8
1964		112·2
1965		112·5
1966		112·3
1967		114.8
1968		121·5
1969		130·5
1970		138·2
1971		141·9
1972		150·8
1973		165·4
1974	1st quarter	178·3
1974	2nd quarter	182·7

Source: *Annual Reports of the Central Bank of Ceylon.*

II. MAIN ECONOMIC DEVELOPMENTS IN SRI LANKA

In the late 1950s the most serious economic problem facing Sri Lanka was the increasing external resources gap[3] (69 million rupees[4] in 1952–56; 297 million rupees in 1957–60). During these years money supply had increased rapidly due to government borrowing from the banking system. The increase in the money supply, however, did not generate inflationary pressure. Instead, it led to an increase in the demand for imports which was financed by running down the considerable foreign exchange reserves left over from the tea boom of 1954–56. As exports remained relatively stagnant or increased very slowly due to poor world market conditions, the increase in imports meant an increase in the external resources gap. The Government reacted to the adverse trend in the balance of payments by imposing restrictions on imports. Import duties and quotas were levied on many commodities, especially on consumer goods other than basic necessities. To supplement the import restrictions, the central bank enforced general and selective credit controls such as an increase in the bank rate, higher reserve requirements, and higher margin requirements on many imports.

An important factor contributing to the increase in money supply during a major part of the period of this study was government borrowing from the banking system (Table 2) to finance the growing budget deficit (500 million rupees during the fiscal year, 1960–61; by fiscal year 1970–71 it had increased to 1,327 million rupees). The increase in the budget deficit was mainly due to the increase in transfer payments (of which the food subsidies were the most important item) and more active government involvement in the provision of social services. The principal lender to

TABLE 2

MONEY SUPPLY AND GOVERNMENT DEFICIT FINANCING

	Money Supply	Government transactions with the banking system Central Bank Loans and Securities	Commercial Banks Securities (in millions of rupees)	Total
1959	1,178	514	330	844
1960	1,209	760	336	1,096
1961	1,289	903	357	1,260
1962	1,343	1,081	428	1,509
1963	1,506	1,228	422	1,650
1964	1,622	1,358	423	1,781
1965	1,716	1,347	455	1,802
1966	1,659	1,529	441	1,970
1967	1,808	1,652	377	2,029
1968	1,913	1,960	387	2,347
1969	1,883	2,064	303	2,367
1970	1,967	2,220	638	2,858
1971	2,149	2,261	689	2,950
1972	2,481	2,472	736	3,208
1973	2,778	2,590	498	3,088
1974 1st quarter	2,869	2,476	482	2,958
1974 2nd quarter	2,873	2,616	485	3,101

Source: Annual Reports of the Central Bank of Ceylon.

the Government was the central bank and the main instrument of lending was the treasury bill. The total value of treasury bills outstanding was subject to a ceiling which could be raised only by Act of Parliament. But, with the persistence of large budget deficits, the treasury bill ceiling was raised from time to time. Thus, during the fiscal year 1959–60, the authorised limit on treasury bills was raised twice by parliament to 450 million rupees in October 1959 and to 650 million rupees in August 1960. By July 1972 the authorised limit had risen to 2,500 million rupees.[5]

With imports being restricted and money supply expanding, the monetary authorities became concerned with inflation although the Consumer Price Index showed only a very mild increase in the early 1960s. Thus the central bank argued that:

> In previous years the increase in consumer demand generated by the monetary expansion was substantially met out of an expanded volume of imports which in turn was made possible by the running down of external reserves. The increased supplies of imported goods served, to a large extent, to protect the general level of prices in Ceylon from pressures of the monetary expansion. In 1961, with the sharp contraction in the volume of imports, the situation has altered basically. Given the continuance of the expansionary factors in the monetary field, the contraction in the supply of goods implies rising pressures on prices and costs.[6]

Inflation would not have become a major issue during the period of this study if output had increased rapidly. Between 1959 and 1973, Gross National Product at constant (1959) prices increased by approximately 4·15 per cent per annum; but when allowance is made for population growth, the increase is only about 1·80 per cent.

The Government's anti-inflationary strategy consisted of switching periodically from the banking system to non-bank sources for the financing of the budget deficit. The principal non-bank sources were the Employees' Provident Fund and the Insurance Corporation. As for the central bank, it held the view that, while a restrictive monetary policy would help to bring down the prices, it might also act as a disincentive to domestic producers by reducing the availability of credit. Hence the central bank followed a policy of encouraging bank credit to productive ventures while discouraging credit to activities not directly related to production or considered to be non-essential. In practice, however, the decrease in credit for non-productive or non-essential purposes was not large enough to offset the increase in credit for productive or essential purposes and consequently, bank lending increased (from 526 million rupees in 1961 to 1,243 million rupees in 1968) despite the enforcement of selective credit controls.

In the late 1960s, with the rather sharp rise in the Consumer Price Index, the central bank became more seriously concerned with the inflationary impact of increased commercial bank lending, and therefore fixed credit ceilings to limit the increase in certain types of commercial bank loans and advances. The main items which were exempted from the ceilings included export bills, loans under the Agricultural Credit Scheme, tea factory modernisation loans, and medium- and long-term loans for industry and agriculture. The credit ceilings which were in operation from October 1968 to April 1972 did not result in a reduction in commercial bank lending to the private sector. Instead, there was a slight increase in bank lending during the period of this operation (the annual average rates of increase for 1959–68 and 1969–71 were approximately 11·38 per cent and 12·36 per cent respectively). But, although the credit ceilings did not produce a reduction in bank credit, they certainly induced a larger proportion of it to flow into productive uses. For example, loans and advances to agriculture and industry as a proportion of total bank loans averaged 39 per cent in 1969–71 compared with 21 per cent in 1965–68. The ceilings were lifted with effect from 1 April 1972 as the central bank felt that 'some expansion in bank credit to the private sector would be consistent with the objective of monetary stability'.[7] Commercial banks, however, were asked to refrain from increasing credit for non-essential purposes over the level of such credit as on 31 March 1972. After the credit ceilings were lifted, bank lending to the private sector shot up once again, increasing at an annual average rate of 20 per cent from April 1972 to April 1974. This rapid expansion of commercial bank credit necessitated central bank intervention and credit ceilings were re-introduced in May 1974. In announcing the new credit restrictions, the central bank reiterated its position that the purpose of the credit ceilings was to prevent the increase in credit for non-essential purposes and not to restrict credit for productive or essential purposes.

While the above developments were taking place in the domestic monetary scene, the external resources gap continued to increase (from 225 million rupees in 1960–62 to 330 million rupees in 1964–66) mainly due to a marked decline in the terms of trade (from 142 in 1960–62 to 109 in 1964–66). The increasing external resources gap was an eye opener to the Government that import restrictions were not the answer to Sri Lanka's foreign exchange problems. There were two main considerations influencing government policy in the mid-1960s. Firstly, it was recognised that import restrictions had been carried to their maximum and that, therefore, it was becoming increasingly difficult to introduce further restrictions. Secondly, the need was felt for a liberalisation of imports of raw materials and capital equipment to meet the requirements of domestic agriculture and industry. Therefore, a change in government policy was felt necessary to correct the balance of payments situation. As a first step, following the British devaluation, the Sri Lankian rupee was devalued by 20 per cent in 1967. Commenting on the devaluation, the central bank stated:

> . . . while the new rate was a good basic rate, it was not sufficiently realistic to permit the liberalization of a substantial range of imports. A unitary rate at a further depreciated level might have met the situation in some respects, but in other respects it might have created further difficult problems in the domestic economy. Thus, for instance, a 20 per cent devaluation was felt to be inadequate to meet the problem of other exports. Similarly, on the imports side, while a 20 per cent devaluation gave a sufficient mark up in the costs of a wide range of essential imports, it was insufficient to permit an adequate liberalization of imports, especially for growing sectors of the economy. Hence some system of multiple rates appeared to supply the answer to Ceylon's problem.[8]

The above considerations led to the adoption of the Foreign Exchange Entitlement Certificate Scheme (FEECS) in 1968. The essence of the FEECS is the establishment of a dual exchange rate system. The official exchange rate governs one set of transactions. For example, basic essentials such as foodstuffs are imported at the official exchange rate. Similarly, transactions involving the export of tea, rubber, and coconut products also come under the official rate. All other transactions with the outside world are governed by a second exchange rate (known as the FEEC rate) which is higher than the official rate.[9] The FEEC rate was initially fixed at 44 per cent but was raised to 55 per cent in July 1969 and further raised to 65 per cent in November 1972. All individuals who wish to make transactions with the outside world have to obtain Foreign Exchange Entitlement Certificates from the central bank. Producers of minor (non-traditional)[10] export products enjoy a subsidy under this scheme since they are entitled to foreign exchange at the higher FEEC rate. Finally, import quotas on intermediate and investment goods were abolished under the FEECS. Instead, those who wish to import these goods are permitted to do so at the FEEC rate.

As a result of the FEECS there was a considerable increase in non-traditional export products as well as in tourism. But the balance of payments continued to be unfavourable. Indeed, the balance of payments problem has become so severe in recent years that the Government has been forced to resort to heavy short-term borrowing from abroad, thereby imposing an enormous debt-servicing burden on the economy in the short-run.

To sum up, Sri Lanka presents the picture of an economy plagued with a severe balance of payments deficit, a slow rate of economic growth, and continuing inflation. The slow rate of economic growth along with the relative unwillingness on the part of the unemployed young to accept certain types of employment, such as farm work, has created considerable unemployment in the economy.[11] To achieve a higher rate of economic growth and a reduction in unemployment, it is necessary to have more imports of intermediate and investment goods; but in view of the chronic balance of payments deficit, there is only very limited scope for increasing imports. Therefore, the Government has adopted several strategies to overcome the foreign exchange bottleneck. These include export promotion with heavy emphasis on non-traditional exports,[12] reduction in the budget deficit (by reducing the food subsidies), reduction in food imports, and encouragement to grow more food domestically.

III.   THE MODEL

The model described here is based on the monetarist or quantity theory approach to inflation. The general monetarist view is that inflation is caused by money supply expanding more rapidly than real output. However, we have gone beyond the simple monetarist interpretation by also adding several structural variables to our model.

Two important assumptions underlying the model should be made explicit. First, the exchange rate is fixed; second, all imports are assumed to be subject to restrictions.

There is nothing remarkably original about the present model. In fact, it is very similar to the models used by Schotta, Jr. [1966], Kieran [1970], Baker and Falero, Jr. [1971], and Prais [1961]. But two important differences between our model and previous ones deserve mention. First, earlier models were solely concerned with the determination of nominal income. In these models the domestic price level is determined by international prices and hence is treated as an exogenous variable. But once import restrictions are brought into the picture, money supply can influence the domestic price level, depending on what happens to real output. Second, in contrast to previous models, we have treated exports as an endogenous variable determined by foreign real income and the ratio of foreign to domestic prices.

To describe the model, let us start with the following money supply equation:

1. $M_t^s = f(R_t, G_t, C_t)$

Where M^s = money supply

   R = international reserve
   G = government borrowing from the banking system
   C = commercial bank credit to the private sector.

The level of international reserves during period t is given by the following identity:

2. $R_t = R_{t-1} + B_t + B_{ft}$

    Where B = balance of payments deficit
           B_f = net foreign borrowing.

The demand for real cash balances is given by

3. $(M^d/P)_t = f(Q_t, P_t^{\bullet})$

    Where M^d = demand for nominal cash balances
           Q = real income or output
           $P^{\bullet}$ = anticipated rate of inflation
           P = price level

Interest rates have been omitted from equation (3) as preliminary tests revealed their lack of statistical significance.[13] $P^{\bullet}$ is a proxy for the cost of holding real balances and is defined as[14]

4. $P^{\bullet} = f(\dot{P}_{t-1} \ldots \dot{P}_{t-n})$

    Where $\dot{P}$ = rate of change in the price level.

The price level responds to changes in $M^{\bullet}$ and M^d/P. Substituting (3) for M^d/P and adding two new variables—wages (w) and import prices (Pm_1)—we derive the following price equation[15]

5. $\dot{P}_t = f(\dot{M}_t^{\bullet}, \dot{Q}_t, \dot{P}_t^{\bullet}, \dot{W}_t, \dot{P}m_{1t})$

    Where a dot above a variable denotes rate of change.

Real output is determined by[16]

6. $Q_t = f(G_{et}/P_t, C_t/P_t, Im_{2t}/Pm_{2t})$

    Where G_e = government expenditure
             Im_2 = value of imports of intermediate and investment goods
             Pm_2 = the weighted import price index of intermediate and investment goods.

The balance of payments deficit is defined as

7. $B_t = X_t - (Im_{2t} + Ic_t + K_t)$

    Where X = exports
           Ic = imports of consumer goods
           K = total capital payments.

Finally, the demand for exports is given by

8. $X_t = f(Y_{ft}, P_{ft}/P_t)$

    Where Y_f = foreign real income
           P_f = foreign prices.

Endogenous variables: M^d, $M^{\bullet}$, P, $P^{\bullet}$, Q, B, R, and X.
Exogenous variables: G, C, G_e, P_f, Y_f, W, Pm_2, Pm_1, Im_2, I_c and K.

The working of the model can be described as follows. Starting from a position of equilibrium in the economy, consider the effects of an increase in $M^{\bullet}$ due to, say, an increase in government borrowing from the banking system (G). When the government spends its borrowings (i.e. when G_e

increases), there will be an increase in Q (according to equation 6) which in turn raises the public's demand for real balances (equation 3). Other things remaining the same, the change in the price level ($\dot{P}$) depends on $\dot{M}^s$ and $\dot{M}^d$ (see equation 5); if $\dot{M}^d < \dot{M}^s$, $\dot{P} > 0$; if $\dot{M}^d = \dot{M}^s$, $\dot{P} = 0$; and finally, if $\dot{M}^d > \dot{M}^s$, $\dot{P} < 0$. Other things constant, the change in P affects the demand for X (equation 8) and thus influences B (equation 7). The resulting change in R (equation 2) will lead to a corresponding change in M^s (equation 1) unless the monetary authorities undertake offsetting action.[17] Thus, theoretically, the system is interdependent.

Although the above model is based on simultaneous equations, in the statistical analysis that follows we have estimated the key equations separately. This might introduce some bias into our estimates. In defence, we would argue that, since we are dealing with annual data for the most part of the analysis, the number of observations is too small to attempt a simultaneous equation estimation. Moreover, some economists such as Teigen [*1964*] have argued that the ordinary least squares method yields results roughly comparable to those obtained from the two-stage least squares method.

IV. STATISTICAL ANALYSIS

Before presenting the statistical results, it is necessary to discuss the data used in this study. The following is a complete list of the data:

1. M^s = currency plus demand deposits held by the non-bank public (excluding the government)
2. R = total external assets net of Sterling Loan Sinking Funds
3. G = government borrowing from the central bank and commercial banks
4. C = commercial bank loans and advances to the private sector
5. P = Colombo Consumer Price Index (1952 = 100)
6. Pm_1 = Import price index of consumer goods, intermediate goods, and investment goods (weighted by the volume of imports in each category for the period 1963–66)
7. Pm_2 = Import price index of intermediate and investment goods (weighted by the volume of imports in each category for the period 1963–66)
8. Pm_3 = Import price index of intermediate goods
9. Im_2 = value of imports of intermediate and investment goods
10. Im_3 = value of imports of intermediate goods
11. G_e = sum of government consumption and investment expenditure (national income data)
12. Q = Gross National Product at constant (1959) factor cost prices
13. X = volume of exports
14. W = minimum wage rate index of workers in Wages Boards Trades —i.e. combined index for workers in agriculture, industry and commerce
15. Y_f = foreign real income—countries selected are the U.K., U.S.A., Canada, Japan, European Common Market countries (Belgium, Luxembourg, France, German Federal Republic,

Italy and Netherlands), Australia, New Zealand, South Africa, Iran, United Arab Republic, and India[18] (the weights used to construct the Y_f series are the shares of the respective countries in Sri Lanka's exports[19] for the period 1963–66)

16. P_f = cost of living index of countries given in (15) above. The weights used are the shares of the respective countries in Sri Lanka's exports for the period 1963–66.

Data on (1) to (13) are from *Monthly Bulletins and Annual Reports of the Central Bank of Ceylon*. Data on wages (*W*) are from the *Annual Reports of the Commissioner of Labour* and *Monthly Labour Review*. Data on Y_f and P_f are from *Direction of Trade: A Supplement to International Financial Statistics*, published by IMF and IBRD.

Although nothing definite can be said about most of the data used here, we feel more uncomfortable with, for example, the price and wage data than with others. Ceylon does not have a general wholesale price index. The only price index available for our purposes and the one used in this study is the Colombo Consumer Price Index which suffers from the following weaknesses. First, it is based on a budget survey of working class families in Colombo and may not be truly representative of the whole country. Second, it contains several items which are subsidised or subject to price control. Finally, the Colombo Consumer Price Index has not undergone a major revision[20] since it was first set up in 1952. Like the Consumer Price Index, the wage rate index used in this study also has several shortcomings. First, it is a minimum wage rate index and may not be an accurate indicator of movements in wages actually paid in an industry or sector. For example, actual earnings may record a sharp increase in some years while the minimum wage rate index remains constant or moves very slowly. Second, the minimum wage rate index applies only to the plantations and a few selected sectors of the economy.[21] It does not apply to most of the new manufacturing industries which have appeared since the early 1960s.

The expected rate of inflation ($P^{\bullet}$) series was derived as follows:[22]

$$P_t^{\bullet} - P_{t-1}^{\bullet} = \beta(\dot{P}_{t-1} - P_{t-1}^{\bullet}), \ 0 < \beta < 1$$

where β is the coefficient of price expectation. This formulation implies that $P^{\bullet}$ can be constructed as an exponentially weighted average of price changes in past periods. This technique assumes the following geometrically declining distributed lag:

$$P^{\bullet} = \sum_{i=0}^{\infty} \beta(1-B)^i \dot{P}_{t-1}$$

By trying out different β's, we can construct the associated $P^{\bullet}$ series and choose the β which gives the highest R^2. In this study the β which maximised R^2 was approximately 0·66.

Finally, it should be noted that we have used three import price variables in the price equation. Theoretically, Pm_1 is the most appropriate variable because it includes the prices of all imports. But the presence of consumer subsidies or price controls might tend to obscure the influence of Pm_1 on the domestic price level. Therefore, we have also used two other import price variables—Pm_2 and Pm_3 (for definitions, see p. 29). As the subsequent analysis indicates, the three import price variables do not seem to have had the same impact on the domestic price level.

The main statistical results are summarised in Table 3. Equation (1) shows that G is significant at the 90 per cent level only. Non-bank borrowing by the Government appears to have reduced the statistical significance of G. C is significant at the 95 per cent level. R is not significant at all and has a negative sign, thus indicating that the increase in money supply has occurred despite the decline in foreign exchange reserves. In equation (3), Q is the only significant variable. The poor performance of P^e in equation (3) may be explained in terms of the relative stability of the price level[23] during a major part of the period of this study. In the three price equations, $\dot{M}^s$ is not significant at all. $\dot{P}m_1$ and $\dot{P}m_2$ are significant at the 90 per cent level whereas $\dot{P}m_3$ is significant at the 95 per cent level. The lower explanatory power of $\dot{P}m_1$ and $\dot{P}m_2$ is probably due to price controls

TABLE 3

RESULTS OF REGRESSION ANALYSIS (1959–73: annual data)

---

1   $M_t^s = 115 \cdot 2429 + 0 \cdot 6653\ G_t{}^* + 0 \cdot 5814\ C_t{}^{**} - 0 \cdot 1026\ R_t$ $R^2 = 0 \cdot 51$
                    $(1 \cdot 812)$ $(2 \cdot 206)$ $(0 \cdot 713)$ D.W. $= 0 \cdot 76$

3   $M^d/P_t = -2 \cdot 7621 + 0 \cdot 7847\ Q_t{}^{**} - 0 \cdot 2617\ P_t^e$ $R^2 = 0 \cdot 83$ D.W. $= 0 \cdot 93$
                        $(2 \cdot 415)$ $(0 \cdot 903)$

5.1 $\dot{P}_t = 20 \cdot 3482 + 0 \cdot 1168\ \dot{M}_t^s + 0 \cdot 2064\ \dot{W}_t{}^* + 0 \cdot 2963\ \dot{P}_t^{e*} + 0 \cdot 2043\ \dot{P}m_{1t}{}^*$
                      $(0 \cdot 772)$ $(1 \cdot 893)$ $(1 \cdot 975)$ $(2 \cdot 216)$
         $+ 0 \cdot 0973\ \dot{Q}_t$ $R^2 = 0 \cdot 42$ D.W. $= 2 \cdot 29$
         $(0 \cdot 683)$

5.2 $\dot{P}_t = 31 \cdot 4537 + 0 \cdot 1459\ \dot{M}_t^s + 0 \cdot 1875\ \dot{W}_t{}^* + 0 \cdot 2148\ \dot{P}_t^{e*} + 0 \cdot 1567\ \dot{P}m_{2t}{}^*$
                      $(0 \cdot 815)$ $(1 \cdot 945)$ $(2 \cdot 134)$ $(2 \cdot 168)$
         $+ 0 \cdot 1624\ \dot{Q}_t$ $R^2 = 0 \cdot 40$ D.W. $= 2 \cdot 17$
         $(0 \cdot 698)$

5.3 $\dot{P}_t = 18 \cdot 1394 + 0 \cdot 0665\ \dot{M}_t^s + 0 \cdot 1958\ \dot{W}_t{}^* + 0 \cdot 2715\ \dot{P}_t^{e*} + 0 \cdot 3946\ \dot{P}m_{3t}{}^{**}$
                      $(0 \cdot 736)$ $(1 \cdot 870)$ $(1 \cdot 939)$ $(2 \cdot 654)$
         $+ 0 \cdot 1051\ \dot{Q}_t$ $R^2 = 0 \cdot 53$ D.W. $= 2 \cdot 28$
         $(0 \cdot 629)$

6.1 $Q_t = 106 \cdot 8749 + 1 \cdot 8326\ G_{et} + 0 \cdot 6468\ C_t{}^{**} + 0 \cdot 5499\ Im_{2t}/Pm_{2t}{}^*$
                    $(1 \cdot 064)$ $(2 \cdot 217)$ $(1 \cdot 803)$
                           $R^2 = 0 \cdot 50$ D.W. $= 1 \cdot 23$

6.2 $Q_t = 123 \cdot 4115 + 0 \cdot 7184\ G_{et} + 0 \cdot 6512\ C_t{}^{**} + 0 \cdot 7468\ Im_{3t}/Pm_{3t}{}^{**}$
                    $(1 \cdot 259)$ $(2 \cdot 218)$ $(2 \cdot 205)$
                           $R^2 = 0 \cdot 66$ D.W. $= 1 \cdot 40$

8   $X_t = 50 \cdot 6738 + 0 \cdot 5193\ Y_{ft}{}^{**} + 0 \cdot 1423\ P_t/P_{ft}$ $R^2 = 0 \cdot 63$ D.W. $= 0 \cdot 91$
              $(2 \cdot 608)$ $(0 \cdot 739)$

---

t ratios are given within parentheses
R^2 = coefficient of determination adjusted for degrees of freedom
D.W. = Durbin-Watson statistic
**   = significant at the 0·05 level
*   = significant at the 0·10 level

TABLE 4

PRICE EQUATIONS WITH LAGGED OUTPUT VARIABLES (1959–73: annual data)

5.4 $\dot{P}_t = 27\cdot8914 + 0\cdot0735\ \dot{M}_t^* + 0\cdot1674\ \dot{W}_t^* + 0\cdot2639\ \dot{P}_t^{e*} + 0\cdot1485\ \dot{P}m_{1t}^*$
$\phantom{5.4\ \dot{P}_t = 27\cdot8914}(0\cdot734)(1\cdot903)(2\cdot078)(2\cdot226)$
$\phantom{5.4\ \dot{P}_t = }+0\cdot0693\ \dot{Q}_{t-1}R^2 = 0\cdot40\text{D.W.} = 2\cdot26$
$\phantom{5.4\ \dot{P}_t = }(0\cdot648)$

5.5 $\dot{P}_t = 48\cdot7336 + 0\cdot1548\ \dot{M}_t^* + 0\cdot2481\ \dot{W}_t^* + 0\cdot2093\ \dot{P}_t^{e*} + 0\cdot1629\ \dot{P}m_{2t}^*$
$\phantom{5.5\ \dot{P}_t = 48\cdot7336}(0\cdot638)(1\cdot985)(2\cdot164)(1\cdot989)$
$\phantom{5.5\ \dot{P}_t = }+0\cdot1304\ \dot{Q}_{t-1}R^2 = 0\cdot43\text{D.W.} = 2\cdot30$
$\phantom{5.5\ \dot{P}_t = }(0\cdot684)$

5.6 $\dot{P}_t = 19\cdot2629 + 0\cdot1148\ \dot{M}_t^* + 0\cdot1837\ \dot{W}_t^* + 0\cdot1928\ \dot{P}_t^{e*} + 0\cdot2135\ \dot{P}m_{3t}^{**}$
$\phantom{5.6\ \dot{P}_t = 19\cdot2629}(0\cdot716)(2\cdot074)(2\cdot187)(2\cdot393)$
$\phantom{5.6\ \dot{P}_t = }+0\cdot2124\ \dot{Q}_{t-1}R^2 = 0\cdot52\text{D.W.} = 2\cdot24$
$\phantom{5.6\ \dot{P}_t = }(0\cdot946)$

See footnotes in Table 3

on imported consumer goods and to the rather erratic behaviour of the import price index of investment goods. The high level of statistical significance of $\dot{P}m_3$ is not altogether surprising in view of the heavy dependence of domestic industries on imported raw materials. Even as late as 1973, approximately 67 per cent of the raw material requirements of domestic industries was met through imports.[24] $\dot{P}^e$ is significant only at the 90 per cent level. W is also significant only at the 90 per cent level, thereby indicating that the cost-push element has not been a strong factor in inflation during this period. Q is not significant and has a positive sign (also see Table 4). Perhaps its poor performance may be due to our inability to separate real output originating in the 'subsistence' sector from that originating in the 'monetary' sector.[25] In equation (6), G_e is not significant probably because a large proportion of government expenditure has gone into consumption rather than into investment.[26] C and Im_2/Pm_2 are significant at the 95 and 90 per cent levels respectively. The results show a considerable improvement when Im_3/Pm_3 is used. Finally, in the export demand equation Y_f is significant at the 95 per cent level. But the relative price variable is not significant at all probably because domestic inflation was not strong enough to have an adverse effect on the international competitiveness of Sri Lanka's exports.

Our analysis of the money–price relationship suffers from at least two weaknesses. First, the use of annual data is not very helpful in examining any lagged relationship that might exist between money supply and inflation. Second, as mentioned in the introduction, inflation really became a serious issue only after about 1967. Therefore, we decided to take a closer look at the more recent period January 1967–June 1974, to determine the extent to which monetary expansion has contributed to inflation. The method used is a distributed lag analysis based on quarterly data. The import price variables had to be left out due to lack of quarterly data on a continuous basis. Similarly, the wage variable was also omitted as quarterly data showed very little or slow movement most of the time.

Only two independent variables were selected for consideration—$\dot{M}^*$ and $\dot{P}^*$. Although the latter variable did not perform well in the earlier analysis, we still included it to find out whether price expectations had anything to do with the recent inflation.[27] The money supply data are seasonally adjusted.

The distributed lag analysis used here is borrowed from Almon [1965]. The reported polynomial lag distribution is the one among distributions with similar shapes for which the coefficients of the transformed lag variables in the least squares regression had the largest t-statistic values. This procedure for choosing among polynomial lag distributions would appear to be a better method than choosing on the basis of R^2 or because a given polynomial lag distribution best approximates an unconstrained lag.

TABLE 5

PRICE EQUATION (January 1967–June 1974: quarterly data)
CONSTRAINTS: Second degree polynomial

$$\dot{P}_t = 14.67830 + \sum_{i=0}^{9} m_i \dot{M}^*_{t-i} + 0.29367\, \dot{P}^*_t \qquad R^2 = 0.46732$$

		(2·03823)	D.W. = 2·31
m_0 =	−0·02148	(−0·34796)	
m_1 =	0·01063	(0·66109)	
m_2 =	0·02552	(1·05381)	
m_3 =	0·03615	(2·02435)	
m_4 =	0·04820	(2·67814)	
m_5 =	0·05647	(3·46229)	
m_6 =	0·06889	(3·67863)	
m_7 =	0·05792	(3·28457)	
m_8 =	0·03080	(2·39562)	
m_9 =	0·01006	(0·58173)	
m_i =	0·32316	(2·56935)	

See footnotes in Table 3

Table 5 presents the results of regression analysis based on a second degree polynomial lag distribution. $\dot{P}^*$ is still significant only at the 90 per cent level. The influence of $\dot{M}^*$ is negative in the first quarter but becomes positive thereafter. Two points can be made about the money–price relationship. First, the rate of monetary expansion has exerted a significant influence on the recent inflation. Second, the impact of monetary expansion is felt only after a fairly long lag. In fact, only about 15 per cent of the total response is felt in the first year. Finally, R^2 is quite low, thereby making it clear that several other relevant variables have been omitted from the regression analysis.

V. CONCLUSION

The findings reported in this study should be treated as highly tentative due to its obvious weaknesses. First, some of the data used here are extremely crude and leave a lot to be desired. Second, the period covered is also relatively short, thereby making it difficult to offer any firm generalisations. Subject to the above limitations, the principal conclusion of this study is that money supply has exerted a significant influence on the recent inflation. In other words, the Government has been forced to print more money to finance the growing budget deficit (resulting from increased transfer payments such as food subsidies and greater government participation in social welfare programmes) and this in turn has exerted upward pressure on the price level. However, the case for the monetary interpretation of inflation should not be overstated for the following reasons. Firstly, money supply has not been the sole factor contributing to inflation. Several other factors such as import prices also appear to have been important determinants of inflation. Secondly, although money supply has been important during the period, 1967–74, its influence on the domestic price level for the longer period, 1959–74, has been negligible. Finally, this study is unable to contribute very much to our understanding of the unfavourable effects of inflation on exports. Although our finding in this respect is negative, further research is necessary before we could reach definitive conclusions.

NOTES

1. The monetarist interpretation of inflation has been subjected to considerable empirical testing. Almost all of these studies, of course, are invariably related to the monetarist-structuralist controversy. See, for example, Harberger [1963], Diaz-Alejandro [1965], Hynes [1967], Diz [1970], Argy [1970], Teh-Wei Hu [1971], Koot [1972], and Vogel [1974].

2. The Consumer Price Index used in this study tends to underestimate the rate of inflation for several reasons, some of which are mentioned in section IV.

3. The external resources gap is equal to total foreign exchange earnings (goods and services) minus the sum of total import payments (goods and services) and total capital payments. Figures on total capital payments prior to 1968 are only for the net change in short-term liabilities on account of credit imports, and these relate mainly to imports of rice from Burma and flour from Australia. But after 1968 all data on short-term credit imports were included in the category of total capital payments.

4. Unless otherwise mentioned, all the figures given in this section are from the *Annual Reports and Monthly Bulletins of the Central Bank of Ceylon.*

5. At this writing, the authorised limit is still at 2,550 million rupees.

6. *Annual Report of the Central Bank of Ceylon (1961)*, p. 24.

7. *Annual Report of the Central Bank of Ceylon (1972)*, p. 109.

8. *Annual Report of the Central Bank of Ceylon (1969)*, p. 21.

9. The Sri Lankian rupee is now tied to the pound sterling, although for a brief period (November 1971 to July 1972) it was pegged to the U.S. dollar.

10. These are exports other than tea, rubber and coconut products.

11. For an interesting discussion of these issues, see the ILO Mission Report [1971]; also see M. Lipton [1972].

12. For example, the Convertible Rupee Account Scheme which was started in January 1973 was conceived as a measure of providing further incentives for the export of non-traditional items, by the grant of a proportion of foreign exchange earnings as freely convertible currency to the exporter.

13. Adekunle [1968] also found interest rates to be insignificant in his demand for money equations for Sri Lanka.

14. For a discussion on the relevance of P^e to price determination, see Harberger [1963] and Friedman [1970].

15. Strictly speaking, we should have substituted (1) and (6) for $\dot{M}^s$ and $\dot{Q}$ in the price equation (5); but we avoided doing this because it would have involved us in a

degrees of freedom problem since we are dealing with a limited number of annual data for the most part of the analysis.

16. In Mundell [*1965*], Q is related to G_e only; but we also included C and Im_2/Pm_2 to examine their impact on Q.

17. In this discussion we have ignored P^e by confining ourselves to a once and for all increase in M^s. However, if the monetary authorities keep on increasing M^s, price expectations will come into play and can become an important factor in inflation.

18. Together these countries account for about 70–75 per cent of Sri Lanka's exports.

19. This weighting procedure has also been used by Houthakker and Magee [*1969*].

20. The only significant revision made during the period we are interested in is the change in weights in 1968.

21. These include coconut manufacturing, engineering, printing, match manufacturing, motor transport, tea export, building, dock harbour and port transport, rubber export, and cinema trades. Source: *Annual Reports of the Commissioner of Labour.*

22. On this derivation, see Nerlove [*1958*].

23. On this point, Johnson [*1963: 126*] has argued that 'the public only becomes sensitive to inflation after a certain threshold of price increase has been passed, or that recognition that the situation has been characteristically inflationary comes only with a very long lag'.

24. *Annual Report of the Central Bank of Ceylon (1973)*, p. 69.

25. Vogel [*1974*] found that lagged rates of change in Q performed better than the current rate of change in Q. He interpreted this to mean that some measure of permanent real income is superior to current real income. With the limited number of annual observations we have, it is difficult for us to construct a permanent income series. But we lagged $\dot{Q}$ to see whether it would show an improvement in the results. As shown in Table 4, $\dot{Q}$ is still insignificant.

26. According to national income data, in 1962–64 the ratios of government consumption and investment expenditures to GNP at current prices were about 15 per cent and 5 per cent respectively, whereas in 1971–73 the ratios were approximately 14·5 and 4 per cent respectively. Source: *Annual Reports of the Central Bank of Ceylon.*

27. To conserve the degrees of freedom, we have not applied the Almon technique to determine the influence of $\dot{P}^e$ on $\dot{P}$.

REFERENCES

Adekunle, J. O., 1968, 'The demand for money: an international comparison', *Indian Economic Journal*, Vol. XVI, No. 1.

Almon, S., 1965, 'The distributed lag between capital appropriations and expenditures', *Econometrica*, Vol. 33, No. 1.

Argy, V., 1970, 'Structural inflation in developing countries', *Oxford Economic Papers*, Vol. 22, No. 1.

Baker, A. H. and Falero, F. Jr., 1971, 'Money, exports, government spending and income in Peru, 1951–66', *Journal of Development Studies*, Vol. 7, No. 4.

Diaz-Alejandro, C. F., 1965, 'Exchange Rate Devaluation in a Semi-Industrial Country: The Experience of Argentina, 1955–61', *Massachusetts Institute of Technology Monographs in Economics*, No. 5, Cambridge, Mass.: M.I.T. Press.

Diz, A. C., 1970, 'Money and prices in Argentina, 1935–62', in *Varieties of Monetary Experience*, ed. by D. Meiselman, Chicago: University of Chicago Press.

Friedman, M., 1970, 'A theoretical framework for monetary analysis', *Journal of Political Economy*, Vol. 78, No. 2.

Harberger, A. C., 1963, 'The dynamics of inflation in Chile', in *Measurement in Economics: Studies in Mathematical Economics and Econometrics in Memory of Yehuda Grunfeld*, ed. by C. Christ, Stanford, California: Stanford University Press.

Houthakker, H. S. and Magee, S. P., 1969, 'Income and price elasticities in world trade', *Review of Economics and Statistics*, Vol. LI, No. 2.

Hynes, A., 1967, 'The demand for money and monetary adjustments in Chile', *Review of Economic Studies*, Vol. XXXIV (3), No. 99.

International Labour Office, 1971, *Matching Employment Opportunities and Expectations: A Programme for Action for Ceylon.* 1. The Report of an Inter-Agency Team Organised by the International Labour Office. 2. The Technical Papers, Geneva, International Labour Office.

Johnson, H. G., 1963, 'A survey of the theories of inflation', *Indian Economic Review*, Vol. VI, No. 4.

Johnson, H. G., 1964, 'Fiscal policy and the balance of payments in a growing economy', *Malayan Economic Review*, Vol. IX, No. 1.

Kieran, M., 1970, 'Monetary policy and the business cycle in postwar Japan', in *Varieties of Monetary Experience*, ed. by D. Meiselman, Chicago: University of Chicago Press.

Koot, R. S., 1972, 'Price expectations and monetary adjustments in Uruguay', *Social and Economic Studies*, Vol. 21, No. 4.

Lipton, M., 1972, 'Ceylon: The Role of the Inter-Agency Mission', *South Asian Review*, Vol. 5, No. 3.

Mundell, R. A., 1965, 'Growth, stability and inflationary finance', *Journal of Political Economy*, Vol. LXXIII, No. 2.

Nerlove, M., 1958, *The Dynamics of Supply: Estimation of Farmers' Response to Price*, Baltimore, Johns Hopkins Press.

Prais, S. J., 1961, 'Some mathematical notes on the quantity theory of money', *International Monetary Fund Staff Papers*, Vol. 8, No. 2.

Schotta, C. Jr., 1966, 'The money supply, exports and income in an open economy: Mexico, 1939–1963', *Economic Development and Cultural Change*, Vol. XIV, No. 4.

Teh-Wei Hu, 1971, 'Hyperinflation and the dynamics of demand for money in China', *Journal of Political Economy*, Vol. 79, No. 1.

Teigen, R. L., 1964, 'Demand and supply functions for money in the United States: some structural estimates', *Econometrica*, Vol. 32, No. 4.

Money, Prices and the Balance of Payments: Indonesia 1968–73

by Bijan B. Aghevli*

I. INTRODUCTION

In this paper, a model of Indonesia's monetary sector is developed and estimated econometrically, in order to provide an analytical framework for studying the behaviour of key monetary variables. The model will enable us to quantify the relationships between money, income and prices in a macroeconomic context. The estimation results are used for projecting the appropriate rate of monetary expansion consistent with targeted rates of growth of real income and prices. In the absence of adequate and reliable statistics, it is not possible to construct a detailed disaggregated model of the economy. The framework employed is thus relatively simple and highly aggregated.[1] While these factors weaken the reliability of the model for accurate forecasting purposes, the estimation results can be used for projecting the appropriate rate of monetary expansion consistent with targeted rates of growth of real income and prices. This procedure can provide a very useful and independent check on the appropriate course of monetary policy, augmenting the other information available to the policy makers.

The model consists of four main sections: demand for real money balances, supply of nominal money, government budget, and balance of payments. It is argued that the balance of payments and government budgetary and monetary policies affect the level of reserve money and lead to changes in nominal money supply. On the other hand, the demand for money on the part of the public is a demand for real balances. The level of prices adjust to bring about monetary equilibrium. In this study, real income is regarded as exogenous. Clearly, monetary developments do affect the real sector since severe contractions of money supply would affect economic activity adversely. But as long as the excess demand for money is not too large, the level of income is determined mostly by crop conditions, technological advance, and other factors which are outside the monetary sector.

The Indonesian economy, especially its monetary aspects, has undergone dramatic changes in the last two decades. It is not, therefore, feasible to rely on an econometric model which is based on annual series going far back into the past for projection purposes. A quarterly model is, therefore, constructed, on the basis of quarterly observations from recent years (1968:1 to 1973:4) which are characterised by a marked stability of prices

* International Monetary Fund and The London School of Economics. The author is grateful to P. R. Narvekar for valuable comments and suggestions and to Fredes Pham for research assistance. The views expressed in this paper are not necessarily those of the IMF.

and rapid rate of economic growth. A complete system of equations is estimated simultaneously using the two-stage least squares method. The model tracks the movement of various economic variables quite well.

In section II the demand for real balances is derived. The supply of money is analysed in section III. Government budget and balance of payments are discussed in sections IV and V, respectively. The complete model is estimated and utilised for projections of appropriate monetary expansion in section VI. Section VII presents brief concluding remarks.

II. DEMAND FOR MONETARY ASSETS

Monetary assets play a doubly important role in developing countries since they are not only used for transaction purposes, but are also the major form in which savings are held. In the absence of a well-developed capital market the public holds its savings either in the form of real goods or monetary assets. It is therefore important for the monetary authorities to create enough additional money to meet the increased demand for such assets in each period. If too rapid, monetary expansion would lead to high rates of inflation, whereas an inadequate expansion would dampen the demand for goods and services.[2]

Total liquidity is composed of currency, demand deposits, and quasi-money. Prior to 1968, narrow money (currency plus demand deposits) constituted the major portion of total liquidity. Since then, however, the volume of quasi-money has grown substantially. There is no consensus in the literature as regards the appropriate definition of money. Although traditionally money has been defined in the 'narrow' sense, a number of economists, most notably Milton Friedman, have used the 'broad' measure of money in their empirical work. Allan Metzler has argued that whichever form of money proves to behave in a more stable fashion in relation to variables in the real sector, should be considered the appropriate one.[3] In order to choose the appropriate definition on the basis of this criterion, the demand for real balances is specified in terms of both narrow and broad money.

Assume that the public adjusts its real holdings of any form of monetary asset to the desired level according to a partial adjustment mechanism. That is, the public adds to its previous stock of money balances a fraction λ of the difference between the desired demand and the actual supply of the previous period. Let (M/P) denote the actual stock of real balances and the superscript D denote the desired stock. The partial adjustment mechanism can then be specified in the following form:

(1) $\Delta \log (M/P)_t = \lambda[\log (M/P)_t^D - \log (M/P)_{t-1}]$

$$0 < \lambda < 1$$

Next assume that the desired demand for the real monetary asset $(M/P)^D$ is a function of real income, Y, rate of inflation, π, and the interest paid on quasi-money, r, as follows:

(2) $\log (M/P)_t^D = a_0 + a_1 \log (Y) + a_2\pi + a_3 \log (r)$

The public measures the opportunity cost of holding money relative to goods by the expected rate of inflation, $\pi^\bullet$. It can be assumed that the public adjusts its expectations according to the following relationship:

(3) $\Delta\pi^\bullet = \alpha(\pi_t - \pi^\bullet_{t-1}); \; 0<\alpha<1$

The above formulation implies that the public adjusts its expectations of inflation according to the difference between the actual inflation rate and the expectations entertained in the previous period. An analysis of the Indonesian data indicates that the adjustment coefficient is very close to unity.[4] The actual rate of inflation can thus be used as a close proxy for expected inflation since the public seems to adjust its expectations as to the inflation rate very rapidly to the actual rate. The rate of interest on quasi-money is included since any rise in this variable will induce the public to adjust its portfolio from goods and narrow money to quasi-money.

Substituting equation (2) into (1) and manipulating we get:

(4) $\log(M/P)_t = a_0\lambda + a_1\lambda \log(Y)_t + a_2\lambda \, \pi_t + a_3\lambda \log(r)_t +$
$$(1-\lambda)\log(M/P)_{t-1}$$

The income elasticity, a_1, is expected to be positive, whereas the inflation coefficient a_2 is expected to be negative to reflect the opportunity cost of holding money balances relative to real goods. The coefficient a_3 would be negative for the narrow definition of money and positive for the broad definition of money, reflecting the fact that the relative attractiveness of quasi-money changes as the interest paid on time and savings deposits changes. The above relationship is used to estimate the demand for real balances, with both narrow and broad definitions of money.

III.   SUPPLY OF MONEY

Under a fractional reserve system, the nominal supply of narrow money as well as broad money is determined by changes in reserve money and the money multiplier. In this framework, a rise in reserve money results in a rise in the supply of liquidity as banks expand credit with additional reserves. The supply of narrow money, NM, and of broad money, BM, can be written according to the following identities, where RM denotes the stock of reserve money and m_1 and m_2 denote the money multipliers for narrow and broad money, respectively.[5]

(5) $NM \equiv RM \left\{ \dfrac{\dfrac{D+T}{R}\left(1+\dfrac{D}{C}\right)}{\dfrac{D+T}{R} + \dfrac{D}{C}\left(1+\dfrac{T}{D}\right)} \right\} \equiv m_1 . RM$

(6) $BM \equiv RM \left\{ \dfrac{\dfrac{D+T}{R}\left[1+\dfrac{D}{C}\left(1+\dfrac{T}{D}\right)\right]}{\dfrac{D+T}{R} + \dfrac{D}{C}\left(1+\dfrac{T}{D}\right)} \right\} \equiv m_2 . RM$

In this framework the money multiplier is a function of the ratios of demand deposits to currency, (D/C), of quasi-money to demand deposits,

(T/D) and of total deposits to reserves, $(D+T)/R$. We can, therefore, analyse the changes in money multipliers, m_1 and m_2, by analysing their components. In the absence of a comprehensive model of the banking sector in Indonesia and adequate statistics, it is difficult to analyse the variations in the ratio of total deposits to reserves $(D+T/R)$. The ratio is therefore treated as an exogenous variable determined by the banking sector. It should be noted, however, that an increase in the (T/D) ratio would increase the $(D+T/R)$ ratio since the reserve requirements on quasi-money are less than the reserve requirements on demand deposits. The (T/D) and (D/C) ratios are determined as the public shifts its monetary assets between currency, demand deposits and quasi-money according to its preference and the relative attractiveness of these assets. It is, therefore, crucial to study the portfolio preference of the public for these various assets.

It is to be expected that the income elasticity of demand for quasi-money would be higher than the income elasticity of demand deposits, which in turn would be higher than the income elasticity of demand for currency. That is, as income rises, the public would use more checks for transaction purposes, increasing its desired demand deposit-currency ratio. Also, as income rises, from low levels as in Indonesia, savings may be expected to rise more than proportionally. Since in Indonesia savings are held mostly in time and savings deposits, the desired ratio of quasi-money to demand deposits would rise along with the rise in real income. Another factor contributing to variations in the desired ratio of quasi-money to demand deposits is the interest paid on time and savings deposits. As it increases, the public would shift its portfolio in favour of quasi-money. The desired ratio of demand deposits to currency, denoted by $(D/C)^D$, and the desired ratio of quasi-money to demand deposits, denoted by $(T/D)^D$, can then be written in the following log-linear form where r denotes the rate of interest paid on savings and time deposits.

(7) $$\log (D/C)^D = d_0 + d_1 \log (Y)$$

(8) $$\log (T/D)^D = e_0 + e_1 \log (Y) + e_2 \log (r)$$

Assuming that the public adjusts its ratio of demand deposits to currency and of quasi-money to demand deposits to the desired levels according to a partial adjustment mechanism similar to the demand for real balances (equation (1)), the following estimable equation can be derived, where ϕ and γ denote the partial adjustment coefficients for (D/C) and (T/D) respectively.

(9) $$\log (D/C)_t = d_0\phi + d_1\phi \log (Y) + (1-\phi) \log (D/C)_{t-1}$$

(10) $$\log (T/D)_t = e_0\gamma + e_1\gamma \log (Y) + e_2\gamma \log (r) + (1-\gamma) \log (T/D)_{t-1}$$

Identities (5) and (6) can be utilised to determine the relative importance of contributions of the money multiplier and reserve money to changes in the money supply. A study of the data for the period 1968:1 to 1973:4 reveals that 99 per cent of change in narrow money and 87 per cent of changes in broad money can be attributed to changes in reserve money.

Changes in the money multiplier hardly contributed to changes in narrow money and only marginally to changes in broad money. This does not imply that there were no variations in the components of the money multiplier; as can be seen from Charts 7, 8 and 9, $(D+T/R)$ and the (T/D) ratio both rose with a trend over the period 1968–71 before stabilising over the last few years, while the (D/C) ratio rose with a small trend over the entire period. Changes in the (D/C), (T/D) and $(D+T/R)$ ratios, however, did not affect the average and marginal multiplier for narrow money appreciably, as can be seen from Chart 10. The average multiplier for broad money rose over this period but the marginal multiplier remained relatively stable.

Since changes in reserve money were the main factor responsible for changes in money supply, an alternative formulation of money supply is developed where the marginal money multiplier is assumed to remain stable over time. Assume that an increase in reserve money in period t will increase the money supply by $m_1 k$ in the first period and the effect will diminish in subsequent periods according to the following geometric lag structure, where M denotes the stock of narrow or broad money.

$$(11) \qquad M_t = m_0 + m_1 k \sum_{i=0}^{\infty} (1-k)^i \, RM_{t-i}; \; 0 < k < 1$$

Using a Koyck transformation, we derive the following equation to be estimated for narrow as well as broad definitions of money.

$$(12) \qquad M_t = m_0 k + m_1 k \, RM_t + (1-k) M_{t-1}$$

The above equation can be utilised as an alternative formulation to estimate the supply of narrow and broad money. In so far as the money multiplier continues to behave in a stable fashion, this simpler formulation would be preferable for projection purposes. In this framework, changes in money supply are projected by the changes in reserve money. Changes in reserve money are, in turn, linked to government monetary policy, budgetary policy and the private sector's balance of payments according to the following identity.

$$(13) \qquad \Delta RM \equiv GDR - GDE + B.P. + \Delta CNG$$

where GDR = government domestic revenue
            GDE = government domestic expenditure
            $B.P.$ = private sector's balance of payments
           ΔCNG = changes in central bank credit to non-government sector

In the following sections government domestic revenue and the private sector's balance of payments will be explained while government expenditure and changes in credit to the non-government sector are treated as exogenous policy instruments.

IV. GOVERNMENT BUDGET

For the decade prior to 1968 Indonesia was experiencing very high rates of inflation, which were generated by the government's budgetary policy. During that period the authorities engaged in substantial deficit financing in order to close the gap between government expenditure and revenue. The excessive creation of money induced higher prices leading to an increase in government expenditure. Since government revenues lagged substantially behind price developments, the authorities were forced to finance larger deficits by further creation of money. This self-perpetuating process of inflation soon reached the hyper-inflation stage in 1966.[6] After the overthrow of the Sukarno government, the new authorities introduced a vigorous stabilisation programme in late 1966 and were able to bring down inflation to an acceptable rate by 1968. Since then Indonesian budgetary policy has been geared to a balanced budget criterion. The authorities have adhered to this principle by eliminating overall budget imbalances on an annual basis. Since a large portion of government revenue in recent years has been from foreign sources (i.e. tax on oil corporations and foreign aid and loans), however, the balanced budget policy has still resulted in substantial increases in reserve money. To the extent that the government budget affects the monetary sector, it is the domestic deficit that is relevant, the domestic deficit being defined as the excess of domestic expenditures over domestic revenue.

The 'balanced budget policy' of the Indonesian authorities can be written as the following relationship, where GFR and GFE denote government's foreign revenue and expenditure, respectively.

$$(14) \qquad GDE - GDR = GFR - GFE$$

In this framework, government foreign revenue, GFR, is determined exogenously to the system. Moreover, there are no reliable data available for the breakdown of total government expenditure into domestic and foreign categories. We will therefore estimate only government domestic revenue for which data are available.

Government domestic revenue is composed of direct and indirect taxes on domestic residents. Clearly, the level of income is the most important factor determining revenues, although they are also dependent to some extent on the targets set by the authorities. Due to the lag involved in the assessment of certain taxes and a heavy dependence on foreign trade, however, nominal taxes are slow in responding to a rise in the price level. That is, as long as taxes are based on previous price levels, high rates of inflation will reduce the government domestic revenue, once the effect of the rise in nominal income is taken into account. In the following equation, government domestic revenue is specified as a log-linear function of nominal income and the rate of inflation.

$$(15) \qquad \log(GDR) = g_0 + g_1 \log(YP) + g_2\pi; \, g_2 < 0 < g_1$$

V. BALANCE OF PAYMENTS

The balance of payments comprises imports, non-oil exports, oil exports and the balance of payments on capital account. In this section, oil exports and the balance on capital account are regarded as exogenous, and only imports and non-oil exports are estimated econometrically. Import and export (excluding oil) prices are determined in the world markets and are treated as exogenous variables. Indonesia's foreign trade is relatively free of restrictions. Therefore, it can be assumed that at given world prices exports are determined by supply conditions, whereas imports are determined by demand conditions. In order to carry out the analysis on a macro level, both import and export functions are estimated in aggregated form.

The fraction of Indonesia's output which is exported can be written as a function of export prices relative to domestic prices and income. That is, as the relative price of exports rises, it becomes more profitable to divert production from domestic to foreign markets. The income coefficient, x_2, could be positive or negative, depending on the income elasticity of domestic demand for exportable goods. If the domestic demand for exportables rises more (less) than proportionally as income rises, x_2 will be negative (positive) and less (more) of the output will be exported. Let X and P_x denote the volume and price of exports. We can then write the following supply equation:

$$(16) \qquad \log(XP_x/YP) = x_0 + x_1 \log(P_x/P) + x_2 \log(YP)$$

The above equation is solved for the value of exports, XP_x, and rewritten as follows:

$$(17) \qquad \log(XP_x) = x_0 + x_1 \log(P_x/P) + (1 + x_2) \log(YP)$$

The demand for imports is a function of total demand for goods and services and the price of imports relative to domestic prices. The level of income can be used as a proxy for total demand. Real imports, Z, as a fraction of real income, Y, can then be written as a function of real income, Y, and the ratio of import prices, P_z, to domestic prices, P, as follows:

$$(18) \qquad \log(Z/Y) = z_0 + z_1 \log(Y) + z_2 \log(P_z/P)$$

The coefficient z_2 is negative whereas the coefficient z_1 could be positive or negative depending on income elasticity of demand for imported goods. Since imported goods generally tend to have a larger income elasticity than domestically produced goods, it would be expected that the coefficient z_1 be positive. Equation (18) can be written in the following form for estimation purposes.

$$(19) \qquad \log(Z) = z_0 + (1 + z_1) \log(Y) + z_2 \log(P_z/P)$$

VI. COMPLETE MODEL OF THE MONETARY SECTOR

In this section the complete model of the monetary sector is stated and estimated. The model comprises the following relationships which were developed in the previous sections.

Demand for real balances
Narrow money

$$(20a) \quad \log(NM/P)_t = a_0\lambda + a_1\lambda \log(Y)_t + a_2\lambda\pi_t + a_3\lambda \log(r)_t +$$
$$(1-\lambda)\log(NM/P)_{t-1}; \ a_1 > 0 > a_2, a_3; \ 1 > \lambda > 0$$

Broad money

$$(20b) \quad \log(BM/P)_t = a_0\lambda + a_1\lambda \log(Y)_t + a_2\lambda\pi_t + a_3\lambda \log(r)_t +$$
$$(1-\lambda)\log(BM/P)_{t-1}; \ a_1, a_3 > 0 > a_2; \ 1 > \lambda > 0$$

Balance of payments
Non-oil exports

(21) $\log(XP_x)_t = x_0 + (1+x_1)\log(YP)_t + x_2\log(P_x/P)_t;\ x_2,\ x_2 > 0$

Imports

(22) $\log(Z)_t = z_0 + (1+z_1)\log(Y)_t + z_2\log(P_z/P)_t;\ z_1 > 0 > z_2$

Government domestic revenue

(23) $\log(GDR)_t = g_0 + g_1\log(YP)_t + g_2\pi_t;\ g_1 > 0 > g_2$

Supply of money (Formulation I)
Narrow money—reserve money identity

(24a) $NM \equiv RM \left\{ \dfrac{\dfrac{D+T}{R}\left(1+\dfrac{D}{C}\right)}{\dfrac{D+T}{R}+\dfrac{D}{C}\left(1+\dfrac{T}{D}\right)} \right\}$

Broad money—reserve money identity

(24b) $BM \equiv RM \left\{ \dfrac{\dfrac{D+T}{R}\left[1+\dfrac{D}{C}\left(1+\dfrac{T}{D}\right)\right]}{\dfrac{D+T}{R}+\dfrac{D}{C}\left(1+\dfrac{T}{D}\right)} \right\}$

Ratio of demand deposits to currency

(25) $\log(D/C)_t = d_0\phi + d_1\phi\log(Y)_t + (1-\phi)\log(D/C)_{t-1};$
$$d_1 > 0;\ 1 > \phi > 0$$

Ratio of quasi-money to demand deposits

(26) $\log(T/D)_t = e_0\gamma + e_1\gamma\log(Y)_t + e_2\gamma\log(r)_t + (1-\gamma)\log(T/D)_{t-1};$
$$e_1,\ e_2 > 0;\ 1 > \gamma > 0$$

Supply of money (Formulation II)
Narrow money

(27a) $NM_t = m_0 k + m_1 k\,RM_t + (1-k)\,NM_{t-1}$

Broad money $m_1 > 0;\ 1 > k > 0$

(27b) $BM_t = m_0 k + m_1 k\,RM_t + (1-k)\,BM_{t-1}$

Reserve money identity
(28) $RM_t \equiv XP_x - ZP_z - GDR + H$
                     where
                     $H \equiv GDE + \Delta NCG$

The variables are defined below:

Endogenous variables
    NM = stock of narrow money
    BM = stock of broad money

YP = level of nominal income
P = level of prices
π = rate of inflation
XP_x = non-oil exports in nominal terms
ZP_z = imports in nominal terms
Z = imports in real terms (nominal imports deflated by import prices)
GDR = government domestic revenue
D/C = ratio of demand deposits to currency
T/D = ratio of quasi-money to demand deposits
RM = reserve money

Exogenous variables
Y = real income ($Y = YP/P$)
P_x = export price index
P_z = import price index
r = rate of interest paid on time and savings deposits
H = residual term in the reserve money identity composed of government domestic expenditure, GDE, and changes in credit to non-government sector, ΔNCG
All lagged variables.

DIAGRAM 1

FLOW DIAGRAM OF THE MONETARY SECTOR

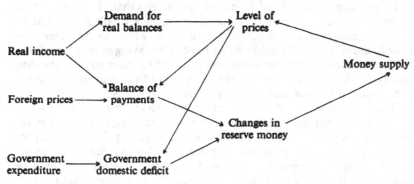

In order to demonstrate the workings of the model, the main characteristics of the system are represented in a flow diagram (Diagram 1). For expository purposes, consider a rise in government expenditure financed by the creation of reserve money. Assuming that the (D/C), (T/D) and $(D+T/R)$ ratios remain relatively stable, this will result in a rise in money supply. To the extent that the rise in money supply exceeds the rise in the demand for money, prices will rise and reduce real balances to the desired level. Clearly, changes in prices and nominal income will also affect the balance of payments and government domestic revenues. The system will adjust simultaneously in order to bring about a monetary equilibrium.

The above simultaneous system is linear in parameters but non-linear

in endogenous variables. It can be shown that estimation by the method
of two-stage least squares will provide us with consistent estimators for
the parameters of the system.[7] The estimation results are given in Table 1
where the ratio of coefficients to standard errors are given in parenthesis
underneath the coefficients.

The demand for real balances is a stable function of real income, the
inflation rate and lagged real balances for narrow as well as for broad
definitions of money. It is difficult to choose between the two specifications
of demand for real balances on the basis of the fit of the equations since
the $\bar{R}^2$ coefficient is 0·99 for both definitions of money supply. All of the
coefficients were significant at 0·05 confidence level except the interest
elasticity which was insignificant. The interest rate variable was eliminated
since its exclusion did not change the other coefficients appreciably.

The short-run income elasticity of narrow money is 0·67 which exceeds
the short-run income elasticity of broad money which is 0·49. This reflects
the fact that the partial adjustment coefficient of narrow money (i.e.
$\lambda = 0·31$) exceeds the partial adjustment coefficient of broad money
(i.e. $\lambda = 0·21$) implying that adjustments in real balances due to a rise
in income will, in the short run, be reflected in holdings of narrow money
to a greater extent than in holdings of quasi-money. Long run income
elasticities of demand for real balances for narrow and broad money can
be calculated from the short-run income elasticities and partial adjustment
coefficients.[8] The value of long-run income elasticity for narrow and broad
definitions of money are 2·18 and 2·29, respectively. As expected, the
long-run income elasticity of broad money exceeds that of narrow money
but by a very small margin. Both of these values are rather high but by
no means unusual for a developing country in which in the absence of
other financial assets, the public holds most of its saving in monetary form,
and in which, moreover, the monetised sector of the economy is expanding
rapidly. In the absence of an independent proxy to capture the monetisation effect, the income elasticity will be biased upwards.[9]

The supply elasticity of exports with respect to income is close to unity,
which implies that the export sector grows in the same proportion as the
rest of the economy. The coefficient of the relative price term (i.e. the
ratio of export prices to domestic prices) is also significant, indicating
that the supply of exports is responsive to price changes. It should be
pointed out that both price indexes for exports and imports are not very
reliable. The income elasticities of imports are well above unity, indicating
that the demand for imports rises more than proportionally as income rises.

The income elasticity of government domestic revenue exceeds unity
which implies that as income rises these revenues rise more than proportionally. The coefficient of inflation is negative and significant implying
that higher rates of inflation reduce the real value of domestic revenues,
as expected.

The rise in the ratio of demand deposits to currency and quasi-money
to demand deposits is explained mostly by the rise in real income and the
lagged endogenous variables. The coefficient of interest rate paid on time
and savings deposits is significant indicating that this variable had a
pronounced impact on the determination of the (T/D) ratio. Both (D/C)

TABLE 1

INDONESIA: ESTIMATION RESULTS, 1968:1 TO 1973:4[a]

Equation	Endogenous variable	Constant	Lagged endogenous	Log (r)	Log (Y)	Log (YP)	Log (P_x/P)	Log (P_m/P)	π	RM	R^2
(20a)	Log (NM/P)	−0·459 (3·2)	0·690 (9·7)	b	0·675 (3·3)				−0·570 (4·4)		0·99
(20b)	Log (BM/P)	−0·213 (1·8)	0·788 (13·4)	b	0·486 (2·3)				−0·798 (6·0)		0·99
(21)	Log (XP_x)	−3·280 (3·5)				1·127 (8·8)	0·846 (4·7)				0·96
(22)	Log (Z)	−2·697 (10·4)			2·317 (6·5)	2·317 (6·5)		−1·107 (3·3)			0·67
(23)	Log (GDR)	−0·480 (12)			1·325 (23·0)				−0·485 (2·2)		0·96
(25)	Log (D/C)	−0·390 (3·2)	0·410 (2·4)		0·460 (3·2)						0·85
(26)	Log (T/D)	−0·740 (2·6)	0·810 (12·5)	0·190 (2·9)	0·410 (1·6)						0·97
(27a)	NM	−2·332 (0·7)	0·463 (5·9)							0·705 (8·01)	0·99
(27b)	BM	−35·156 (3·9)	0·422 (4·4)							1·189 (6·9)	0·99

[a] Due to lack of adequate data, imports in real terms (equation (4)) were estimated for the period 1968:1 to 1973:2. The values in parenthesis are the ratio of coefficient to standard errors. All of the coefficients are at least significant at 0·025 except the coefficient of real income in equation (26) which is significant at 0·075 confidence level. For sources of data see Statistical Annex.

b The interest elasticity of this equation was not significantly different from zero. The exclusion of the interest rate variable does not affect the results appreciably.

and (T/D) ratios will affect the money multiplier through the identities (24a) and (24b) according to the first formulation of the money supply. Assuming a stable money multiplier, however, the supply of money for narrow and broad categories is estimated in equations (27a) and (27b) based on the second formulation of money supply. As the results indicate, the constant term for narrow money is not significantly different from zero which implies that the average as well as the marginal multiplier remained constant over this period. The constant term in the broad money equation, however, is negative and significant, implying that the marginal multiplier remained relatively constant while the average multiplier rose over the period. The rise in the average money multiplier for broad money is due to the rise in (D/C), (T/D) and $(D+T/R)$ ratios, since all of these ratios affect the money multiplier given in identity (24b) in a positive fashion. On the other hand, the rise in the (T/D) ratio decreases the money multiplier for narrow money and counteracts the effects of the rise in the (D/C) and $(D+T/R)$ ratios, leading to a stable average as well as marginal multiplier for narrow money.[10]

The above estimation results can be used to make projections for the appropriate rates of growth of money supply. Given target rates of growth of real income and prices, the model will provide us with a rough estimate of the level of money stock which will not result in excess demand for or supply of money. The model of the monetary sector developed in this paper is highly aggregated and the data used for estimation is not fully reliable. Moreover, any forecasting of the endogenous variables will depend on the future behaviour of the exogenous variables which cannot be predicted accurately. Hence, the projection results should be regarded only as a rough guide for policy-making to be used in conjunction with other available information. Based on the past performance of the economy, it is assumed for illustrative purposes that real income will grow at an annual rate of 7 per cent. Hypothetical target rates of inflation are given in Table 2. It should be emphasised that these rates are only rough estimates and not predictions with any degree of certainty. The appropriate levels and rates of growth of narrow and broad money are calculated on the basis of the parameters of equations (20a) and (20b).

As the results in Table 2 indicate, the long-run rate of growth of reserve money, narrow money and broad money consistent with 7 per cent real growth and 18 per cent inflation is around 30 per cent. The model utilised for projection is basically a short-term model and it should be updated as new observations become available. Since the model is estimated only for a period of six years, it cannot be expected that forecasts for periods longer than a year would be accurate at all.

It should be noted that the above projected growth rates of monetary variables are rather high. This is mainly due to high long-run income elasticity of demand for real balances. As was pointed out previously, the high income elasticity could be attributed partially to monetisation of the economy. To the extent that monetisation will not take place in future as rapidly as it has done in the recent past (which was characterised by a marked stabilisation of prices, rehabilitation of productive activity and, therefore, by growing confidence), the estimated income elasticity would

TABLE 2

INDONESIA: PROJECTIONS OF MONETARY VARIABLES

	Actual 1974	Projected 1975
Real rate of growth[a]	7·7	7
Rate of inflation[a]	33	16
Stock of narrow money[b]	942	1,261
	(41)	(34)
Stock of broad money[b]	1,401	1,832
	(42)	(31)
Stock of reserve money[b]	750	980
	(39)	(31)

[a] Real rate of growth and inflation rates are hypothetical target values, expressed in percentage terms. Inflation rates are based on changes in the level of prices from the end of one year to the end of the following year. On the basis of annual averages, the corresponding rates of inflation for the above would be 40% and 18% respectively.

[b] Stock of narrow money, broad money, and reserve money are the projected stock at the end of the year in billions of rupiah. The numbers in parentheses indicate percentage growth rates.

be biased upwards. The above projections should therefore be viewed as upper bounds.

VII. CONCLUSION

In this paper a relatively simple model of Indonesia's monetary sector was developed and estimated using quarterly series for the period 1968:1 to 1973:4. The model performed two functions. Firstly, we were able to analyse the behaviour of key economic variables for the past six years. As the graphs of fitted and actual values of endogenous variables indicate, the model performed very well in this regard. Secondly, the results of the model were used to make projections for the appropriate rates of growth of narrow money, broad money and reserve money.

The model developed in this paper is a first attempt for Indonesia and the results should be treated with caution. As new data become available, the model can be improved and updated. Even at this stage, however, the model does provide us with independent estimates of monetary variables which can be used in conjunction with other available information for policy-making purposes. Moreover, the model will enable us to examine the internal consistency of monetary, budgetary and balance of payments policies.

STATISTICAL ANNEX

Data Sources and Definitions

The data used in this paper were obtained from the following sources:

A. *International Financial Statistics*, International Monetary Fund, Washington, D.C.

B. *Indonesian Financial Statistics*, Bank Indonesia, Jakarta
C. *Indikator Ekonomi, Monthly Statistical Bulletin*, Biro Pusat Statistic, Jakarta

The data in the above sources is frequently revised by the Indonesian authorities (IA). Where available, the most recently revised series were used. A list of variables and their definition is given below.

The following variables are given in billions of current rupiahs:

C = currency, Source B and IA
D = demand deposits, Source B and IA
QM = quasi-money (sum of time, savings and foreign exchange deposits), Source B and IA
$NM = C+D$ = narrow money, Source B and IA
$BM = NM+QM$ = broad money, Source B and IA
RM = reserve money, Source B and IA
GR = government revenue (total), Source B and IA
GDR = government domestic revenue, Source B and IA
GE = government expenditure (total), Source B and IA
YP = nominal income (gross domestic product)

The national income series are the only series used in this paper which are not available on a quarterly basis. Consequently, the nominal income series is derived by first taking a linear interpolation of the annual series for real income subject to the condition that their sum for each year should add to the corresponding annual value.[11] The quarterly real income series were then inflated by the Jakarta cost of living index (P), subject to the condition that the sum of quarterly values for nominal income add up to corresponding annual value. Jakarta cost of living index was used since the series is available on a quarterly basis whereas GNP deflator is available only on an annual basis. This should not affect the result, however, since the two price series, namely, Jakarta cost of living and GNP deflator move in a parallel fashion.[12]

XP_x = nominal non-oil exports, Source A and C
ZP_z = nominal imports, Source A and C

The following definitions are given for various price variables:

P = Jakarta cost of living index (September 1966 = 100), Source B and IA
r = rate of interest paid on deposits with maturity of one year or more expressed on annual basis in percentage terms
ER = exchange rate, expressed in terms of number of rupiahs per \$US1
P'_x, P'_z = index of export and import prices in U.S. dollars (1970:1 = 100). These series were calculated based on a value weighted index of non-oil exports and imports. The value and volume of exports and imports for different categories were obtained from Source C.
P_x, P_z = index of export and import prices in rupiahs. These series were calculated based on the following relationships:

$$P_x = ER.P'_x$$
$$P_z = ER.P'_z$$

NOTES
1. Highly aggregated models of this type have been successfully constructed for a number of countries. See for instance Aghevli [*1975*], Aghevli and Khan [*1976*], Khan [*1975*] and Otani and Park [*1976*].

2. For earlier studies regarding the relationship between money and prices in Indonesia see H. W. Arndt, J. Gurley, and R. M. Sundrum and G. L. Hicks.

3. For a thorough survey of the theoretical and empirical issues relevant to the demand for money see John H. Boorman [*1972*].

4. The expected inflation rate can be generated for a range of values for a. The appropriate a can then be chosen according to the criterion of maximising the likelihood function. The maximum likelihood value of a was between 0·9 and 1, implying an almost instantaneous adjustment of the public's price expectations. This high value of a could be partially due to the fact that Indonesia had undergone a period of very rapid inflation from 1960 to 1968, and the public was over-compensating in its expectations of inflation based on its previous experience.

5. We can write the following identities:

    (a) $NM = C + D$
    (b) $BM = C + D + T$
    (c) $RM = R + C$

Dividing (a) and (b) by (c) and manipulating results in equations (5) and (6) in the text.

6. For a dynamic analysis of this self-perpetuating process of hyper-inflation in Indonesia see Aghevli and Khan [*1977*].

7. See H. H. Kelijian [*1971*].

8. Long-run income elasticity, a_1, is calculated by dividing the short-run income elasticity, $a_1\lambda$, by the partial adjustment coefficient, λ.

9. It should be noted that the price stability of the late sixties after a period of very high inflation could have contributed to the relatively high income elasticity of money. That is as the public's confidence was restored, they started to hold most of their savings in monetary form. A closer analysis of the data suggests, however that even in mid-seventies, the value of income elasticity did not change, suggesting that the economy is still experiencing rapid monetisation.

10. In order to verify the effects of (D/C), (T/D) and (D+T)/R ratios, the derivatives of identities (24a) and (24b) can be taken with respect to the above ratios. It can easily be established that

$$\frac{dm_1}{d(D/C)} > 0 \qquad\qquad \frac{dm_2}{d(D/C)} > 0$$

$$\frac{dm_1}{d(T/D)} < 0 \qquad\qquad \frac{dm_2}{d(T/D)} > 0$$

$$\frac{dm_1}{d(D+T)/R} > 0 \qquad\qquad \frac{dm_2}{d(D+T)/R} > 0$$

11. For a description of this method see Diz [*1970*].

12. It should be noted that the construction of GNP price deflator is, to a large extent, based on the Jakarta cost of living index. It is not therefore surprising that the above two price variables move parallel to each other.

REFERENCES

Aghevli, B. B., 1975, 'The Balance of Payments and Money Supply Under the Gold Standard Regime: U.S. 1879–1914', *American Economic Review*, March.

Aghevli, B. B. and Khan, M. S., 1976, 'Credit Policy, Price and Output in Developing Countries', paper presented at the Conference on 'Macroeconomic Policy and Adjustment in Open Economies' at Ware, England, April 28–May 1, 1976.

Aghevli, B. B. and Khan, M. S., 1977, 'Inflationary Finance and the Dynamics of Inflation: Indonesia 1951–1972', *American Economic Review*, June.

Arndt, H. W., 1965, 'Banking in Hyperinflation', *Bulletin of Indonesian Economic Studies*, October.

Boorman, J. H., 1972, 'The Evidence on Demand for Money, Theoretical Formulation and Empirical Results', in *Money Supply, Money Demand, and Macroeconomic Policy*, edited by Boorman, J. H. and Havrilesky, T. M., Boston.

Diz, Adolfo C., 1970, 'Money and Prices in Argentina, 1935–62', in D. Meiselman, ed., *Varieties of Monetary Experience*, Chicago: University of Chicago Press.

Gurley, J., 1969, 'Notes on the Indonesian Financial System', mimeo, Jakarta, September.

Hicks, G. L., 1967, 'The Indonesian Inflation', *The Philippine Economic Journal*, second semester.

Kelijian, H. H., 1971, 'Two-Stage Least Squares and Econometric System Linear in Parameters but Non-linear in Endogenous Variables', *Journal of American Statistical Association*, June.

Khan, M. S., forthcoming, 'A Monetary Model of Balance of Payments: The Case of Venezuela', *Journal of Monetary Economics*.

Metzler, A. H., 1963, 'The Demand for Money, The Evidence from the Time Series', *Journal of Political Economy*, June.

Otani, I. and Park, Y. C., 1976, 'A Monetary Model of the Korean Economy', *IMF Staff Papers*, March.

Sundrum, R. M., 1973, 'Money Supply and Prices—A Reinterpretation', *Bulletin of Indonesian Economic Studies*, November.

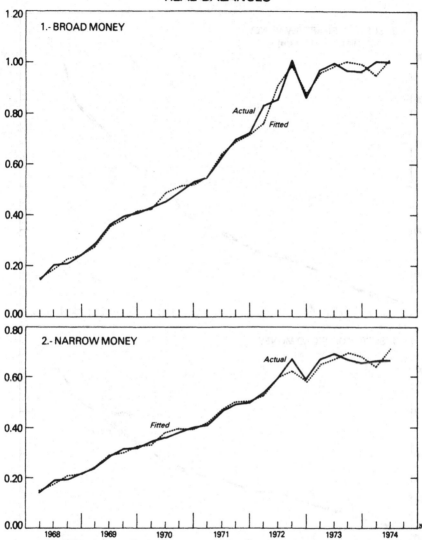

INDONESIA
REAL BALANCES

INDONESIA
MONEY SUPPLY

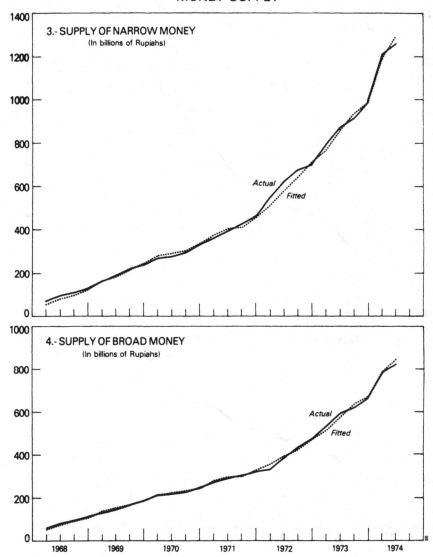

INDONESIA

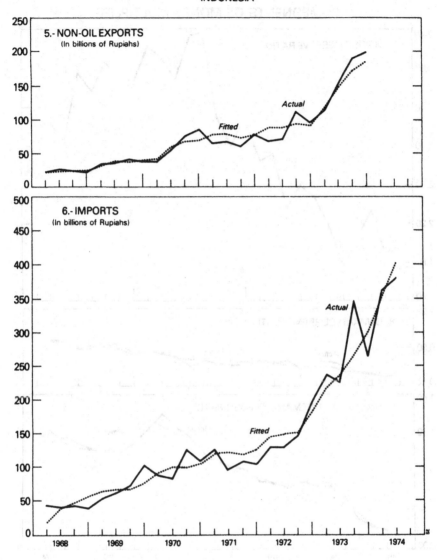

5.- NON-OIL EXPORTS
(In billions of Rupiahs)

Fitted

Actual

6.- IMPORTS
(In billions of Rupiahs)

Actual

Fitted

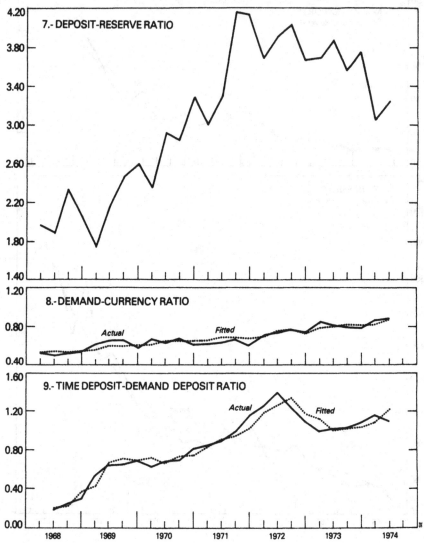

INDONESIA
COMPONENTS OF MONEY MULTIPLIER

INDONESIA

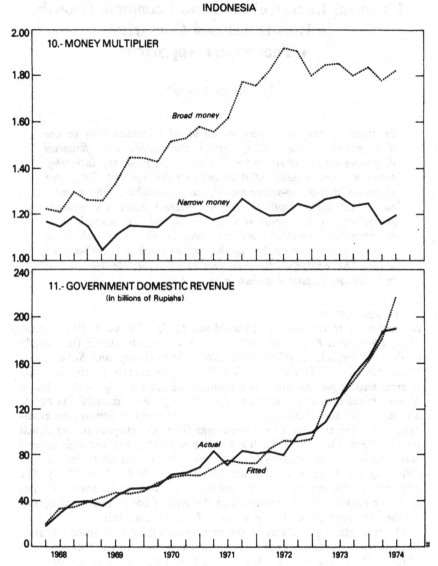

10.- MONEY MULTIPLIER

Broad money

Narrow money

11.- GOVERNMENT DOMESTIC REVENUE
(In billions of Rupiahs)

Actual

Fitted

1968   1969   1970   1971   1972   1973   1974

Financial Intermediation and Economic Growth in Less-Developed Countries: A Theoretical Approach

by Vicente Galbis*

In stressing the importance of financial intermediation in the development of the LDCs, neither the approach of financial deepening nor that of real interest rates has clarified the relationship between financial intermediation and real development. This paper shows—within a two-sector model, but extendable to the n-sector case—that high (equilibrium) real interest rates are growth-promoting, even if total real savings is interest insensitive (a controversial empirical question), because they bring about an improvement in the quality *of the capital stock in a well-defined sense. The analysis also has implications for the theories of inflation and income distribution in the LDCs.*

1. INTRODUCTION

A number of recent writings [*Khatkhate, 1972; McKinnon, 1973; Shaw, 1973; Bhatia and Khatkhate, 1975*] have attempted to clarify the already established hypothesis [*Goldsmith, 1966, 1969; Gurley and Shaw, 1955, 1960; Patrick, 1966; Porter, 1966*] that improvements in the financial intermediation process are a precondition of economic growth. What is at issue is the development at an appropriate pace of financial savings as an alternative to consumption and to reinvestment in low-return enterprises, and the transfer of those savings from the surplus to the deficit sectors [*Khatkhate, 1972*]. Such a transfer appears to call for high interest rate policies as opposed to low interest rates to stimulate investment, following the Keynesian tradition [*McKinnon, 1973; Shaw, 1973*]. The emphasis of the theory of development in the context of the LDCs has therefore switched from concern with the lack of basic investment opportunities, to emphasis on the removal of financial constraints.

The theoretical postulates of the new approach rest on some 'stylised' facts, to use a Kaldorian expression, concerning the nature of the economies of the LDCs [*McKinnon, 1973, Chapters 1–3*]. First, developing economies are fragmented economies where the co-existence of old and modern technologies with strikingly different degrees of efficiency in using scarce physical and human resources result in enormously wide disparities in the rates of return to different investments. It makes therefore little sense in

* The author would particularly like to thank Prof. John Williamson, Warwick University (England) and Messrs. Deena R. Khatkhate and Delano P. Villanueva for their helpful suggestions on an earlier draft of this paper. However, they are absolved of any responsibility for remaining errors. The views expressed here do not necessarily represent those of the International Monetary Fund.

these economies to talk about an aggregate production function and uniform inputs; the spirit of the Cambridge school acquires particular relevance in the fragmented developing economy. Secondly, an important property of a large number of the more modern production processes is that they require comparatively large lump-sum investments so that indivisibilities in physical capital become an important element to be reckoned with in the process of development. These two facts concern properties of production processes.

A third element in the picture is the importance of self-financing of investment. Financial intermediation is in a rudimentary state, imposing serious financial constraints on external investment in new technologies which yield high rates of return, while investment proceeds in the older, self-financed sectors which yield low rates of return. It follows that improvements in the process of financial intermediation which tend to shift financial and real resources from the older low-yield investments to the new investments are likely to result in a dramatic acceleration in the overall rate of economic growth. Naturally, some costs will have to be incurred in the process, as development of the financial system is not a costless endeavour. However, it may well be that financial development is a prerequisite, if not a major determinant, of the take-off into self-sustained economic growth.

Finally, the role played by most governments in LDCs needs to be taken into account. In general, this has not been encouraging at all as a proliferation of regulations based on misguided principles has contributed significantly to the malfunctioning of the financial system and, to the inefficient use of real resources. Take for instance the widespread practice of regulating interest rates which credit institutions may pay for their deposit liabilities, which has resulted in very low rates being paid in the official markets, with the notable exceptions of Taiwan and South Korea. This has generally led (i) to a widening of the existing gap between the demand for and the supply of funds, thereby contributing to open or repressed inflation and (ii) to the perpetuation of an unofficial non-institutionalised financial market, itself a symbol of the segmentation of the economy.

Disparities in rates of return on different assets are not the exclusive property of LDCs. Technological advances even in today's more developed countries offer a more or less temporary advantage to those innovators who introduce them into the production process. So far as a country's economy shows signs of intense dynamism, such disparities may not only be unavoidable but necessary to fuel the entrepreneurial dynamism which characterises the process of economic growth [*Schumpeter, 1911*]. What is at issue in the case of developing economies, however, is the inability to profit from technological advance because of the constraints imposed by the nature of the financial processes.

This paper investigates the nature of the financial constraint in the fragmented developing economy. The analysis is simplified by assuming that the economy consists of two kinds of productive units which operate with quite different technological processes (and hence different real returns) and are subject to different financial constraints. Reality is undoubtedly much more complicated. However, the theoretical framework of this paper is sufficient to derive some important conclusions with regard to the influence of financial intermediation on the process of economic growth.[1]

Section 2 specifies a two-sector model of capital intermediation in a fragmented developing economy and discusses its basic properties. Section 3 discusses the effects of interest rate fixing on the efficiency of investment outlets, inflation, and the distribution of income. Finally, section 4 summarises the main conclusions and relates them to conditions in the LDCs.

2. A TWO-SECTOR MODEL OF FINANCIAL INTERMEDIATION AND GROWTH

The model specified below captures in an essential way the main elements of the fragmented developing economy. Two production sectors with widely disparate technologies are assumed to represent in aggregate form the 'average' technology within each of two sectors into which the economy can be broken down.[2] Sector 1 is the backward or less efficient sector. Sector 2 is the modern or technologically advanced sector. For simplicity, it is assumed that both sectors produce the same output which is sold at a uniform price. This has the advantage that it emphasises the importance of differences in technologies. Even though changes in the composition of the output are also concomitant to the process of development, the model here does not centre on this other aspect. The two sectors are also different in their financial behaviour, but this is more conveniently explained as the various pieces of the model are fitted together.

(a) Technological conditions

Following standard theory, the production functions of the two sectors are specified in general form as follows:

(1) $$Y_1 = F_1(K_1, L_1)$$

(2) $$Y_2 = F_2(K_2, L_2)$$

These are assumed to be continuous and twice differentiable. The functions F_1 and F_2 embody technological factors such as mechanically different production processes, economies of scale, and embodied human capital.

It is assumed for simplicity that competitive conditions exist in each sector in the sense that productive factors are paid according to their marginal productivities. These determine, for instance, the returns to capital as follows:

$$\partial Y_2 / \partial K_1 = r_1$$

$$\partial Y_2 / \partial K_2 = r_2$$

In this context, the assumption that sector 2 embodies a technology with higher rates of return to the production factors than that of sector 1 means:

(3) $$r_2 > r_1$$

Equation (3) is a fundamental empirical assertion concerning the wide disparity in technological efficiency in underdeveloped countries. Since F_1 and F_2 represent quite different technologies to produce the same physical output (meaning that a unit of Y_1 is identical to a unit of Y_2), the greater return to capital in sector 2 does not imply a smaller wage rate. On the contrary, it appears to be empirically demonstrable that technologies with higher rates of return to capital typically also embody higher returns to labour for the same capital–labour ratio. In other words, it is also an empirical assertion that $w_2 > w_1$.[3] Though this paper does not focus on the labour aspects of the fragmented economy, the significance of this assumption is clearly to reinforce any conclusions derived from the disparity between the rates of return to capital in the two sectors.

The empirical assertion concerning the disparity of technologies 1 and 2 can easily be translated into a proposition concerning the growth of income. Under the assumption that the factors of production are fully employed and that they are paid their marginal productivities, Euler's theorem ensures the following income determination equation:

$$(4) \qquad Y = Y_1 + Y_2 = r_1 K_1 + w_1 L_1 + r_2 K_2 + w_2 L_2.$$

Equation (4) can be used to describe the result of redistributing capital from the backward to the advanced technological sector. Under the assumption that capital is fully employed and is given (at any moment in time) $K = K_1 + K_2$. An increase in K_2 at the expense of K_1, leaving K constant, would imply a rise in Y, since this change in the structure of capital would be in favour of the higher capital returns (as $r_2 > r_1$) associated with K_2. This simple result provides the clue to understanding the efficiency aspects of an improvement in the allocative mechanisms of savings and investment.

The process of income growth can now be seen in this simple framework as one of growth of inputs and redistribution of the inputs toward the more advanced technologies, i.e. those technologies that provide for higher rates of return to the factors of production.

The growth of capital inputs is related to investment in capital goods. For simplicity it may be assumed that the rate of depreciation is zero. Then

$$(5) \qquad \dot{K}_1 = I_1$$

$$(6) \qquad \dot{K}_2 = I_2$$

(b) *Savings, investment and financial intermediation*
The basic aggregate expenditure identity within this model is as follows:

$$(7) \qquad Y = C + I = C_1 + C_2 + I_1 + I_2,$$

where $C = C_1 + C_2$ and $I = I_1 + I_2$.

The determinants of expenditures by sector 1 are first specified. As regards consumption, it is assumed for simplicity that it is a simple linear function of income:

$$(8) \qquad C_1 = c_1 Y_1; \; 0 < c_1 < 1$$

Savings is defined as the difference between income and consumption—a residuum—so that

$$S_1 = Y_1 - C_1 = (1 - c_1) Y_1 = s_1 Y_1$$

where $0 < s_1 = (1 - c_1) < 1$.

Thus the functions C_1 and S_1 are not independent and the equilibrium of the model can be discussed in terms of either of the two.

The decision to invest by members of sector 1—the backward sector, which is further characterised as being composed of small self-financing units with no access to borrowing in the capital market[4]—depends on two rates of return, namely, the real rate of return on their own investment and the real rate of return on available financial assets. For simplicity, it is assumed henceforth that the only available financial asset is a deposit with the commercial banks. Complications arising from the existence of a securities market would not alter the essence of the arguments nor the conclusions derived from the model as both forms of intermediation are essentially similai.[5] The investment function is as follows:

$$(9) \qquad I_1 = H_1(r_1, d - \dot{P}^*/P)Y_1;$$

$$\partial H_1/\partial r_1 > 0; \ \partial H_1/\partial (d - \dot{P}^*/P) < 0;$$

where d is the rate of interest on commercial bank deposits (assumed for simplicity to be the weighted average of all bank deposit rates) and $\dot{P}^*/P$ is the expected rate of inflation.

The assumption that sector 1 is a self-financed sector with no access to borrowing implies that $Y_1 > C_1 + I_1$, i.e. $I_1 < S_1$, since units in sector 1 can save in the form of bank deposits. Indeed, ex-post savings-investment must be related by the following identity:

$$(10) \qquad S_1 = I_1 + d(M_1/P)/dt$$

where $d(M_1/P)/dt$ is the accumulation of bank deposits in real terms by units in sector 1, or sector 1's real financial savings.

Identity (10) is the fundamental budget constraint of sector 1 and it means that the accumulation of financial savings by this sector is not independent of the consumption and investment decisions within that sector. This follows from Walras law.[6] Thus, for instance, a decrease in $(d - \dot{P}^*/P)$, which implies *ceteris paribus* an increase in I_1, means a smaller $d(M_1/P)/dt$ than it otherwise would have been. This completes the demand specifications for sector 1.

The consumption behaviour of individuals in sector 2 is assumed to be of the same simplistic type as in sector 1:

$$(11) \qquad C_2 = c_2 Y_2; \ 0 < c_2 < 1$$

This function explains real savings in sector 2 as a residual:

$$S_2 = Y_2 - C_2 = (1 - c_2)Y_2 = s_2 Y_2.$$

There are two sources of investable physical resources which may contribute to the growth of the capital stock in sector 2. First, there is its own non-consumed output, S_2. Second, there is the real physical counterpart of the increase in financial claims by units in sector 1, i.e. $d(M_1/P)/dt$, the difference between output in sector 1 and its own total absorption of physical resources for consumption and self-financed investment. In sum, the supply of investable resources in sector 2 is given by

$$(12) \qquad I_2^s = S_2 + d(M_1/P)/dt,$$

where S_2 is the non-consumed output from sector 2 and $d(M_1/P)/dt$ is the real value of the output produced but not used in sector 1.

The crucial question which arises now is whether the working of the economy can ensure that all these investable funds are effectively financed and invested by units in sector 2. Note first that, unlike in sector 1, units in sector 2 must invest their whole savings in the form of physical goods, thereby keeping no savings of their own in the form of financial assets. Moreover, if full utilisation of resources is to be maintained, sector 2 must also be able to invest the surplus of investable resources procured by sector 1. It therefore follows that sector 2 could neither finance the payment for the surplus of investable resources from sector 1 nor satisfy its complementary need for financial assets without recourse to bank credit.

Two separate but interrelated issues are thus distinguishable in the analysis of the determinants of equilibrium in the market for investable resources in sector 2. First there is the issue of the underlying technological characteristics of the economy which support the demand for investment. Second, there is the question of whether this basic demand is constrained, and in what way, by the financial characteristics of the economic environment.

As regards the first question, the technological conditions of the fragmented economy provide a clear-cut clue to the solution of the problem. It has been discussed earlier in this paper that real rates of return to capital in the technologically advanced sector can be exceedingly large. Moreover, they are not likely to be substantially reduced by even the largest amounts of investment, except in the very long run, i.e. when the economy becomes more mature. This is yet another way to state that the economy is starved for modern forms of capital and advanced technology. In these circumstances, it could not be expected that there will be a lack of basic demand for investment. On the contrary, one should expect that the demand for investable resources will largely exceed the supply. Nevertheless, a full understanding of this proposition also requires the specification of the financial constraints.

The decision to invest by units in sector 2 is not essentially different from that of units in sector 1; it is also based on the relative rates of return affecting this decision:

$$(13) \qquad I_2^D = H_2(r_2, b - \dot{P}^*/P) Y_2;$$

$$\partial H_2/\partial r_2 > 0; \quad \partial H_2/\partial(b - P^*/P) < 0;$$

where $b - \dot{P}^*/P$ is the real rate of interest on bank loans, a cost to investors who finance their investments by borrowing. What appears to be a crucial difference is that r_2 is rather large compared with $b - \dot{P}^*/P$, so that a substantial edge exists for investment in this sector. As noted above, it appears empirically useful to think of I_2^D as being vastly greater than I_2^S under the conditions prevailing in a fragmented economy where an entrepreneurial élite is already in place.

Another crucial difference regarding the demand for investment in sector 2 as compared with sector 1 is that its validation is subject to the availability of credit. As noted earlier, investors in sector 2 cannot satisfy their complementary demand for financial assets nor pay for their investment in excess of their own saving unless they have access to bank credit. Assume for simplicity that all their financial assets are required for transactions purposes alone. Then the following simple incremental demand for financial assets by individuals in sector 2 may be postulated:[7]

(14) $d(M_2/P)^D/dt = \gamma I_2^D$

The monetary authorities are assumed to control the incremental supply of money through the manipulation of the various policy instruments.

(15) $dM_2^s/dt = d\bar{M}_2^s/dt$

Now the role of financial intermediation and of monetary policy in the process of transferring real resources from the backward to the advanced sector can be analysed. It will be shown that various possible mechanisms of adjustment between the supply of and the demand for investment in modern technologies—and the failure or the success of monetary policy to do this within a stable financial environment—have crucially different implications for economic growth.

3. INFLATION, INCOME DISTRIBUTION AND GROWTH
Figure 1 pictures the market for investable resources in the technologically advanced sector in any given period. The kinked shape of the supply of investable resources is the result of the underlying assumptions of the model (equation (12)). Sector 2 invests at least its own surplus of physical resources since units in this sector cannot do better by putting it to alternative uses, namely, financial savings or investment in inferior technologies. This is represented by the intercept of the I_2^s curve with the horizontal axis, which is equal to S_2. The supply of investable resources from sector 1, on the other hand, depends crucially on the real rate of interest on financial savings as this represents an opportunity cost of self-investment in this sector. For simplicity it has been assumed in drawing Figure 1 that all savings of sector 1 are reinvested in that sector if the real rate of interest on financial savings is zero, and that no investment takes place in that sector if the real interest rate on financial savings rises to the level $(b - \dot{P}^*/P)_0$.[8] (The latter boundary results from the limitedness of yields on self-financed, backward types of investment.) No further increases in the supply of investable resources to sector 2 are possible, given the assumption that consumption behaviour is independent from the real rate of interest on financial assets and the return on physical investment. This simplifying assumption—which effectively implies that aggregate investment depends only on income and the distribution of income between the two sectors—could be altered to take into account the more

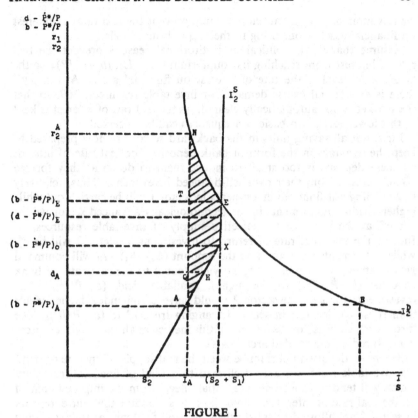

FIGURE 1

general case in which individuals respond to rises in the real rates of interest on financial savings by reducing their propensity to consume [*Porter, 1966: 350–51; McKinnon, 1973*]. If this were so (a controversial empirical question), the conclusions of the model would be reinforced.

The demand for investable resources in sector 2 is a marginal efficiency of investment curve representing the various desired volumes of investment in any given period which can be profitably undertaken at various rates of real borrowing costs. As borrowing costs increase, fewer firms can undertake profitable investments. Thus the curve has a negative slope. Its position is displaced to the right compared to that in Sector 1 as a result of the assumption that the 'average' rate of return in the technologically advanced sector is very high. Technological innovations tend to shift this curve to the right.

It will be observed that the technological assumptions underlying the model are not sufficient by themselves to undermine the existence of an equilibrium solution in the financial market. For an equilibrium, E, between the supply of and demand for investable resources is possible provided that the real cost of borrowing can rise to the level $(b - \dot{P}*/P)_E$. However, various circumstances—either legal, political or institutional, as

well as monetary mismanagement—may prevent the real rates of interest
on financial assets from rising to their equilibrium levels.

Assume that legal, political or institutional reasons prevent the real
rate of interest from reaching its equilibrium level. Let $(b - \dot{P}^*/P)_A$ be the
'acceptable' level of the rate of interest on financial assets. At this level
there is a potential excess demand for investable resources, AB, so that
the market is not automatically cleared. As the real rate of interest is kept
at this lower level, two basic consequences can be observed.

First, not all saving units in the backward sector are now prepared to
keep their savings in the form of bank deposits; the real rate of interest
on these deposits is too small to induce them to do so as they foresee
higher returns from their own self-financed investments. Thus, relatively
low-yielding self-financed investments in sector 1 will be carried out while
higher-yielding investments in the technologically advanced sector will be
cut off at the point of the effective supply of investable resources, A.
Indeed, the marginal rate of return to investment in sector 2 will be r_2^A,
while investments in sector 1 in the amount $(S_2 + S_1) - I_A$ will command
yields ranging from their marginal yield (equal to the real rate on bank
deposits, $(b - \dot{P}^*/P)_A$) to the highest available yield, $(b - \dot{P}^*/P)_0$. The
investments foregone in sector 2 would have commanded higher yields
than those carried out in sector 1, ranging from r_2^A to $(b - \dot{P}^*/P)_E$. The
'producer's surplus' lost as a result of this inefficient allocation of resources
is measured by the shaded area NAXE.

Secondly, the disequilibrium between the real supply of and the demand
for investable resources may itself lead to a kind of financial instability
which will tend to exacerbate the initial effects from the imposed control
on the real rate of interest on financial assets. Assume that entrepreneurs
in sector 2 are allowed to satisfy their demand for loans at the prevailing
borrowing cost. This means that with a price level of P at time t the
incremental supply of money dM_2^s/dt is such that it equals the effective
incremental demand for money $d(M_2/P)^d/dt$ which is provided by the
following relation:

(16) $(d(M_2/P)^d/dt)_A = \gamma H_2(r_2, (b - \dot{P}^*/P)_A) Y_2.$

A peculiar state of simultaneous real and financial disequilibria results
from this situation. On the financial side, the excess demand for loans is
translated into a pressure for the banks to raise their lending rates, but
this may be prevented for legal, political or institutional reasons.[9] On the
real side, the excess demand for investable resources tends to drive the
price level upward. To the extent that the upward pressure on lending
rates materialises—as it is also fuelled by inflation and the consequent
attempt of lenders to adjust to inflationary expectations—this tends to
ease the state of disequilibria. However, inflation aggravates directly the
potential disequilibria by reducing the *real* rates of interest on financial
assets. In the event, unless there is a credit restriction such that it brings
back the effective demand to the effective supply at the prevailing real
rate of interest on financial assets, the system will not by itself have a
tendency toward equilibrium. Resolution of the disequilibria will depend
on the upward flexibility of interest rates in response to the disequilibria

and the ability of the monetary authorities to effectively restrict the supply of credit.

It should be noted that, with an inflexible structure of interest rates, the kind of equilibrating credit restriction implied by the foregoing analysis is a system of credit rationing.[10] Assume that by denying a sufficient amount of loans to prospective borrowers at the prevailing real rate of interest on financial assets, $(b - \dot{P}^*/P)_A$, the banking system brings down the effective (i.e. credit-rationed) demand for investable resources to the level of the effective supply, I_A. Two consequences follow from this credit restriction. First, inflationary conditions are suppressed. Secondly, as $\dot{P}^*/P \to 0$ there is an increase in the real interest rate on financial assets. This results in an increase in the supply of investable resources to, say, H. At this new level of the supply of investable resources the authorities are required to ease correspondingly the initial tightening of the credit rationing measures to allow the effective demand for investable resources to reach the level of the expanded supply. If this action were delayed, the initial credit crunch would be followed by a period of under-utilisation of investable resources (in the amount QH), until the ease was established.

In the light of the above considerations it appears that credit rationing is in the nature of a second-best policy in a country with a rigid structure of interest rates on financial assets. Price level stability resulting from credit rationing ensures that real interest rates on financial assets are as high as they can be—given the restriction on nominal rates—with the consequent release of investable resources from the backward self-financed sectors of the economy. Optimal policy is, of course, to let interest rates rise to the level at which the supply of and demand for investable resources is equated, resulting in stability of the price level and making unnecessary the use of credit rationing devices. These propositions can be elucidated further by analysing the effects of interest rate restrictions on the distribution of income and economic growth.

Assume that starting from an initial equilibrium situation, at E, with no inflation and no credit rationing and with an equilibrium rate of interest on financial assets, a restriction is imposed on the interest rate at the level $(b - \dot{P}^*/P)_A = I_A A$. Assume also that an effective credit rationing system is simultaneously introduced so that an inflationary outbreak is avoided ($\dot{P}^*/P = 0$). For simplicity, assume that both before and after this change banks were forced to charge the same rate for their loans as they pay for their deposits. (Relaxation of this assumption is discussed below.) The effect of the interest rate and credit rationing restrictions is to reduce the volume of investable physical resources effectively traded in the capital market from $(S_2 + S_1)$ to I_A, resulting as already noted earlier in a loss of producer's surplus equal to the shaded area in Figure 1. The real income lost by individuals in sector 1 is given by the area TEXA which is equal to the difference between the equilibrium interest rate foregone and the average rate of return to investments carried on in sector 1 multiplied by the amount of self-investment in sector 1. The real income lost by individuals in sector 2 is given by the area TEN, equal to the difference between the average rate of return foregone by prospective investors which are rationed out of the market and the equilibrium cost of borrowing, multiplied by the volume of investment foregone in sector 2.[11] These losses may be only part of the overall real cost, as they only measure the opportunity costs of capital, not of labour. To the extent that inferior technologies are also associated with lower labour productivity, a real loss may also ensue on this account.[12]

In terms of equation (4), it may be seen that a decrease in d or a rise in the expected rate of inflation, $\dot{P}*/P$, has the effect of impeding the process of real transfer of capital resources from sector 1 to sector 2 (and with it the transfer of labour resources). This means that K_1 will be rising faster than it would at the equilibrium rate at the expense of the growth of K_2. (Indeed the conditions depicted in Figure 1 would require $K_1 = 0$ for optimal growth.) Given the technological assumption that $r_2 > r_1$, this implies that the level of aggregate income will be growing at a slower pace than would be possible at the equilibrium rate of interest on financial assets.

In addition to the direct effect on economic growth from the failure of financial intermediation to secure the optimal allocation of investable resources in each period, other effects may result from the implications regarding the distribution of income. This can again be explored with the use of Figure 1. Assume as before that the banks charge a rate of interest for their loans equal to $I_A A$ and that an effective credit rationing system is monitored through the guidance of the monetary authorities to prevent the outbreak of inflation. If the system of credit rationing were perfectly efficient (see note 11 on page 71 below), the marginal rate of return to investments in sector 2 would be $I_A N$, with the average return being even higher. The distribution of income would be altered in favour of those entrepreneurs who would obtain the loans at a rate of interest below the equilibrium level, thereby reaping some 'windfall profits'. But the banks themselves could be the principal beneficiaries to the extent that they would respond by widening the spread between lending and deposit rates to take advantage of the effective situation of excess demand for loans. Indeed, under the simple assumptions made here, banks could, in principle, raise the lending rate up to the level r_2^A while at the same time keeping the deposit rate at $I_A A$, appropriating all windfall profits. The losses would be suffered by those potential entrepreneurs in sector 2 who would be rationed out of the loan market and by the would-be bank depositors in sector 1 who would now be resigned to undertake their own self-financed lower-yielding investments.

If the assumption of a perfectly efficient credit rationing system is dropped in favour of the more palatable alternative hypothesis that banks have better information about, and give more importance to the net worth of creditors than about the returns from their prospective investments, then something more definite may be said concerning the distribution of income. However, it is not within the scope of this aggregate model to get but a glimpse of the consequences for economic growth derived from the implied redistribution of income toward the already affluent and possibly toward the banks themselves. This would require a detailed theory concerning the economic behaviour toward consumption and investment of the various economic groups—entrepreneurs and labourers—and bankers involved in each sector of the economy. Nevertheless, a further note on the implications of this theory for the behaviour of the banks as financial intermediaries is in order.

It has been assumed throughout the foregoing discussion that some legal, political or institutional restrictions were operating to prevent the interest rates on bank deposits and loans from reaching their equilibrium levels. However, it has also been noted that the banks could benefit, together with their preferred customers, from restrictions on interest rates paid on deposits, provided that limitations on lending rates are not imposed. It follows, therefore, that the banks as financial intermediaries have a veiled interest in perpetuating, if not initiating themselves, whatever restrictions there might be on deposit rates and in establishing a less-than-perfect credit rationing system by discriminating against customers with limited initial endowments.

All the above-mentioned considerations regarding the public and private behaviour leading to low interest rates merit further and more specific attention in a study of the influence of financial intermediation on economic development.[13]

4. CONCLUSIONS

The theory of financial intermediation in the context of LDCs presented above has proceeded on the assumption that the economies of LDCs are fragmented economies with wide disparities in the rates of return to physical investments and with substantial indivisibilities of physical capital. In this context, it has been demonstrated that improvements in the process of financial intermediation—such as those brought about by higher (equilibrium) real interest rates—which shift resources from the traditional low-yielding investments to investments in the modern technological sectors may result in a dramatic acceleration in the overall rate of economic growth [compare with Porter, 1966: 552-55].

In the experience of many LDCs, with notable exceptions such as those of Taiwan and South Korea [Chandavarkar, 1971], interest rates on financial assets appear to have been most of the time below equilibrium levels, a proposition which applies even more clearly to the real rates of interest, given the relatively high rates of inflation in most of these countries. This means that a state of excess demand for funds has generally prevailed. Appropriate correction of such imbalance would have required that interest rates rise to reach their equilibrium level.[14] It appears that this correction failed to materialise both because of misguided interest rate intervention policy and oligopolistic behaviour on the part of the banking and financial intermediation system.

The two consequences from this state of financial disequilibrium, which have been observed variously in LDCs, were: (a) perpetuation of high rates of inflation and (b) the establishment of some sort of credit rationing system. As credit rationing became necessary in many of these countries to halt increasing inflationary pressures, the issue turned to the efficiency and the practical implementation of rationing devices which are in the nature of a second best policy. However, the experience has been generally not encouraging in this area as this requires a comprehensive system of financial guidelines, which has rarely been set up, to ensure that firms with the highest potential rates of return have access to external finance rather than allocating financial resources according to conventional criteria such as the 'creditworthiness'—the initial capital endowment—of the prospective borrowers [*Park, 1973; Bhatia and Khatkhate, 1975*]. An all-too-frequent result of official credit rationing has been to encourage the further development of traditional curb markets operating outside the purview of the monetary authorities, with consequences for the allocation of resources which run contrary to the official design. Another consideration to be taken into account is that credit rationing could be converted into a force increasing the oligopolistic power of the banking system. The distribution of income has also deteriorated as a result of low interest rate policies and credit rationing.

It is important to stress that the above conclusions do not hinge on the simplifying assumption, made in this paper, concerning the insensitivity of the consumption function to interest rates. On the contrary, if consumption behaviour were sensitive to interest rates in LDCs,[15] it would tend to reinforce the arguments developed here. The rise in interest rates, by discouraging consumption, would increase the surplus of investable resources, thereby raising the rate of capital accumulation and mitigating inflationary pressures.

Introduction of a securities market into the model would not alter its basic conclusions. Securities may be viewed as a short cut to financial intermediation in that the savers pass their surplus funds directly to investors rather than depositing with the banks for them to lend to investors. Relative risk factors, costs of collecting information, and government regulations will influence the portfolio choice preferred by savers and investors as to the form of supply and use of funds [*Wai and Patrick, 1973*].

NOTES
1. The approach here is inspired by, but contrasts sharply with, McKinnon's [*1973, Chapter 6*]; it has similar implications and, hopefully, greater clarity. Surprisingly, he attempted to develop his basic propositions from a one-sector aggregative 'model' of economic growth, by assuming that the problem of financial intermediation could be discussed in terms of an 'average' rate of return to physical assets [*p. 59*]. Thus, he shut the door on the analysis of the effects of what he himself vaguely called 'improvements' in the quality of the capital stock and the financial intermediation process. Instead, he followed the path of neo-classical theorists which he himself criticised [*Chapter 5*].
2. 'Average' is used here to indicate that each of the two sectors is itself composed of productive units widely different among themselves. This makes possible the specification, which is made later on (section 3), of a declining marginal efficiency of investment in each sector. A similar notion was introduced by McKinnon [*1973: 63–64*] within his one-sector model.
3. To demonstrate that the existence of different technologies can result in a positive correlation between profits and wages across sectors, assume that the production functions are of the Cobb–Douglas type:

(1.a) $Y_1 = A_1 K_1^\alpha L_1^{1-\alpha}$
(2.a) $Y_2 = A_2 K_2^\beta L_2^{1-\beta}$

The rates of return to capital and labour are as follows:
$r_1 = \partial Y_1/\partial K_1 = \alpha Y_1/K_1; r_2 = \partial Y_2/\partial K_2 = \beta Y_2/K_2;$
$w_1 = \partial Y_1/\partial L_1 = (1-\alpha)Y_1/L_1; w_2 = \partial Y_2/\partial L_2 = (1-\beta)Y_2/L_2,$

and it is possible to simultaneously have

$$r_1 < r_2; \ w_1 < w_2$$

for the same values of the capital labour ratio, $K_1/L_1 = K_2/L_2$, if A_2 is sufficiently larger than A_1.

4. This extreme assumption is made for convenience, though it is recognised that in the real world some amount of borrowing may be undertaken by these units. The argument would then have to be modified to characterise this sector as a surplus sector *or net* supplier of funds, with gross flows running both ways [*Khatkhate, p. 547*].

5. One of the differences is that the securities market may provide a system of direct finance, while the intermediation through the banking system is indirect [*Wai and Patrick, 1973*]. However, the main difference between the role of the banking system and that of the securities market is that the latter acts as a purely intermediation market while the former is the source of expanding primary liquidity needed in order to finance the continued growth in income. This point is clarified below.

6. Alternatively, one could have specified a demand function for financial assets and let I_1 be determined as a residual. Such a demand function would take the general form:

$$(M_1/P)^d = L_1(Y_1, r_1, d - \dot{P}^*/P); \ \partial(M_1/P)^d/\partial Y_1 > 0;$$

$$\partial(M_1/P)^d/\partial r_1 < 0; \ \partial(M_1/P)^d/\partial(d - \dot{P}^*/P) > 0;$$

It is easy to show that this function implies (9), given the budget constraint (10). Nevertheless, McKinnon [*1973, Chapters 6 and 9*] appears to have overlooked this simple law in discussing the structure of his one-sector model.

7. This simplifying assumption is made here in order to avoid the complications arising from the interest sensitivity of the transactions demand for money.

8. For simplicity, it is assumed henceforth until page 68 that bank lending and deposit rates are strictly equal. Alternatively, the argument could be developed under the more realistic assumption that lending rates are above deposit rates by some constant fraction. But even this proportionality assumption could and indeed should be discarded to take account of the quasi-monopoly position of the banks.

9. The outcome will depend on the nature of the constraint. For instance, some countries have regulations concerning maximum deposit rates payable by the banks while lending rates are not controlled, thereby allowing for a response of lending rates to market forces. This situation is further analysed on pages 68–69 below.

10. The basic conclusion is in complete agreement with the literature on the role of money in LDCs. According to Park [*1973: 411*]: 'The effects of changes in the stock of money are transmitted to the real economy in part by portfolio substitution but primarily by credit rationing, which appears to be the most direct and powerful channel of monetary policy.'

11. This argument assumes that banks are fully efficient in their system of loan rationing in the sense that they provide loans only to those entrepreneurs who make investments with the highest rates of return. Clearly, this is a very strong assumption since banks may not be able to collect enough information to determine which entrepreneurs and which investments obtain the highest yields and, more important, it is not at all sure that they have an incentive to behave in a socially optimum way. Instead, banks may look at the creditworthiness of their customers primarily in terms of their net worth, which might not be correlated with the productivity of their investments. The failure of the credit rationing system as an *allocation* mechanism in this sense would further increase the producer's surplus loss.

12. This argument refers to the medium or long run. In the short run one would have to consider the possible loss of employment as a result of the transfer of labour to the advanced technological sector.

13. Another area which would require re-elaboration and integration in the framework presented here is that of international capital movements, because access to foreign borrowing by banks and large corporations provides an alternative source of finance at world-determined interest rates.

14. This conclusion is in agreement with McKinnon's [*1973*], though the reasons behind it are different.

15. It appears that no conclusive evidence is available in this area.

REFERENCES

1. Bhatia, Rattan J. and Deena R. Khatkhate, 1975, 'Financial Intermediation, Savings Mobilization and Entrepreneurial Development: The African Experience', IMF, *Staff Papers*, Vol. 22, 1, March.
2. Chandavarkar, Anand G., 1971, 'Some Aspects of Interest Rate Policies in Less Developed Economies: The Experience of Selected Asian Countries', IMF, *Staff Papers*, Vol. XVIII, No. 1, March.
3. Goldsmith, Raymond W., 1966, *The Determinants of Financial Structure*, Paris: Organization for Economic Cooperation and Development.
4. Goldsmith, Raymond W., 1969, *Financial Structure and Development* (Yale University Press).
5. Gurley, John G. and E. S. Shaw, 1955, 'Financial Aspects of Economic Development', *American Economic Review*, Vol. 45, September.
6. Gurley, John G. and E. S. Shaw, 1960, *Money in a Theory of Finance*, Washington: Brookings Institution.
7. Khatkhate, Deena R., 1972, 'Analytic Basis of the Working of Monetary Policy in Less Developed Countries', IMF, *Staff Papers*, Vol. XIX, No. 3, November.
8. McKinnon, Ronald I., 1973, *Money and Capital in Economic Development*, Washington: The Brookings Institution.
9. Park, Yung Chul, 1973, 'The Role of Money in Stabilization Policy in Developing Countries', IMF, *Staff Papers*, Vol. XX, No. 2, July.
10. Patrick, Hugh T., 1966, 'Financial Development and Economic Growth in Underdeveloped Countries', *Economic Development and Cultural Change*, Vol. 14, January.
11. Porter, Richard C., 1966, 'The Promotion of the "Banking Habit" and Economic Development', *Journal of Development Studies*, July.
12. Schumpeter, J. A., 1934, *Theory of Economic Development* (in German, 1911). First English version, 1934.
13. Shaw, Edward S., 1973, *Financial Deepening in Economic Development*, Oxford University Press.
14. Wai, U. Tun and Hugh T. Patrick, 1973, 'Stock and Bond Issues and Capital Markets in Less Developed Countries', IMF, *Staff Papers*, Vol. XX, No. 2, July.

Securities Markets in Less-Developed Countries

by P. J. Drake*

The view has long prevailed among economists that, in less-developed countries, securities markets would be difficult to create, costly (in both budgetary and opportunity senses) to establish and maintain, and of little economic benefit.[1] The virtual neglect of securities markets in the literature of development economics reflects a general academic attitude that the subject is unimportant. Opinion in underdeveloped countries and international agencies has been similar to that of academics, save for the 'institution building' attitude sometimes found among politicians and officials.

On the other hand, few economists have been blind to the obvious association between financial development[2] and economic growth, long known but little documented until recent years.[3] Perhaps Goldsmith's pioneering empirical work has prompted the search for cause and effect relationships in the joint growth historically of financial and real economic variables. Perhaps disenchantment with trade, aid and planning policies is leading development economists to look more closely at all aspects of financial policy [Wai and Patrick, 1973: 253]. Whatever the spur, there has lately been a burgeoning of interest in financial development and capital market operations appertaining to less-developed countries. Intelligent examination is now directed at the possibility that 'there might be something' in capital market development;[4] and coherent analysis of this possibility is conducted within frameworks which provide for the simultaneous consideration also of trade, investment and exchange rate policies [Shaw, 1973; McKinnon, 1973].

So far as specifically *securities* markets are concerned, the small amount of relevant academic literature gives no enthusiastic endorsement to their promotion. Policy conclusions are tentative and caution predominates. The most recent and comprehensive published work in this field concludes 'our study has drawn attention to the dangers of expecting capital markets (as we have defined them) to have a sizeable and rapidly increasing effect on the process of development in the LDC's in the foreseeable future. This does not imply that policies to develop capital markets should not be used, but it should be recognised that their effects are limited. We support a positive and comprehensive but gradualist approach to capital market development by the government authorities.'[5] While this is essentially the right approach, it could be advanced with more vigour and conviction. The inherent obstacles to securities market development seem to have been overplayed, and the prospects for beneficial community response to positive policies correspondingly understated, in the limited literature. In

* Professor of Economics, the University of New England, Armidale, New South Wales, and Hallsworth Fellow, University of Manchester (1976). I am grateful to P. C. I. Ayre and M. L. Treadgold for their helpful comments on a draft of this paper.

this paper, therefore, an attempt is made to redress the balance, and to stimulate further enquiry and discussion, by taking a more optimistic attitude towards the prospects for, and the possible benefits of, securities market development in the poorer countries.

The first section reviews the likely advantages of a well-functioning securities market, the second considers the constraints on market development which may be expected in any backward economy, the third refers briefly to market structure and performance as observed in some under-developed countries. Section IV details measures for the promotion of issues and trade in securities, Section V discusses the costs of conscious market promotion.

I. BENEFITS OF A SECURITIES MARKET

The worth of a securities market may be indicated chiefly by answers to the following questions:

(a) Does its existence augment the quantity of real saving from any given national income?
(b) Does it increase net capital inflow from abroad?
(c). Does it increase the productivity of investment by allocating investible funds in descending order of expected yield?[6]
(d) Does it cheapen the cost of providing the investor with resources?

These are the general questions which must be asked of any form of financial development[7] (and in answering them any consequential effects on the distribution of income and wealth should not be overlooked). There are also more particular developmental benefits which may be derived from a securities market, as distinct from all other financial forms. These will be noted after first discussing the four general questions as they relate specifically to the development of securities markets.

(a) *The Savings Ratio*

The mere provision of financial institutions and of opportunities for acquiring financial assets will not *per se* raise the rate of saving in an economy. But there are some grounds for expecting savings to respond favourably to financial development (including the opportunity to acquire bonds and/or equity securities). First, the provision of financial assets divorces individual acts of saving from acts of investment, over both time and place. Individual saving may thus occur '. . . without the need for a concomitant act of investment' [Porter, 1966: 349]. Second, the yield promised or anticipated on security ownership may be sufficiently great to attract net saving of income that would otherwise have been consumed. Third, net saving may occur because of other attractive features of securities ownership, e.g. the possibility (though fraught with risk) of capital gain, or the protection of savings against inflation.

The first two points are sound so far as the general provision of financial assets is concerned, but how strongly do they argue specifically for the issue and marketability of securities? U Tun Wai and Patrick [*1973: 257*] incline to the generalisation that the existence of a securities market '. . . has relatively little effect on the aggregate rate of private savings at the

level of development of most LDC's' because there are sufficiently close
financial substitutes to satisfy most would-be owners of financial assets.
On the third point, those disposed towards risk taking may participate in
direct business investments of their own, or of relatives or friends. Although
U Tun Wai and Patrick [*1973: 257–58*] concede that the liquidity of publicly traded shares may attract '. . . to that level of risk those savers who
would not be willing to accept the illiquidity of investment in their own or
their friends' projects', they do not judge this attribute to be aggregatively
important enough to influence the savings rate. They base their qualified
generalisation on 'scattered evidence' [*1973: 257–58*] which is not directly
cited. But there is alternative evidence (discussed directly in Section II
below) which suggests that small savers *are* attracted by the opportunity
to acquire corporate securities: in most cases probably because of the
prospect of capital gain, although the liquidity and yield attributes of the
securities cannot be disregarded [*Drake, 1969b; Arowolo, 1971*]. It is, at
the very least, arguable that a portion of the funds which have been
subscribed to corporate shares and debentures in the developing countries
would not otherwise have been saved and invested locally.

(b) *International Capital Flows*
Financial improvements certainly facilitate international capital flows but
it is doubtful whether they have hitherto attracted to underdeveloped
countries any foreign capital which was not already so destined, for
other reasons. The much more important likelihood is that local financial
development will deter capital outflow by providing attractive financial
assets, especially negotiable securities, in the home economy.

(c) *The Allocation of Investible Resources*
Any financial development which causes investment alternatives to be
compared with one another is bound to produce allocational improvement
over a system of segregated, 'compartmentalised' [*Porter, 1966: 352*]
investment opportunities. Moreover, just as the availability of financial
assets makes saving independent of any concomitant act of investment, so
too does finance divorce investment acts from the ability of investors to
save. With the aid of external finance, the entrepreneur may be able to
undertake those discrete and lumpy investments which embody technological improvements and give rise to increased productivity.[8] But a securities
market is not the only avenue of external finance for a firm, nor the only
means by which prospective investment alternatives may be compared.
The question at issue is whether a market improves the allocational
machinery over and above the functioning of banks and other institutional
lenders.

In contrast to financial institutions, the securities market does not
intermediate and provides no institutional assessment of the competing
claims for finance as is made, for example, by the loan officers of banks.[9]
The disposition of investible funds via the securities market is made in
accordance with the apparent profit prospects of the companies which
compete for share and debenture issues. Unfortunately, relative profit
rates (adjusted for risk) may not reflect relative efficiencies between firms

because profit rates may be distorted by market imperfections arising from
monopoly power, tariff protection, import quotas, credit rationing and so
forth. In such circumstances the allocative effect of the securities market
may even be harmful [*Wai and Patrick, 1973: 258*]. If these imperfections
did not exist, it might appear that the securities market would allocate
investible funds neutrally, in strict accord with expected investment yields.
In fact, however, the knowledge of individual saver-subscribers, acting
en masse, is necessarily inadequate to make sharp marginal evaluations
of the profit prospects of alternative investments. Accordingly, the
marketability of new issue securities tends to be weighted in favour of
large, well-known, long-established and successful firms (often foreign
controlled), and against newer, smaller, domestic enterprises [*Wai and
Patrick, 1973: 258*]. Moreover, organised securities markets rarely assist
fund raising by agricultural enterprises, tending rather to be the exclusive
preserve of metropolitan industrial and commercial firms. But the disposition of bank and institutional credit may be biased in exactly the same
directions.

The allocative effect of the securities market is even more complex than
the previous paragraph suggests. For example:

> It can be argued that in LDC's only the most creditworthy firms can sell
> their securities via a capital market, that these firms also have prime access
> to bank loans, and hence that such firms have greater freedom of choice
> between different sources of finance (in terms of availability of funds),
> for example, between bank loans and security issues. Development of
> capital markets provides no reallocation of resources to such firms. We
> have to examine instead where the buyers of securities obtain their funds,
> and how they would have used them alternatively; and how the lending
> bank derives its loanable funds, and to what use it would have put them
> alternatively. [*Wai and Patrick, 1973: 259.*]

Without this information the allocative effects of the securities market
cannot be identified.

In the light of the discussion to this stage, one cannot come to any
firm conclusion as to whether or not a securities market would improve
upon the allocational machinery provided by the financial institutions.
The most that can be said is that, since the securities market constitutes
an additional avenue of borrowing and lending, the capital market is
wider than hitherto and should function more competitively.

(d) *The Costs of Finance*

Inasmuch as securities markets enlarge the financial sector—promoting
additional and more sophisticated financing—they increase the opportunities for specialisation, division of labour and reduction of costs in financial
activities.

Securities markets need not be costly to operate. The issue of shares and
debentures can be carried out with relatively small costs of advertising,
postage and clerical wages; subsequent trading of securities requires little
more than a meeting place, telephones and clerks. Further discussion of
these costs will be deferred to the final section. Suffice it to say that
securities markets cannot be presumed either to be wasteful of administra-

tive resources or to be more expensive than financial intermediaries in handling a given amount of finance.

Beyond these broad ways in which securities markets, and other financial developments, may assist economic growth, are the developmental benefits which may be derived more particularly from the existence of a securities market. First, the securities market provides a first-rate breeding ground for the skills and judgment needed for entrepreneurship, risk bearing, portfolio selection and management. These capacities may develop in the proprietors and managers of firms 'going public'; in those who conduct stock broking, underwriting and new issue activities; and in the managers of financial institutions and individuals who trade in stocks and bonds. All such individuals perforce must improve their knowledge of finance and their ability to evaluate risk and seize opportunities.[10]

Second, active securities markets serve as an 'engine' of general financial development and may, in particular, accelerate the integration of unorganised or traditional financial systems (sometimes referred to as 'curb markets') [*Shaw, 1973: 135–38*], with the organised and institutional financial sector. Shares and bonds may directly displace traditional assets such as gold and stocks of produce or, indirectly, they may provide portfolio assets for unit trusts, pension funds and similar financial institutions which raise savings from the traditional sector.

Third, the existence of a securities market enhances the scope, and provides institutional mechanisms, for the operation of monetary and financial policy. In the last few years volatility of capital internationally, flexibility of exchange rates and new theoretical ideas (about the nature and purpose of monetary policy) have called discretionary monetary policies into question if not disrepute (especially for open underdeveloped economies). Nevertheless, it remains true that national central banks require influence over interest rates and the size and composition of the assets of an economy's financial institutions. A flourishing securities market is invaluable for the implementation of general official financial policy, which is less damaging to resource allocation than are selective controls.

II. FACTORS LIMITING THE DEVELOPMENT OF SECURITIES MARKETS

It is necessary first to distinguish between government and corporate securities. In most countries enough government securities seem to be available to provide the basis for a market in such paper [*Wai and Patrick, 1973: 270*]. (In a later section some discussion will be devoted to securing an appropriate supply-demand balance of government paper.) But both the supply of, and the demand for, corporate securities is, by nature, very limited in most underdeveloped economies.

(a) *Supply*

This section concentrates on the basic economic and institutional reasons for the dearth of corporate securities. To begin with, underdeveloped economies are dominated by agriculture, which is usually organised on smallholder lines; where corporate agricultural enterprises exist, they are usually foreign controlled with their shares predominantly held abroad.

Public utilities commonly provide power, transpoi t and communication services, while the industrial sector is small and weak.

The activities (industrial, commercial, extractive) which are in private hands and would be large enough to warrant the corporate form of business organisation, are commonly owned and controlled abroad. Foreign companies generally have little need or desire to raise capital locally, unless persuaded or obliged to do so by local authorities (see below, pp. 84–85). The remaining domestic corporate concerns are often not in need of further capital, or are unwilling or unable to raise funds by public subscriptions.

Family, or clan, companies are common in underdeveloped countries and it has often been observed that such firms are reluctant to admit outside capital, and risk dilution of control.[11] Some such firms have attained what they regard as optimum size and do not wish to expand their operations. Maniatis draws attention to the further practice, common in Greece, of *premature diversification* in which profits are siphoned out of industrial companies into non-industrial activities (family trusts, real estate, etc.) before the original company reaches full industrial maturity [*Maniatis, 1971*]. Thus possible equity issues are frustrated not only because the industrial company's expansion is arrested, but also because the activities into which funds are diverted are not carried out by public companies.

Firms which are bent on expansion may finance it with retained profits and/or bank credit. Bank overdrafts, nominally short term, are so continuous as to be long-term in effect. Good banking connections permit this system of finance to be perpetuated [*Wai and Patrick, 1973: 288*] (indeed interlocking ownership and direction between banks and other companies is very common in underdeveloped countries) and may lead to a dependence on bank finance which the banks may not wish to curtail. This pattern probably owes much to artificially low bank rates of interest. Cheap bank finance is much sought after and is rationed to favoured borrowers, who benefit at the expense of those who unsuccessfully seek bank credit and the bank depositors whose funds earn inadequate—if not negative—real rates of interest.[12]

These practices lead in general to low ratios of equity to debt in the capital structure of firms. Maniatis has argued, at some length, that this seemingly weak capital structure puts firms which desire to raise equity funds by new issues of shares into a 'vicious circle'. The firm's unsatisfactory equity: debt ratio makes the new issue appear too risky and unattractive for potential subscribers, but only new subscription capital could improve the equity: debt ratio.[13] Although this argument may seem intuitively persuasive, it is unsupported by empirical evidence. It cannot therefore be asserted that firms with thin equity structures will invariably be unable to float share issues successfully. Much less can one generalise, from this view of undercapitalised firms, that any willing company will find it difficult to promote a successful issue of equity in an underdeveloped country: as we shall soon see, there is strong evidence to the contrary.

Fundamentally, the limited supply of private securities in underdeveloped countries is related to the small size and limited investment horizons of many local businesses. It will inevitably take time for such firms to reach the point of raising funds through public share and debenture issues, thus providing the necessary augmentation of the supply of private paper. Meanwhile, it might in some countries be desirable for development banks, etc., to raise funds by issuing shares and debentures publicly, or for governments to increase their own borrowing beyond the amounts needed to finance public sector investment, and re-lend to undercapitalised local firms [*Drake, 1969a: 218–20*].

It is therefore sometimes argued that the whole machinery of public companies, issuing shares and bonds which are traded on the stock exchange, is inappropriate to underdeveloped countries where there is likely to be, for some time, a preponderance of firms which are too small to approach the public capital market and depend upon self-finance or institutional finance for expansion. In these circumstances, a case can perhaps be made for long-term bank financing, in the traditional way of the continental banks which provide equity capital, often substantial, to firms. Moreover, it has recently been suggested that financial institutions—either public or private—might sell their own bonds abroad and employ the proceeds in making long-term loans to domestic enterprises [*McKinnon, 1973: 176–77*]. Whilst there is something to be said for these approaches *in conjunction with* the development of a securities market, they seem to be inadequate substitutes for the machinery of share issues and trading. In the first place, in the absence of a securities market the investments (equity and debenture type) made by banks and other institutions will lack liquidity—with a conseqential diminution of the flexibility and an increase in the costs of bank operations; second, total reliance on institutional finance would close off the important entrepreneurial avenue of direct appeal to the public; finally (as will be discussed later), it cannot be presumed that institutional lending will be conducted at lower real social cost than fund raising via the securities market. And we shall see in Section IV, that there are measures at hand which would encourage the issue of marketable securities.

(b) *Demand*

There are a number of *a priori* reasons for expecting the demand for securities to be limited in an underdeveloped economy. The arguments which are well put by Maniatis [*1971: 603–05*][14] are:

  (a) individual savings accrue in the main to unsophisticated people, who are financially inexperienced and have conservative attitudes towards money. Such people are apathetic towards advanced forms of wealth holding and this threshold of insensitivity will be overcome only gradually and most likely through a fairly protracted learning process [*Maniatis 1971: 604*].

  (b) share ownership by individuals tends to be confined to those with high incomes who may spread their risks through diverse portfolios (this risk spreading is not possible for those with limited funds to invest and for whom transactions costs are high); there is not a sufficiently large class of well-to-do to sustain a corporate securities market in an underdeveloped country;

   (c) the generally underdeveloped financial system means that there is
       little or no institutional demand for securities;
   (d) price uncertainty reinforces the traditional preference for money
       over financial assets which fluctuate in value;
   (e) accurate information is scarce and the costs of obtaining it are
       inordinately high; market regulation is limited. Hence, investment
       in securities is extremely risky and in the nature of a racecourse
       gamble.

No widespread empirical evidence has yet been marshalled in support
of these arguments (nor does Maniatis document his assertions about
limited demand for securities in Greece). While they seem intuitively
sensible, there is enough contrary argument and fragmentary evidence to
suggest that it would be wrong to regard the characteristics just described
as universal constraints on securities demand.
   Experience in Malaysia/Singapore casts a lot of doubt on arguments
(a) and (b). In the course of a stock market boom in those territories
between September 1961 and June 1964, 24 industrial and commercial
companies were offered in public subscriptions considerably more than
the $M128m which in total they had sought for new issues of shares and
debentures.[15] It is plain beyond all doubt that the subscriptions for these
securities came mainly from local sources. Most applications were in
the names of locally domiciled Chinese: these were chiefly individual
subscribers, although some were apparently buying on behalf of syndicates.
From data about the geographical distribution of applications, it is
evident that interest in securities investment was concentrated in the
wealthier urban centres (Singapore, Kuala Lumpur and Petaling Jaya,
Ipoh, Penang). But it is also clear that the subscribers were by no means
confined to the high-income class. Very many subscriptions were for small
blocks of shares, and the occupational range of subscribers descended
through the clerical lower-middle-class to domestic servants, gardeners
and labourers. Even after allowance is made for massive speculative
behaviour in the Malayan boom, a wide distribution of 'steady' share
ownership remained (e.g. Malayan Tobacco's share register maintained
38,000 different names three months after the initial post-issue speculative
trading had died down).
   Similar, though not so striking evidence of public interest in acquiring
industrial securities comes from Nigeria. In the period 1959–66 (prior to
the economic disruption caused by the civil war in 1967/68) £N14·5m
was subscribed to twenty new issues made by fifteen companies; of the
total sum, £N5·5m (38·1 per cent) was raised in ordinary shares.[16]
Participation by Nigerians in the share issues was at an encouraging level
and was well maintained throughout the period: five issues each attracted
over 1,000 Nigerians (the highest recorded number of local subscribers
being 2,150 for the £1 ordinary shares issued by Nigerian Cement Co.
Ltd.), while Nigerian individuals took up between 38 per cent and 72 per
cent of the value of subscriptions in six issues [Arowolo, 1971: 456].
   In the light of such evidence, one must have reservations about believing
that the attraction of securities ownership is confined to a very narrow,

high-income section of the population the rest of which may become interested only through 'a fairly protracted learning process'.

The proposition (c) that there is little demand by financial institutions for securities relies on the conventional view, based on earlier observations, that there is but a small number and range of financial institutions in most underdeveloped countries. Nowadays this view hardly accords with the facts, as a number of recent studies attest [Sowelem, 1967; Drake, 1969a; Rozenthal, 1970; Emery, 1971]. Because of the rapid financial development which has occurred in many less-developed countries since the mid-1960s, one may reasonably expect that financial institutions will provide a growing source of demand for securities, both corporate and government, of a wide range of maturities. In Section IV, policy measures by which institutional demand for securities may be augmented will be discussed. It is here apposite to observe that the emergence and growth of institutions such as pension funds, insurance companies and unit trusts (which would be greatly encouraged by a free market interest rate policy) provide the means whereby small amounts of individual saving may be gathered together into sums large enough for the institutions to channel into securities purchases. This form of financial intermediation also provides for the spread of risks which is otherwise impossible within the individual small portfolio.

The observation (d) that price uncertainty leads savers to prefer money over financial assets which fluctuate in value, does not necessarily hold when a country is experiencing inflation and/or exchange rate uncertainty. Irrespective of fluctuations, if the trend of share prices is upward, equity investment may be preferred to holding money which is losing real value.[17]

Finally, the scarcity of accurate information about corporate behaviour and prospects leads.to 'Lack of confidence [which] is probably the most important inhibition to capital market development' [Wai and Patrick, 1973: 285]. This is a real and severe problem which has certainly not been exaggerated; indeed, apart from U Tun Wai and Patrick, few writers have made enough of this difficulty, which will be discussed more fully in a later section.

III. MARKETS OBSERVED

This is not the place to recount in detail the structure and performance of securities markets in individual countries.[18] In this rather brief section, we attempt to distil some general observations about market patterns and behaviour in less developed countries, drawing particularly on data provided by U Tun Wai and Patrick [1973: especially 265–68, 306–17].

The most notable characteristic of LDC securities markets is the great, and often increasing, importance of government as both issuer/seller and buyer of securities. So far as new issues are concerned, government securities accounted for 60–80 per cent of total new issues of securities 1965/70 in 13 countries surveyed by U Tun Wai and Patrick [1973: 265]. Moreover, the government share of new issues was the greater, the lower the ratio of total securities issues to GNP; conversely, in countries where the ratio of new issues to GNP was high '... private issues are predominant and are purchased mostly by business corporations and individuals' [*Wai and Patrick, 1973: 267*]. In general, the supply of government securities is now sufficient to meet current domestic demand for them[19] [*Wai and Patrick, 1973:.270*].

Government is also the major buyer of securities (often of its own debt) either directly or through its sinking funds, pension funds or agencies, such as public corporations and government banks. Central banks are powerful buyers often, apparently, in order to shore up the market in government paper. Of private sector buyers, commercial banks are the most important (frequently to meet the requirements of official liquidity standards) followed by other financial institutions, businesses and, lastly, individuals.

Private sector issuers are manufacturing and commercial companies and, to a lesser extent, financial enterprises (though commercial banks seldom issue new securities). The finance sector is, as one would expect, more active in trading paper than issuing it. On the whole however, private securities are very limited in supply [*Wai and Patrick, 1973: 270, 312–13*].

In the century before 1914 a major element in the growth of the London stock exchange was the issue and subsequent trading of the securities of railway, tramway, canal, dock, gas, electricity and water companies, operating in Britain and in the colonies [*Morgan, 1965: 136–38*]. In the less-developed countries of today, such activities invariably belong in the government sector where they are not financed by shareholders and rarely by the issue of debentures or bonds.

U Tun Wai and Patrick [*1973: 273*] notice, further, that many new securities are issued by private placement so that the volume of truly public issues made by companies is small; Malaysia/Singapore, however, provides an exception.

The turnover of securities is typically low in underdeveloped countries. In the main, new issues are bought for holding rather than trading. U Tun Wai and Patrick [*1973: 271–72*] found that only in China (Taiwan), Malaysia/Singapore and Mexico was the ratio of securities turnover to GNP at all substantial. Occasional and intermittent sharp accelerations of turnover have been observed in connection with speculation. Instances of substantial share speculation (possibly including manipulation of the share market) are not uncommon and have occurred in Malaysia/Singapore, Korea, Brazil, Colombia, China (Taiwan) and Hong Kong [*Wai and Patrick, 1973: 280, 286–88; Drake, 1969b*].

The narrow and fragmented markets just described are very susceptible to discontinuities in supply and demand—and also to manipulations—which produce wide price fluctuations. These conditions may make equity securities unattractive to investors. Maniatis goes even so far as to argue that generally increasing the yields on equities would not lead to an increase in the demand for them so long as sharp price fluctuations, and the consequent risks, persist [*Maniatis, 1971: 599*]. On the other hand, one cannot expect any sustained augmentation of equity supply and demand, sufficient to iron out discontinuities, to occur unless and until the general yield of equities relative to other assets is increased. It seems, indeed, that an increase in yields is a necessary—though not sufficient—condition for improved functioning of the equities market.

To sum up this section: the securities markets of underdeveloped countries are characterised by a limited number, volume and variety of stocks traded; and by a narrow range of participants, with government often dominant. Turnover activity is low, except when speculation erupts. The value of corporate new issues floated publicly is not significant in relation to GNP or real investment. Government issues are much more substantial but are taken up largely by captive buyers. We turn in the next section to a consideration of policy measures which might increase the size, range, activity and usefulness of securities markets.

IV. MEASURES TO DEVELOP SECURITIES MARKETS

It is surely obvious that the securities market in an underdeveloped country should be viewed and assessed in relation to the country's limited economic and financial development. Consequently, any specific measures for fostering the growth of the securities market should be introduced as part of a general programme for economic and financial development. This view is well argued by U Tun Wai and Patrick [1973: 281–84, 301] (who refer also to necessary legal and political improvements) and there is no need for detailed repetition here. Suffice it to single out for emphasis the importance of curbing inflation and freeing interest rates, if securities markets are to germinate and flourish [Wai and Patrick, 1973: 280–83; Shaw, 1973, Ch. 5; McKinnon, 1973, Ch. 7].

Inflation unquestionably has deleterious effects on the real value and the yield of bonds, debentures, etc., whose capital values are expressed in fixed money amounts and whose yields are fixed as a given rate of interest. This has led some economists to commend the practice of indexation (i.e. basing the principal and income of such securities on some appropriate price index), and to advocate its adoption in some countries [Wai and Patrick, 1973: 282–83; Ness, 1974: 456]. However, a major practical problem is how far (within the wide range of nominal value assets) to extend the practice of indexation. The indexation of some financial assets would be expected to depress further the capital values and drive up the yields of instruments which are not indexed. It follows that indexation may lead to a change in the composition of demand for various financial assets. The effect of inflation upon equity securities (which have neither capital value nor yield expressed in fixed money terms) is uncertain: it must be presumed that they would be attractive as a 'hedge' but, on the other hand, inflation might undermine the operating profitability of the firms whose shares provide equity securities for investors.

Expert opinion is united against government interference with the pattern of interest rates and allocation of investible funds that would be determined by the free play of market forces. The fullest arguments have been put persuasively by McKinnon [1973] and Shaw [1973][20] and are too long and complex for even brief repetition here. In essence, market determined interest rates would be higher than the rates of interest which prevail currently in the organised financial sectors of most poor countries; it is a different story in the unorganised or traditional finance markets where the true scarcity of capital is reflected in the high rates of interest charged by money-lenders. Organised and unorganised markets are separated by practices (such as interest rate ceilings and collateral rules) which prevent financial institutions from lending to small-scale enterprises. Freer, and higher, interest rates would promote the integration of organised and unorganised finance markets, encourage enterprises and activities other than those which flourish under 'financial repression' and change the factor proportions in production.[21] In McKinnon's words, '. . . high rates of interest for both lenders and borrowers introduce the dynamism that one wants in development, calling forth new net saving and diverting investment from inferior uses so as to encourage technical improvement' [*1973: 15*].

But the liberalisation of interest rates is easier said than done: for it entails the budgetary consequence of a higher service cost on government debt as well as considerable redistribution of interest burdens within the private sector (e.g. in general, urban house mortgages would be dearer while loans to farmers may be cheaper). If securities markets are to develop to any worthwhile extent, governments must abstain from interfering with the interest rates, security prices and yields determined freely by the forces of supply and demand. But wider economic, social and political considerations may lead a government to prefer administered interest rates (and other forms of intervention in the savings and investment process) to capital market development.

There is little doubt that the development of securities markets is stifled by interest rate ceilings and would be encouraged by a more liberal policy about interest rates. For instance, higher interest charges on bank loans would encourage company borrowers to seek equity finance instead. Any net increase in the attractiveness of equities for individual savers would depend upon the added availability and marketability of equity assets outweighing the lure of increased interest obtainable on deposits in banks and other financial institutions. This seems probable and, in any event, the demand of financial institutions (other than commercial banks) for equities would seem likely to increase *pari passu* with any rise in their deposits, as the institutions would be looking for high yielding assets, with prospects of capital gain also.

Specific measures to promote the supply of marketable securities are concentrated on the concessions which may encourage companies to issue shares and debentures. This tactic has been tried in various European countries [*OECD, 1967*] and used with great success in Brazil [*Ness, 1974: 461*]. Stronger measures would be to oblige firms above a certain size to offer shares publicly and to restrict the granting of bank credit to under-capitalised firms, in order to force them to seek equity funds through public issues of shares. But such drastic measures would be difficult to administer, and they clearly conflict with the economic philosophy of the free capital market [*Wai and Patrick, 1973: 289; Maniatis, 1971: 615*].

More realistically, consideration should be given to the policy of requiring foreign corporations to issue some local equity, or encouraging them to do so by penalising overseas borrowing. Such action would certainly be in tune with nationalistic sentiments. 'The rise of economic nationalism in many countries already raises uncertainties as to the continued foreign ownership of many of these companies. The pressures for increased local participation in such companies is not confined to securing the appointment of a few local people as senior personnel who are usually without much responsibility in policy decisions. The offer of shares and securities (sic) on a voluntary basis to local subscribers might provide a safety valve and reduce the risk of nationalization.' [*Arowolo, 1971: 464.*] The Malaysia/Singapore experience suggests that there is likely to be very strong local demand for securities issued by first class international firms [*Drake, 1969b: 81*].

Although foreign firms may be under considerable pressure to issue shares and debentures in the underdeveloped host country, they will not need to do so as long as they continue to have ready access to cheap local bank loans or international capital markets, and/or generate high profits which provide the wherewithal for self-financed expansion. For example, the General Motors–Holden company has flourished in Australia for many years, its growth having been financed principally by retained profits [*Penrose, 1956*]. General Motors–Holden has not issued any equity in Australia (other than the preference shares issued in 1931 to acquire the Holden Company), despite frequent and vociferous demands that it should do so.[22] Moreover, one must have reservations about recommending a policy which, by perhaps restricting capital inflow, might serve also to reduce the total amount of investment resources available to an economy.[23]

Arowolo makes two further proposals in respect of local enterprises. First, he suggests that statutory corporations engaged in essentially 'industrial' activities could offer their securities—either directly or through subsidiaries—to the public (incidentally permitting the public to 'have a more direct say in the management of such enterprises'). Secondly, he argues that when joint ventures are undertaken between government and private interests '. . . the base of equity ownership could be substantially broadened if the government would divest itself of part of the ownership of such ventures as they become successful' [*Arowolo, 1971: 463*].

The demand for securities is much more amenable to official influence than their supply. It may be promoted, firstly, by tax concessions in favour of shareholders. Ness's [*1974*] account of the Brazilian experience provides a rich and detailed illustration of the efficacy with which fiscal incentives may foster the growth of the share market. In brief, the Brazilian incentives included: (a) provisions for shareholders to deduct substantial proportions of the purchase cost of shares from taxable income; (b) provisions for part personal income tax exemption of dividends, and for concessional rates of withholding tax for shareholders in those 'open capital' companies which undertook to achieve a wide dispersion of equity; (c) provisions for individuals and corporations to discharge a proportion of their tax liabilities by subscribing to special mutual funds ('the 157 funds'); withdrawals from these funds could not begin for at least two years. The 157 funds, in turn, were required to invest in company securities, particularly new issues. The generous tax-relief provisions not only swelled the 157 funds but seem also to have encouraged the growth of mutual funds generally. The Brazilian fiscal incentives quickly produced striking increases in the volume of share issues, the number of firms issuing, stock exchange turnover and share prices [*Ness, 1974: 460*].

Second, indexation of the principal and income of nominal value securities, as previously discussed, will enhance the demand for such securities. Third, distinct from giving protection against inflation, government may guarantee the redemption value and dividend rates of certain securities in order to alleviate risk [*Wai and Patrick, 1973: 285*]. Fourth, the demand for securities may be greatly augmented by the imposition of portfolio rules upon banks and other financial institutions. A related measure would be to restrict capital outflow generally or to prohibit/limit the transfer abroad of funds accruing to financial institutions (e.g. premiums on life insurance). If finance houses are required to hold a proportion of their assets in the form of local securities—government or private—a demand for such securities is readily generated, as has been demonstrated, for example, in Malaysia, Kenya and Nigeria [*Drake, 1969a: 180, 186, 213; Arowolo, 1971: 439, 455, 457*].[24] Next, the demand for securities will be stronger the greater is their liquidity, which will be improved by the willingness of a central bank to rediscount private paper, as well as that of government, and to accept securities as collateral for loans to commercial banks [*Wai and Patrick, 1973: 291–92*]. In their turn, the commercial banks will enhance the liquidity of securities if, within reasonable margins, they will accept them as collateral for overdrafts.[25]

Finally, official supervision of trading in the securities markets is imperative if shares and bonds are to become attractive assets. Otherwise, the public may justifiably feel too exposed to the risk of market manipulation and other abuses, and may decline to invest.[26]

The objectives of official regulation and supervision should be: to provide for the full disclosure and wide dissemination of accurate information about the companies whose stocks and bonds are traded; to prevent the various forms of market rigging; to protect the interests of minority shareholders; and to encourage the development of specialised financial services and techniques. For these purposes, adequate legislation for disclosure and shareholder protection as well as some sort of supervisory body are necessary. The latter, however, need not, and should not, be too sophisticated or expensive. U Tun Wai and Patrick [*1973: 286*] warn of the 'danger of regulatory overkill . . . which may actually inhibit capital market development'. It is better to promote disclosure of information and interests, which not only engenders confidence among investors but— by creating a climate of opinion favourable to 'clean' trading—may actually diminish the need for close supervision of transactions.

Honest and capable stockbrokers are necessary if trading is to be clean and efficient but it cannot be taken for granted that brokers will measure up to the required standards. Dissatisfaction with brokers' behaviour has been expressed in many countries—advanced as well as underdeveloped— and has led to a variety of reform proposals.[27] The essence of the problem is that a conflict of interest often arises between the obligations of a broker as an agent—executing share purchases and sales, for commission, on behalf of clients—and the personal economic freedom, and attractions, for the broker to trade on his own account, to underwrite new issues, to act as company promoter or director, etc. Whilst it would be possible legally to restrict brokers to the agency role, it might not be wise to do so in underdeveloped countries where the volume of transactions is not large and where financial skills are scarce. The public and the economy might be better served by brokers who also sustain other financial activities, develop their knowledge and skill accordingly, and ultimately contribute to the spread of financial techniques. For instance, two essential activities in any securities market are the floating and underwriting of new issues, and the 'jobbing' of existing securities [*Drake and Mathews, 1974: 14–15*]. In embryonic markets, at least, brokers are best placed to perform these functions. However, there are no clear-cut and universally desirable boundaries for broker activities, nor is it an easy matter to ensure that brokers always conform to the appropriate activities and canons of conduct in any country. It is essential, therefore, that the roles and responsibilities of brokers be formulated after public discussion, be well publicised subsequently, and be capably supervised.

V. COST OF PROMOTING SECURITIES MARKETS

The conscious promotion of a securities market would have costs. In the first place, a government might spend money directly on what could be described as 'securities markets infrastructure', e.g. buildings, communication facilities, market supervision, staff training, etc.; but these expenditures are not likely to be very large, especially as private enterprise is usually more than willing to undertake the operations, as distinct from the supervision, of the market. Arowolo recounts the occasion in Kenya in 1954 when brokers resisted the idea that government be invited to establish and finance a stock exchange, preferring instead to form a stockbrokers' association which subsequently was incorporated as the Nairobi Stock Exchange [*Arowolo, 1971: 441*]. Similarly, the trading of shares and bonds, albeit in a small way, developed spontaneously in a number of underdeveloped countries as long as one hundred years ago.

A much more important consideration is that the government budget would suffer a fall in revenue as a result of allowing any of the tax concessions outlined in the last section. The opportunity cost of subsidising the development of securities markets in this manner is presumed to be high by U Tun Wai and Patrick [*1973: 290*], although they concede that 'it is difficult to reach a judgment in this matter, as only society can decide whether the trade-off was worthwhile' [*1973: 298*].

In the light of the manifold demands made for urgent government assistance for agriculture, industry, education, health, etc., few governments in underdeveloped countries are likely to give high priority to any substantial inducement to participants in the securities market. This is not just a matter of the latter assistance having an apparently high opportunity cost. Even if an administration judged that a given amount of assistance to the buyers and sellers of securities would be preferable to, say, a subsidy for industry of the same order, it might be reluctant to act accordingly. This is because the incidence of the benefits from government incentives for the issue and purchase of securities seems sure to conflict with a more equal distribution of income, at least in the short run [*Wai and Patrick, 1973: 291, 298*]. Over the longer period, however, a more general participation by the population in financial activity and a more widespread dispersion of share ownership (perhaps fostered by reserving some shares in new issues for local workers or domestic nationals) may be expected to contribute to a more even and acceptable distribution of income. U Tun Wai and Patrick [*1973: 298*] note that the Brazilian stock market boom '. . . may have dispersed ownership somewhat from the highest 5 per cent; it has attracted the so-called middle class (say, the next 15 per cent of the income distribution)'; much the same could be said for Malaysia/Singapore. Moreover, in the absence of a securities market, dependence on bank loans may sustain and exacerbate a mal-distribution of income [*McKinnon, 1973: 73*] for so long as bank credit is available to a privileged and relatively limited clientele.

The social costs (opportunity and distributional) of government assist-ance to those who participate in the securities market should be viewed in relation to the costs of government intervention elsewhere in the economy (to begin with, the administrative and compliance costs of interest rate controls and other forms of capital market repression). When compared with the massive, and often fruitless, government assistance given by tariff protection and subsidy to agriculture and manufacturing industry in so many less-developed countries (to say nothing of the consequent price and output distortions in the product markets), the costs of promoting a securities market may not look so great. In an intervention-ridden world, it is scarcely appropriate to judge a proposed further intervention by the canons of theoretical welfare economics. The provision of a measure of government encouragement for the securities market, which is cheap relative to government subsidisation of other activities, may well be a good gamble on generating savings and enterprise in the longer run.

There remain the resource costs incurred directly in the operation of the securities market. These need not be great, despite Shaw's vehement assertion—unsupported by any evidence—of the contrary opinion [*Shaw, 1973: 145*]. Marble halls, computers, electronic price boards, etc., are not necessary for the conduct of securities trading, especially in small countries. Securities trading has been going on in Singapore, for example, since the late nineteenth century, but not until 1960 did the brokers adopt even a trading room. The Nairobi Stock Exchange has operated, in effect, as a regional exchange serving Kenya, Tanzania and Uganda, yet the method of dealing in securities there is quite simple and does not involve expensive paraphernalia [*Arowolo, 1971: 442*]. A market requires only communica-tion between traders and the accurate recording of transactions. This boils down to a meeting place, telecommunication links between the main cities of a country and with the outside world, and a few good clerks. Financial institutions which require permanent buildings, furniture, equipment and a large staff would seem to be more expensive to operate than simple facilities for issuing, buying and selling securities and recording and publishing their prices.

CONCLUSION

While not providing a key to rapid economic growth, a securities market makes too useful a contribution to be neglected. And as securities markets take root in developing economies, some of the basic retarding features of the backward economy—notably the monopolistic powers of various financiers—may be reduced. If governments eschew authoritarian financial policies and instead cultivate the conditions in which financing can flourish naturally, then securities markets will emerge spontaneously to perform a significant and useful role. There are indeed obstacles, inherent in the nature of poor and backward societies, to the germination and quick growth of securities markets. But it has been argued above that the constraints are not as binding as they appear at first sight and may have been magnified by other writers.

In the right circumstances, it may be justifiable to go a stage further and introduce measures to promote securities markets. More research is needed about market structure, performance and potential in individual countries. The limited empirical work so far conducted gives some grounds for thinking that the development of securities markets may be more feasible and beneficial than has generally been believed. Appropriate supply and demand inducements are available, have proved effective where tried, and do not seem to be prohibitive in cost. On the other hand, it would be foolish to attempt to impose a securities market upon an economy in which complementary economic and financial developments were not occurring. Securities markets will bear promotion only as part of a consistent package of economic policy. It seems most important to awaken official awareness of the benefits of financial development generally and of the need to eliminate economic and financial dualism.

NOTES

1. The term 'securities markets' is used in this paper to denote the markets for those financial instruments/claims/obligations which are commonly and readily transferable by sale—namely, the shares, debentures, etc., issued by companies as well as the bonds, bills, debentures and stock issued by government and public authorities. 'Securities' is used as the generic term for these various forms of financial instruments. The securities market is, therefore, a narrower concept than 'capital market' which embraces all forms of borrowing and lending, whether or not evidenced by the creation of a negotiable financial instrument. For further discussion of concepts and terminology see: Drake and Mathews [1974: 3–7]; Wai and Patrick [1973: 253–57]; Wilson [1966].

2. Which we may define as the expansion and elaboration of financial structure (institutions, instruments and activities) over time.

3. The main contribution is by Goldsmith [1969].

4. As well as works already cited, Patrick [1966], Porter [1966].

5. Wai and Patrick [1973: 301]. Their usage of 'capital markets' approximates securities markets.

6. In its most general form, this question refers to the possible re-allocation of *existing* wealth, as well as to the disposition of new savings. Not all a nation's capital stock is irrevocably committed to particular productive activities and some part of it—most notably precious metals, foreign exchange, excess inventories of foodstuffs and raw materials but also many forms of equipment and vehicles—may be transformed into alternative capital employment. See Patrick [1967: 178–81].

7. A similar approach may be found, for example, in the cited works by Patrick, Porter, U Tun Wai and Patrick.

8. McKinnon [1973: 12–13], puts this argument clearly and persuasively. It relates, of course, to raising the aggregate rate of investment as well as to improving its allocation.

9. However, new issues of shares and debentures are often approved by sponsoring issue houses before being offered in the market place.

10. See also Patrick [1967: 176].

11. For example [Maniatis, 1971: 660–62; Wai and Patrick, 1973: 260–88]. Indeed where outside equity is admitted '. . . unsavory policies detrimental to the interests of the minority (outsider) shareholding groups (with respect to dividend policy, stock manipulation, corporate disclosure, excessive compensation to executives who are family members) are not unknown' [Maniatis, 607]. Such activities will discourage demand for equities issued by family-controlled firms.

12. However, this state of affairs may not survive a liberal reform of interest rates; see pp. 83–84 below.

13. Maniatis [1971: 600–03]. Of course, ploughed-back profits could improve the equity : debt ratio but this would normally require more time than Maniatis probably has in mind.

14. See also Wai and Patrick [1973: 269–70, 276–77].

15. For a detailed account and analysis see Drake [1969b]. A similar experience occurred again in 1973–74 but I have not been able to obtain comparable figures.

16. Arowolo [1971: 456]. At the relevant time £1 Nigerian exchanged at $US2.40.

17. U Tun Wai and Patrick suggest, however, that inflation may increase uncertainty to such an extent that the attractiveness of equity investment is reduced [Wai and Patrick, 1973: 280].

18. For more detailed accounts, refer to the cited articles by Arowolo, Drake, Maniatis, U Tun Wai and Patrick, and Walter L. Ness, Jr.

19. However, exceptions have been observed in particular circumstances: e.g. the occasional shortages of Treasury Bills in Malaysia and Singapore [Drake, Chs. 12, 13].

20. See also Wai and Patrick [1973]; Porter [1966]; Ness [1974].

21. McKinnon [1973, Ch. 3], gives a particularly good account of the economic distortions which are associated with the 'intervention syndrome' and repressed financial markets.

22. The company's associate General Motors Acceptance Corporation has raised large sums by debenture issues in Australia, chiefly to finance credit sales of the motor vehicles, etc., manufactured by the main company.

23. An alternative strategy which, while restraining foreign direct investment, might sustain the total inflow of international capital by encouraging portfolio investment is outlined by McKinnon [1973: 176–77].

24. Arowolo attributes the fact that institutions took up over half of the total of corporate new issues in Nigeria 1959/66 partly to attractive yields and '. . . partly the factor of legislative direction noted above' [1971: 457].

25. cf. Arowolo [1971: 464] for an example from Kenya.

26. See Drake [1974: 528–30] for a description of common forms of market abuse.

27. Several of these, and the rationale and role of brokers, are discussed by Drake and Mathews [1974], and Drake [1974]. See also U Tun Wai and Patrick [1973: 286–88].

REFERENCES

Arowolo, Edward A., 1971, 'The Development of Capital Markets in Africa, with Particular Reference to Kenya and Nigeria', International Monetary Fund, Staff Papers, July.

Drake, P. J., 1969a, Financial Development in Malaya and Singapore, Canberra: A.N.U. Press.

Drake, P. J., 1969b, 'The New Issue Boom in Malaya and Singapore, 1961–64', Economic Development and Cultural Change, October; reprinted in David Lim, ed., Readings on Malaysian Economic Development, Kuala Lumpur: Oxford University Press, 1975.

Drake, P. J., 1974, 'Performance, Responsibility and Control in the Australian Securities Markets', in Hirst, R. R. and Wallace, R. H., eds., The Australian Capital Market, Melbourne, Cheshire.

Drake, P. J., and R. L. Mathews, 1974, 'The Securities Markets', in Hirst, R .R. and Wallace, R. H., eds., The Australian Capital Market, Melbourne, Cheshire.

Emery, R. F., 1971, The Financial Institutions of South East Asia, New York: Praeger.

Goldsmith, R. W., 1969, *Financial Structure and Development*, New Haven: Yale University Press.

McKinnon, Ronald I., 1973, *Money and Capital in Economic Development*, Washington: Brookings Institution.

Maniatis, George C., 1971, 'Reliability of the Equities Market to Finance Industrial Development in Greece', *Economic Development and Cultural Change*, July.

Morgan, E. Victor, 1965, *A History of Money*, Harmondsworth: Penguin.

Ness, Walter L., Jr., 1974, 'Financial Markets Innovation as a Development Strategy: Initial Results from the Brazilian Experience', *Economic Development and Cultural Change*, April.

OECD Committee for Invisible Transactions, 1967, *Capital Markets Study: General Report*, Paris.

Patrick, Hugh T., 1967, 'Financial Developemnt and Economic Growth in Under-developed Countries', *Economic Development and Cultural Change*, April.

Penrose, Edith T., 1956, 'Foreign Investment and the Growth of the Firm', *Economic Journal*, June.

Porter, Richard C., 1966, 'The Promotion of the "Banking Habit" and Economic Development', *Journal of Development Studies*, July.

Rozenthal, A. A., 1970, *Finance and Development in Thailand*, New York: Praeger.

Shaw, Edward S., 1973, *Financial Deepening in Economic Development*, New York: Oxford University Press.

Sowelem, R. A., 1967, *Towards Financial Independence in a Developing Economy*, London: Allen and Unwin.

Wai, U Tun and Hugh T. Patrick, 1973, 'Stock and Bond Issues and Capital Markets in Less Developed Countries', *International Monetary Fund, Staff Papers*, July.

Wilson, J. S. G., 1966, 'Some Aspects of the Development of Capital Markets', *Banca Nazionale del Lavoro Quarterly Review*, December.

Evolving Open Market Operations in a Developing Economy: The Taiwan Experience

by Deena R. Khatkhate*

Most of the developing countries have been observed, in recent years, to take a variety of policy measures to promote and broaden the market for government bonds, primarily as a means to mobilise savings but also as the basis for using the government bonds for open market operations as an instrument to control the money supply. The general experience, however, had been that policies directed toward the development of bond markets often tended to, more often inadvertently but in some cases intentionally, interfere with the evolution of open market policy. Nowhere has this been more dramatised than in the case of Taiwan. Many of the measures designed both by the monetary authorities as well as the Government, in fact, knocked out the very conditions that would have made for successful open market operations. For one thing, it was made mandatory that transactions in government bonds were at par, in so far as the non-bank public was concerned. For another, though theoretically bond prices were variable in regard to the transactions with banks, their effect was neutralised by their asset management policies, necessitated partly by the institutional factors and partly owing to basic limitations on the government bond as a profitable alternative asset for banks. As a result, the monetary authorities could neither influence the structure of interest rates nor the credit granting capacity of banks. There are, however, enough pointers, due to the recent developments in policies, that the situation may change in the near future.

Historically, the discount rate and open market operations have evolved together as techniques of the central banking policy. If the discount rate affects the price of credit granted by the Central Bank to banks, open market operations tend to carry the impulse to the terms of credit provided by other dealers, besides influencing the ease with which credit is obtained in the market. Thus, when the discount rate is altered, the Central Bank purchases and/or sells securities to reinforce its effects with regard to both the cost and availability of credit. In this sense, discount rate and open market policy are mutually interdependent and complementary to each other[1] which perhaps explains why both of these instruments are incor-

* The author thanks the referee and also Delano P. Villanueva and Vicente Galbis for their comments which helped to improve the presentation of the paper, but absolves them of any errors that remain. The views expressed in this article are the author's own and do not represent in any way those of the International Monetary Fund where he is currently working as an Adviser.

porated together in the central banking statutes of nearly all the developing countries.

Curiously enough, while use has been made very often of the re-discount mechanism in these countries, resort to open market operations has been conspicuous by its almost total absence, thereby leading many academicians, as also central banking practitioners to believe that the incorporation of that monetary policy instrument in the central banking statutes is nothing more than a mere status symbol. The real difficulty, however, in pursuing open market operations in these countries is posed not so much by the lack of any desire on the part of the monetary authorities to use it as by the inchoate stage of the government bond market, which constitutes the basis of open market operations. As a first step toward this, therefore, the authorities in these countries tend to preoccupy themselves with the policies directed toward promotion and broadening of the government bond market. But it so happens that the very considerations which heavily weigh in setting up a bond market come in the way of the use of open market operations as a tool of monetary management.[2] Nowhere has this been so dramatised as in the case of Taiwan. Open market operations as a technique of monetary control was denied any chance to function by the pursuit of a high interest rate policy which, though primarily designed to promote rapid rate of economic growth, high saving ratio and the export performance, also contributed to the development of a market for government bonds.

The rest of the paper is divided into two sections. The first section briefly sketches the institutional background of the development of the government bond market during the late 1950s and the early 1960s, as a prelude to the discussion in Section II about why open market operations could not be evolved in Taiwan.

I. DEVELOPMENT OF THE GOVERNMENT BOND MARKET

If there is to be purchase and sale of securities by the Central Bank for monetary policy purposes, there needs to be not only a market for government bonds of all maturities, but also that the market must be sufficiently broad based. With this objective in view, a real beginning in the cultivation of a market for government bond issues was made in Taiwan in 1959. Until that time the only public obligations were the Patriotic Bonds of 1949, bearing interest at 4 per cent per annum. Of these, approximately NT$6 million are still outstanding. Two major steps were taken toward this goal of developing a market for government debt. First, in 1959, the Government issued bonds with maturities of 12–30 months, bearing interest at between 9 and 18 per cent per annum to bring them in line with bank deposits. Bonds with an interest rate of 18 per cent were sold exclusively to the investing public, other than financial institutions, and other facilities such as tax exemption and quarterly payments of interest were also provided [*Irvine and Emery, 1966: 64–70*]. Currently, the tax-free return on government bonds is around 10–11 per cent per annum, which compares favourably with that offered on savings and time deposits of banks.

The second measure was taken by the authorities in 1960 to assure the full liquidity of bonds sold to the non-bank public. At the time when the large quantity of public debt was floated, the authorities had to face the psychological barrier to acquisition of government paper raised by the prolonged experience of hyper-inflation in Mainland China in the pre-war years and in Taiwan during the immediate post-war period. In order to make a dent on this ingrained reluctance of the public to subscribe to bonds, the Government authorised the Bank of Taiwan which, until 1961, was almost functioning as a central bank, to sell bonds and to buy them at par at all times, if returned by any individual holder. This choice was limited only to the public; the financial institutions, mainly banks, were barred from taking advantage of it through close and constant surveillance by the Bank of Taiwan and the Central Bank of China. However, any variation in the sale or purchase price of government bonds to be taken up by the banks was only a hypothetical risk. In actual practice, the banks were persuaded by the Central Bank through continuous consultation to hold a certain stipulated volume of government paper, which was disgorged in the market before maturity, only in exceptional circumstances.

As a result, there was an impressive increase in the total issue of public bonds which could theoretically have been made the basis for purposive open market operations. In addition to the outstanding NT$6 million of Patriotic Bonds issued in 1949, there was a further such issue in 1966 and again in 1968 and of these NT$1·01 billion remained outstanding as at the end of 1972. They too attracted the same interest rate and other conditions as the 1949 issue of Patriotic Bonds. The total amount of Patriotic Bonds outstanding as of the end of 1972 was NT$1·7 billion. Of all the other types of bonds floated since 1959, those issued in 1959 and 1966 had been redeemed. The outstanding amount of the total bonds as at the end of 1972 was around NT$9·6 billion. With the exception of the 1967 issue of these bonds, which bore a tax-free rate of return of 10·4 per cent, all others carried a tax-free interest of 10 per cent.[3]

Equally striking was the diversification of the ownership pattern of government bonds (Table 1). Financial institutions, including the Postal Savings System, held in 1972 about 32 per cent of the total public debt. Comparing this with the corresponding proportion of 61–67 per cent during the period 1963–66, it might appear that the institutional holdings plummeted rather sharply, perhaps indicating their waning interest in the government bonds. However, this development has to be viewed against the institutional background of the issue of government bonds in Taiwan. At the beginning, the authorities could persuade the institutions more easily to purchase the bonds, while the non-bank public was not ready for such investment. As the public confidence was built up, the non-bank holdings began to grow both in the absolute and relative sense, which accounted for pulling down the proportion of bond holdings by the financial institutions in the total. This was evident from the holdings of 'others' which rose from 48 per cent in 1961 to as high as 60 per cent in 1972. It may be noted, however, that the category 'others' is a catch-all group comprising public and private enterprises and individuals. Though a further breakdown of the holdings of this group was not available, one estimate places the bond holdings on account of private and public enterprises at around 6 and 11 per cent respectively, in 1969. This propor-

TABLE 1

PRELIMINARY ESTIMATES OF OWNERSHIP OF GOVERNMENT BONDS

(Par value; in millions of N.T. dollars and per cent)

End of period	Total amount outstanding	Central Bank		Financial institutions[a]		Insurance companies		Others[b]	
		Amount	Per cent of total	Amount	Per cent of total	Amount	Per cent of total	Amount	Per cent of total
1961	776			385	49·6	21	2·7	370	47·7
1962	1,123	43	3·8	618	55·0	31	2·8	431	38·4
1963	1,539	43	2·8	974	63·3	57	3·7	465	30·2
1964	2,094	21	1·0	1,403	67·0	80	3·8	590	28·2
1965	3,137	56	1·8	2,074	66·0	80	2·6	927	29·6
1966	4,753	61	1·3	2,929	61·6	86	1·8	1,677	35·3
1967	6,625	110	1·7	3,518	53·0	177	2·7	2,820	42·6
1968	8,009	426	5·3	3,801	47·5	188	2·3	3,594	44·9
1969	7,651	192	2·5	3,239	42·3	212	2·8	4,008	52·4
1970	9,030	594	6·1	3,319	36·8	308	3·4	4,809	53·7
1971	9,572	302	3·1	3,153	32·9	497	5·2	5,621	58·7
1972	9,636	217	2·3	3,107	32·2	501	5·2	5,811	60·5

Source: Central Bank of China.

[a] Financial institutions comprising all banks other than the Central Bank, credit co-operative associations, mutual loans and savings companies, Credit Departments of Farmers' Associations and the Postal Savings System.

[b] Includes also holdings by private and public enterprises in addition to individual holdings; data for separate holdings are not available, but it is estimated by one observer that the proportions of government bonds held by private and public enterprises were about 6 and 11 per cent, respectively in 1969. (*The Bond Market in Taiwan* by A. A. Rozenthal, Urban and Housing Development Committee, CIECD, June 1969.)

tion is most unlikely to change radically either upward or downward since then, which makes it quite reasonable to assume that individuals might hold presently about 36 per cent of the total public debt in Taiwan.

The maturity of early issues of these bonds was two and a half years; it was lengthened by steps to the present six years. The amount of maturities, however, did not reflect the effective maturities, even for those who kept the bonds until the redemption date. Government bonds were redeemed in four equal instalments. Thus a purchase of a NT$1,000 bond issued for five years would have at the end of four years a security with the face value of only NT$250, so that the average period for which the amount of a bond remained outstanding was one half of the stated maturity [*CBC, 1970–73*].

II. OPEN MARKET POLICY AS A NON-STARTER

Though the volume of public debt had grown enough to a point when the monetary authorities could have used it for the purpose of regulating domestic liquidity, no attempt was in fact ever made in that direction, despite the emergence of many situations which might have been considered to justify a pursuit of such a policy. Instead they leaned on the re-discount rate changes and direct intervention as their principal monetary policy instruments to control the domestic interest rates and money supply [*McKinnon, 1973: 123–29*]. The hallmark of an open market policy directed toward regulating domestic liquidity is the ability of the central bank to sell and purchase, in the open market, government bonds of different maturities at varying prices and to influence the ease or otherwise of the credit flows from the banking system. In other words, two conditions have to prevail if open market operations are to be a feasible proposition from the point of view of monetary management. First, the structure of interest rates has to be sufficiently variable and second, the assets management policy of banks has to be significantly affected by the action of the Central Bank on the bond prices. It is with reference to these two conditions that the absence of open market operations in Taiwan would have to be analysed.

As observed in Section I, the authorities presumed that the assurance of a nonvariable, but high interest rate was a *sine qua non* of the public's acceptance of the government obligations, and from the very beginning they laid much store by that belief. Through the Bank of Taiwan's intervention, the liquidity of government bonds was fully assured so that the sellers of government bonds could recoup their money value at any time they desired. In short, what they held as bonds were, in fact, 'money' but with a difference in that they bore quite a lucrative rate of interest. By the very nature of this policy of maintaining unchanged prices of government bonds, the authorities denied themselves any chance to vary the structure of interest rates as far as the non-bank public was concerned. Thus, once the interest rate was kept rigidly fixed, the control of the monetary authorities over the quantity of money was greatly weakened. In these circumstances, any net purchase or net sale of bonds, through the mediation of the Bank of Taiwan, was no more than an exchange of one kind of money for another without any impact on the domestic liquidity and therefore aggregate demand. The absence of this instrument to control money supply perhaps did not matter during the early 1960s, as the economy was more or less on an even keel, neither assailed by inflationary forces nor by recessionary tendencies. But when the situation demanded a sharp curtailment of money supply and the authorities had no instrument other than variations in reserve ratios, whose effectiveness was neutralised by the narrow range of its variability [*CBC, 1967: 19*], an instrument to directly control the money stock, such as open market operations, would have come as a blessing.

Apart from the fact that the assurance of full liquidity of government bonds without any risk of capital depreciation divested them of the attribute of the necessary ammunition for open market operations, it did not even succeed in its primary objective of mobilising the savings of the community through the issue of public debt. This was amply evident from the fact that whereas the individuals held as much as NT$38 billion at the end of 1972 by way of fixed and saving bank deposits, which was perhaps the most favoured financial asset in Taiwan, the individual holdings of public debt amounted to hardly NT$3·5 billion (see footnote b to Table 1). The percentage increase of these deposits had also been higher than that of holdings of government bonds by the household sector in the last few years [*CBC, February 1974: 94–100*].

Relative lack of enthusiasm for government bonds has to be explained in terms of the alternative rates of return and the convenience of holding any particular financial asset. The rate of return on government bonds, high and attractive though it seemed, was not much of an inducement to the public, since bank deposits of over two years' maturity had the same features, i.e. tax-free rate of return of 10–11 per cent and in many cases even more, in addition to greater convenience of holding saving and time deposits, rather than government bonds. Historically, the banks in Taiwan had a certain aura around them as a safe haven for savings but more importantly, the savers holding bank deposits could at any time borrow from banks against the security of their deposits at a concessional rate. On the other hand, there was always the fear in the minds of bond holders that the policy with regard to the bond prices might change in future. It follows, therefore, that the rate of return on government bonds, high though it was, needed to be raised further to allow for the relative inconvenience of holding government bonds vis-à-vis bank deposits.

This may perhaps imply that the gimmick of maintaining the prices of government bonds unchanged proved to be unrewarding in the long run, though it paid substantial dividends in the early period of the bond issues. The supposed disadvantages associated with fluctuating bond prices were also exaggerated, even from the point of view of an objective of the authorities which was to mobilise savings through the bond issue. Assuming that the prices of bonds were depressed, *albeit* within reasonable margins, the immediate sellers of these bonds might take a beating, but the new buyers would always gain by investing their funds in the asset whose price had declined. On balance, therefore, the bonds with attractive returns, but with a variable price would have helped the authorities in

Taiwan both to develop the bond market in depth and to harness it for effective open market operations.⁴

The second condition necessary for meaningful and monetary policy oriented open market operations was also non-existent in Taiwan. The government debt owned by the financial institutions did not respond to the needs of an open market policy as purchase and sale of bonds by them were governed by altogether different factors. For one thing, the financial institutions purchased government bonds not on the basis of relative rates of return, but because they were prescribed quotas by the Central Bank at the time of the flotation of every new issue, which they could not afford to turn down. Given a free choice with regard to their asset management policy, they would hardly buy the government bonds, except for liquidity purposes, because the rate on their advances was much higher, in the region of 16–17 per cent, besides the advantages of flexibility in holding non-bond assets. That was why government bonds constituted a very insignificant proportion of their total assets portfolio (see Table 2).

Theoretically, the prices of bonds held by the financial institutions were variable so that the monetary authorities could, if they so desired, have used purchase and sale of securities to control the money supply. In practice, however, even this option was not open to the Central Bank. Assuming that prices of government bonds were varied, thereby affecting the structure of interest rates, the banks would not have been much affected in so far as their lending policy was concerned. As Table 2 shows, bonds constituted on an average 2–3 per cent of their deposits during the period 1959–73, except for the years 1965–68, so that variations that might have occurred in government bond prices, as a result of the open market policy, would have been too small to have any 'locking in' effect on banks. Their credit operations and, therefore, the changes in the money supply would have remained substantially immune from the Central Bank's actions.

In effect, it so worked out that the fluctuations in prices of bonds held by banks remained no more than a hypothetical proposition. Banks, even if they wanted to purchase and sell securities at prices as determined by demand and supply, were precluded from doing so in view of the meagre trading in this market, there being no open transactions in bonds on the Stock Exchange. This meant that the banks could only sell to or purchase from the Central Bank. Here again, banks found it more profitable to borrow from the Central Bank against the collateral of bonds at a rate lower than that paid on bonds than to sell them to the Central Bank.⁴ The sale to the public, on the other hand, was virtually prohibited by the Central Bank, though, through moral suasion, while the purchase of bonds by banks occurred only under pressure, as observed earlier.

Quite apart from the foregoing, the odds against the possibility of pursuing open market operations were compounded by the narrow spectrum of financial assets. There needs to be a wide range of assets, one end of which should be represented by the assets of the shortest maturity, and the other by those of the longest maturity, so that holders of these assets could easily switch funds into assets of different maturity, depending on the degree of fluctuations in the price of each [*Plumptre, 1947: 4–13*].

TABLE 2

CERTAIN ASSET RATIOS OF COMMERCIAL BANKS (INCLUDING CREDIT ASSOCIATIONS) IN TAIWAN[a]

(In millions of new Taiwan dollars)

End of year	Loans and discounts (1)	Public bonds (2)	Corporate debentures (3)	Investments (4)	Total deposits (5)	Ratio of 1 to 5 (in per cent)	Ratio of 2 to 5 (in per cent)	Ratio of 3 to 5 (in per cent)	Ratio of 4 to 5 (in per cent)
1959	4,669	184	37	34	4,965	94·0	3·0	0·7	0·7
1960	5,802	176	44	79	7,165	81·0	3·0	0·6	0·8
1961	7,569	223	66	106	10,506	72·0	2·0	0·6	1·0
1962	9,874	405	74	163	12,320	80·0	3·0	0·6	1·3
1963	13,567	720	38	220	15,763	86·1	4·5	0·2	1·3
1964	17,647	1,016	165	395	20,172	87·4	5·0	0·8	1·9
1965	22,731	1,491	194	486	23,474	96·8	6·3	0·8	2·0
1966	26,404	2,191	1,014	563	29,719	88·8	7·3	3·4	1·8
1967	34,513	2,608	330	669	36,447	94·6	7·1	0·9	1·8
1968	43,519	2,617	444	760	41,608	104·5	6·2	1·0	1·8
1969	53,834	2,190	439	857	44,430	120·1	4·9	0·9	1·9
1970	65,037	2,483	448	1,151	60,375	107·7	4·1	0·7	1·9
1971	83,414	2,492	552	1,421	78,718	105·9	3·1	0·6	1·8
1972	104,701	2,318	707	1,405	107,445	97·4	2·1	0·6	1·3
1973 (Oct.)	140,000	2,720	689	1,693	134,607	104·0	2·0	0·5	1·2

Source: Taiwan Financial Statistics Monthly, The Central Bank of China.

[a] Figures are exclusive of operations of the Bank of Taiwan which, until the 1960s, was acting as a quasi-central bank in so far as purchase and sale of government bonds were concerned.

There was no such diversification in maturity pattern of the government bonds as Treasury bills or any other comparable financial assets did not exist at all. The structure of interest rates, both short- and long-term, therefore, was insulated from any action by the monetary authorities through open market operations.

Though an open market operations policy was shunned for the reasons mentioned above, there seem to be real possibilities for their use in the future in the context of the latest developments in Taiwan. The authorities have now jettisoned their old prejudices about variability of prices of bonds having adverse repercussions on the stability of the bond market. They have introduced a greater degree of flexibility by announcing that the bonds would be traded at free market prices to be determined by the forces of demand and supply so long as orderly conditions were maintained in the market. Along with this, the market for Treasury bills with variable prices was also created. This slow but cautious beginning toward a free and open market for government bonds, including Treasury bills, does not appear so far to have had any adverse impact on the market, though a six- to eight-month period was too short to make any real assessment of the situation. Provided this development continues unabated, time might yet come to consider open-market operations more as a useful monetary policy instrument in a developing country like Taiwan than as an ornament to be ensconced in the almirahs of the central bank statutes.

NOTES

1. A succinct statement on the interrelationship between the bank rate and open market operations is found in Volume II of *A Treatise on Money* by Keynes. '. . . Open market policy can only be employed by a central bank, not as a substitute for, but to reinforce its bank rate policy by making the latter effective; in other words, save in abnormal and unusual situations the aggregate of the central bank's assets is a function of its bank rate. So that by appropriate variations of the latter the whole situation can be controlled.' *A Treatise on Money*, Vol. II, 'The Applied Theory of Money' [*London, 1950: 250–51*]; see also for similar views, R. S. Sayers, *Central Banking After Bagehot* [*Oxford, 1956: 123–28*].

2. Many examples can be cited to provide a basis for this statement. In Pakistan the policy of the central bank to stand ready to purchase government securities at fixed prices has precluded the use of open market operations, though it contributed to the development of a bond market [*R. Soligo, 1967: 37–38, and R. Porter, 1963: 53*]. In India the position is not dissimilar to that in Pakistan, though it is less rigid. The central bank varies the price of open market paper *albeit* within a narrow margin, but the end result is the same. For instance, it is stated that 'in general open market operations have been used in India more to assist the Government in its borrowing operations and to maintain orderly conditions in the government securities market than for influencing the availability and cost of credit' [*Reserve Bank of India Bulletin, 1966: 1160–65*]. A survey for other countries is found in [*P. G. Fousek, 1967*].

3. Porter suggested the same course of action for Pakistan [*R. C. Porter, 1965: 117*].

4. Such a ready access to central bank credit against the security of government bonds is a common phenomenon in India and Pakistan and its consequences for open market operations have also been no different from those in Taiwan. [*Soligo, 1967: 637*; and B. K. Madan in *Commonwealth Banking Systems*, edited by Crick, *1965: 186–242*.]

REFERENCES

1. Crick, W. F., 1965, *Commonwealth Banking Systems*, Oxford.

2. Central Bank of China (C.B.C.), *The Taiwan Financial Statistics Monthly* for 1970, 1971, 1972, 1973, and 1974.
3. Fousek, P. G., 1957, *Foreign Central Banking: The Instruments of Monetary Policy*, Federal Reserve Bank of New York.
4. Irvine, R. J., and Emery, R. F., 1966, 'Interest Rates as an Anti-Inflationary Instrument in Taiwan', *The National Banking Review*, September.
5. McKinnon, Ronald I., 1973, *Money and Capital in Economic Development*, Washington, D.C.
6. Plumptre, A. F. W., 1947, *Central Banking in the British Dominions*, Toronto.
7. Porter, R. C., 1963, 'Liquidity and Bank Lending: The Volume of Bank Credit in Pakistan' (mimeograph), Pakistan Institute of Development Economics, Karachi.
8. Porter, R. C., 1965, 'Narrow Security Markets and Monetary Policy: Lessons from Pakistan', *Economic Development and Cultural Change*, Vol. XIV.
9. Reserve Bank of India, 'Open Market Operations of the Reserve Bank of India', *Reserve Bank of India Bulletin*, June 1966.
10. Soligo, Ronald, 1967, 'Monetary Problems of Pakistan', *Journal of Political Economy*, Vol. 75, Part II, August.

Rural Credit and the Cost of Borrowing: Inter-State Variations in India

by Subrata Ghatak*

1. INTRODUCTION

The purpose of this paper is to examine the nature of inter-state variations in India in the sources, uses and the cost of rural credit. An attempt is made to analyse such differences in terms of the nature of economic activity in different states, the level of economic development, the system of land tenure and some other relevant factors. Next, variations in the nature of growth of the organised agencies like the co-operative credit societies are discussed. Finally, some conclusions are drawn.

2. THE DATA: SOME PROBLEMS

The present analysis was confronted with a number of problems. Firstly, one of the major difficulties is the absence of suitable time series data which could be subjected to rigorous econometric analysis. In some cases, where data are available, they are so scattered that important problems are involved in lumping them together for the purpose of a comparative study. Frequently, existing data could only be used after considerable processing. Secondly, the major surveys carried out in India are informative but unfortunately, on occasions, data available in different surveys are not strictly comparable because of the changes in the boundaries of the different states in the middle fifties. Sometimes, very little information is available on state-wise variations. Thirdly, in the All-India Rural Debt and Investment Survey of 1961–62 [i.e. *AIRDIS*], no detailed information is available on the nature of the activities of professional and agriculturist moneylenders [*RBI, 1965*]. This makes the task of analysing changes in the activities of moneylenders difficult. Fourthly, little up-to-date information is available either on a time series basis or on a cross-section basis about the nature of operations of indigenous financial agencies in the rural sector of the different states. Finally, there is a great dearth of information about the flow of funds in the unorganised rural sector of the different states and although the study of the flow of funds would have been interesting, no attempt is made here to undertake such an analysis.

The enumeration of these difficulties helps explain why a major part of our study is based on data for two years, 1951–52 and 1961–62. However, in the case of the co-operatives, since recent data are available, the analysis of inter-state variations is brought up to date. It is unfortunate that in the massive Report of the All-India Rural Credit Review Committee [*1969*] as well as in the Report of the Banking Commission [*1972*] very little

* Lecturer in Economics, University of Leicester. I am most grateful to Mr. T. J. Byres for his generous help and encouragement in the preparation of an earlier draft of this paper. I am also indebted to Professor Michael Lipton and Mr. Peter Ayre for their criticisms. Errors that remain are solely my responsibility.

information is available about the functions of the unorganised sector. Our study may, therefore, be of some value in turning attention to the necessity to collect new samples in the field of rural credit for analysing inter-state variations.

3. SOURCES OF DATA

The present study is based on data available from the following sources:

1. Reserve Bank of India, *All India Rural Credit Survey* [i.e. *AIRCS*], 1951–52, Vol. I, pt. I, Vol. I, pt. II, Vols. II, III. Bombay.

2. Reserve Bank of India, *Rural Credit Follow-up Surveys*, 1956–60, Bombay.

3. *Reserve Bank of India Bulletin*, September 1965, 'All-India Rural Debt and Investment Survey: 1961–62', pp. 1296–1393.

4. Reserve Bank of India, *Statistical Statements relating to the Co-operative Movement in India*, yearly publication.

5. Government of India. Ministry of Food and Agriculture, *Indian Agriculture in Brief*, New Delhi.

6. Government of India, Ministry of Food and Agriculture, *Area, Production, and Yield Per Acre of Forecast Crops*, New Delhi.

7. Government of India, Ministry of Food, Agriculture, Community Development and Co-operation, *Agricultural Situation in India*, New Delhi, monthly bulletin.

8. Government of India, Office of the Economic Adviser, *Index Numbers of Wholesale Prices in India*.

9. Government of India, *Report of the Banking Commission*, Delhi, 1972.

10. National Council of Applied Economic Research, *Estimates of State Income*, New Delhi, 1967.

11. Reserve Bank of India, *Selected Statistics on Co-operative Credit in India*, Bombay, 1969.

12. Reserve Bank of India, *Organizational Framework for the Implementation of Social Objectives*, Bombay, 1969.

13. Reserve Bank of India, *Report of the All-India Rural Credit Review Committee*, Bombay, 1969.

4. SOURCES OF FUNDS: INTER-STATE VARIATIONS: 1951–52 AND 1961–62

(a) *Description*

The Indian rural money market is characterised by duality and it is interesting to look into the differences as regards the sources available for obtaining rural credit in the different Indian states. In Table 1 it is shown that in 1951–52, in most of the states, moneylenders—both professional and agriculturist—dominated the supply side of rural credit. But the proportions of cultivators' borrowing from moneylenders varied considerably. In Assam, moneylenders accounted for the lowest proportion of borrowing by the cultivators (i.e. about 25%), followed by Punjab (30·7%) and Bombay (about 40%). In parts of present Madhya Pradesh, money-lenders accounted for more than 90% of the total borrowing. The proportion was more than 80% in states like Orissa (87·9%), Mysore (85·9%), Rajasthan (85·8%), Bihar (84·4%) and more than 70% in states like Uttar

TABLE 1

CULTIVATORS' BORROWING ACCORDING TO SOURCES; PERCENTAGES TO TOTAL BORROWINGS

States	Government (1)	Co-operatives (2)	Relatives (3)	Landlords (4)	Agriculturist Money-lenders (5)	Professional Money-lenders (6)	Traders & Commision Agents (7)	Commercial Banks (8)	Others (9)
1. Assam: 1951–2	6·2	0·5	65·7	—	17·6	7·5	0·9	—	1·6
1961–2	4·5	1·7	21·2	—	38·1	10·8	11·0	—	12·7
2. Bengal: 1951–2	1·8	1·3	32·1	3·2	2·1	58·9	0·5	0·1	32·1
1961–2	2·1	5·9	16·4	1·7	28·1	4·0	9·7	—	0·5
3. Bihar: 1951–2	4·7	0·1	5·5	4·9	62·7	7·0	—	—	4·9
1961–2	1·0	2·6	7·5	0·1	21·7	14·8	6·3	0·1	2·3
4. Uttar Pradesh: 1951–2	0·9	2·2	16·5	1·4	35·9	51·8	3·1	—	8·2
1961–2	2·6	16·6	9·2	0·2	0·4	20·0	6·9	0·4	18·7
5. Punjab: 1951–2	14·6	4·2	47·2	3·2	30·9	30·3	—	—	2·2
1961–2	2·1	10·5	13·9	3·8	—	16·5	3·6	—	20·6
6. Rajasthan: 1951–2	0·6	—	10·5	0·5	26·3	85·8	0·4	0·1	1·4
1961–2	0·8	3·8	6·2	—	1·3	23·8	18·3	0·7	0·9
7. Madhya Bharat: 1951–2	8·7	2·4	2·6	0·8	—	81·7	0·5	—	0·8
1961–2									
8. Vindhya Pradesh: 1951–2	1·2	—	1·0	1·0	45·7	48·6	0·4	1·2	11·5
1961–2									
9. Orissa: 1951–2	1·4	2·7	7·0	0·1	5·0	82·9	0·1	—	1·9
1961–2	4·2	16·6	3·8	0·2	15·1	28·8	19·8	—	4·2
10. Madhya Pradesh: 1951–2	12·8	3·1	12·6	0·8	13·9	52·4	2·1	0·4	3·5
1961–2	1·2	17·4	3·4	0·1	34·0	28·1	11·4	0·3	9·4
11. Bombay: 1951–2	4·6	16·2	23·8	0·8	15·6	23·1	10·0	2·4	1·0
Maharashtra: 1961–2	8·3	38·3	15·5	0·3	16·2	8·5	3·6	0·1	4·2
12. Hyderabad: 1951–2	1·8	0·9	9·5	3·2	22·2	50·7	10·6	—	2·8
Andhra: 1961–2	0·5	12·7	1·6	0·4	59·3	9·6	10·2	1·5	11·2
13. Mysore: 1951–2	—	—	5·4	1·1	78·3	7·6	3·9	1·0	1·5
1961–2	6·1	20·6	6·5	1·8	43·1	0·9	9·2	0·6	6·9
14. Madras: 1951–2	2·3	2·2	2·4	0·4	50·7	22·5	15·5	2·5	12·7
1961–2	2·7	16·5	3·6	0·2	59·8	6·8	2·3	1·2	
15. Gujarat: 1951–2	1·1	25·7	21·2	—	5·8	6·3	11·6	—	

Sources: (1) Reserve Bank of India, *All India Rural Credit Survey*, Vol. I, Part 2, p. 24, Bombay, 1957.
(2) *Reserve Bank of India Bulletin*, September 1965.

Pradesh and Hyderabad (now part of Andhra). In other states the proportion varied between 40% to 70%. Again, among the moneylenders, the professional moneylenders (defined as those for whom money lending is the only source of income) supplied 85·7% of the total borrowings of the cultivators in Rajasthan, 82·9% in Orissa, 81·7% in parts of Madhya Pradesh, 77·4% in Bihar, 58·9% in West Bengal and more than 50% in Hyderabad and Uttar Pradesh. On the other hand, their contribution was less than 10% in states like Assam (7·5%) and Mysore (7·6%). By contrast, agriculturist moneylenders[1] provided 78·3% of the total borrowings of the cultivators in Mysore and 50·9% in Madras. In Rajasthan the proportion of borrowing from agriculturist moneylenders was nil. In Punjab, parts of Madhya Pradesh, West Bengal, Orissa and Bihar the proportion was less than 7%. In the case of other states, it varied between 15% and 46%.

By 1961–62 the proportion of borrowing from professional moneylenders had declined significantly in almost all states, with the exception of Assam only where the proportion went up slightly from 7·5% to 10·8% [*RBI, 1965*]. The decline was significant in the case of West Bengal (4% from 58·9%), Bihar (14·8% from 77·4%), Rajasthan (23·8% from 85·8%) and Orissa (28·8% from 82·9%). But in states like Orissa, Madhya Pradesh and Rajasthan, professional moneylenders continued to contribute from one-fifth to one-third of total borrowings of cultivators. But their importance was quite low in states like Mysore, West Bengal, Madras and Maharashtra.

It is interesting to observe that although the importance of professional moneylenders declined in almost all states, the importance of agriculturist moneylenders increased in almost all states except Mysore. The rise in the proportion of borrowing from such moneylenders was significant in states like Bihar (62·7% from 7%), Punjab (30·9% from 0·4%) and West Bengal (28·1% from 2·1%). In Madras also, agriculturist moneylenders accounted for 59·8% of the total borrowings of the cultivators. Taking both types of moneylenders together, it appears that in Maharashtra, moneylenders provided the lowest proportion of loans to cultivators among all the Indian states (24·7%) followed by West Bengal (32·1%). In the case of all other states the proportion was more than 40%, and in states like Bihar the proportion was as high as 77·5%. In states like Andhra and Madras the proportion was greater than 65%.

In 1951–52, relatives played an important part as a source of borrowing, in states like Assam, Punjab, West Bengal, Bombay and Uttar Pradesh, they accounted for 65·7%, 47·2%, 32·1%, 23·8% and 16·5% respectively of total borrowings of cultivators. In the case of other states, excluding Madhya Pradesh, the contribution of relatives was less than 10%. By 1961–62, the share of relatives had declined in many states. The fall was significant in Assam (21·2% from 65·7%), Punjab (13·9% from 47·2%), West Bengal (16·4% from 32·1%) and Bombay (15·5% against 23·8%).

In the organised sector, in both 1951–52 and 1961–62, the share of the government was low and that of commercial banks was insignificant in almost all states [*RBI, 1954, 1956a, 1956b, 1965*]. As regards the role of the co-operatives it may be said that in 1951–52, the share of the co-operatives was very low in most of the states except Maharashtra where they accounted for 16·2% of the total borrowings of the cultivators. In the case of other states, the proportion of the contribution of the co-operatives was either nil (e.g. Mysore) or very low (e.g. Bihar 0·1%, Assam 0·5%, West Bengal 1·3%). In 1961–62, the proportion of total loans borrowed from co-operatives increased in every state. The share of co-operative credit societies was impressive in Maharashtra (38·3%), Gujarat (25·7%) and Mysore (20·6%). On the other hand, there are some other states, in which the development of co-operatives had been very slow. In Assam, Bihar, Rajasthan and West Bengal, a very small proportion of cultivators' loans was borrowed from co-operatives.

Traders and commission agents had increased their share in the supply of rural credit in all states by 1961–62 in comparison with 1951–52, with the exception of Maharashtra and Madras where the share declined substantially. The rise in the share of traders was much more pronounced in states like Orissa, Rajasthan, Assam and West Bengal.

One of the interesting features on the supply side of rural credit is the growth of the share of the sector which is classified as 'others' in all the states. This is most obvious in states like West Bengal and Punjab. In both these states, nothing was borrowed by the cultivators from 'others' in 1951–52 while in 1961–62, others supplied 32·1% in West Bengal and 18·7% in Punjab of the total borrowings of the cultivators. In Rajasthan, also, the share of the 'others' rose from 2·2% to 20·6%. This may lead one to suspect that although the share of professional moneylenders diminished in most of the states between 1951–52 and 1961–62, still some other form of money lending agency, not necessarily professional, was supplying loans to the cultivators under different forms.

(b) *Evaluation*

The description of inter-state variations in the supply side of rural credit between 1951–52 and 1961–62 is interesting in some important respects. Firstly, in almost all states, the decline in the role of professional money-lenders has been observed though this fall is partly counter-balanced by the rise in the share of agriculturist moneylenders. On the whole, the over-all importance of moneylenders has declined with the notable exception of Assam. In 1961–62 the role of moneylenders was not very significant in states like Gujarat, moneylenders supplied only 12·1% of the total loans borrowed by the cultivators. Similarly, in Maharashtra, money-lenders accounted for about 25% of the total borrowings of cultivators. In both these states it is important to note that the decline in the role of moneylenders is associated with the rise of the co-operatives. In states where co-operatives did not make much impact, the hold of money-lenders remained firm (e.g. Bihar) or increased (e.g. Assam). In West Bengal and Rajasthan, co-operatives made little progress, although the domination of the moneylenders *seems* to have declined substantially. This decline may be more apparent than real in view of large increase in the share of 'others' in the supply side and this may well suggest the continuation of the control of the unorganised sector in the rural money market in these two states. Elsewhere, the decline in the share of the money-lenders has been associated with the increase in the share of co-operatives.

The role of the government as well as of the commercial banks remained very small in both periods of our survey. In the organised sector, landlords did not figure as important sources in any period. The role of the other unorganised agencies like traders increased in many states excepting Maharashtra and Madras—the states where the co-operatives are relatively well developed—and this may partly suggest that the growth of the organised sector in the field of rural credit may depend, to some extent, upon the improvement of the efficiency of the co-operative marketing societies. It may also be mentioned that the progress of the co-operatives in states like Maharashtra and Gujarat may be associated with the system of land tenure. It has been suggested that the co-operatives were relatively weaker in those states where a system of landlord-cultivator form of permanent settlement developed and relatively stronger in those states where peasant proprietorship or the owner-cultivator system was prominent [*RBI, 1957: 398–99*].[2] Further, the slower growth of the co-operatives has also been associated with a low level of average borrowing. For example, the lowest level of average borrowing by the cultivator was recorded in Assam and there the share of the co-operatives was lowest in the total supply. In Gujarat, average borrowing was highest and there the co-operatives advanced relatively larger loans than most of the other states. Other factors may also explain the uneven growth of the co-operatives and we shall turn to the analysis of these factors in the discussion of the co-operative credit societies in different states. The conclusions on the supply side are, therefore:

(i) Although the control of moneylenders and other unorganised agencies has diminished between 1951–52 and 1961–62, in most of the states their control over the rural money market in 1961–62 remained fairly strong.

(ii) The progress of the co-operatives has been quite different in different states and co-operatives in eastern Indian states, as well as in Rajasthan, had little impact on the supply side in comparison with states like Maharashtra and Gujarat.

(iii) The growth of an unclassified agency, i.e. 'others', in all the states may suggest that the moneylenders are operating through the back door.

(iv) The increase in the share of traders on the supply side in most of the states may underline the necessity to build up strong marketing societies.

5. BORROWING ACCORDING TO PURPOSE

(a) *Description*

Data on borrowing according to different purposes are presented in Table 2. Unfortunately, these data are regional and, therefore, straight-forward comparison with data for 1961–62 may not be valid. Nevertheless, some idea of the factors affecting the demand side in the different states may be formed even from regional data. The major factors affecting demand for rural credit are family expenditure, current expenditure and capital expenditure. In 1951–52 borrowing for family expenditure was higher in eastern states like Assam, Bengal, Bihar, Orissa and Uttar Pradesh in comparison with western and southern states which would include Maharashtra, Gujarat, Mysore, Madras. On the other hand, the

TABLE 2

BORROWING ACCORDING TO PURPOSES: PERCENTAGE TO TOTAL BORROWING

States	Capital expend-iture on firm	Current expend-iture on firm	Family expend-iture	Per cent Non-farm business expend-iture	Other expend-iture	More than one purpose
	(1)	(2)	(3)	(4)	(5)	(6)
1. Assam–Bengal	29·6	0·3	57·1	2·2	8·6	1·5
2. Bihar–Bengal	21·6	7·4	57·8	3·0	2·5	2·0
3. Eastern Uttar Pradesh	23·5	16·2	49·3	0·6	2·5	1·6
4. Western Uttar Pradesh	28·9	4·1	46·1	2·5	6·0	3·6
5. Punjab–PEPSU	19·4	5·5	48·8	4·3	7·4	14·1
6. Rajasthan	21·0	6·9	42·9	0·3	1·2	24·9
7. Central India	25·6	5·7	38·9	21·0	3·1	4·9
8. Orissa & East Madhya Pradesh	22·4	5·3	57·8	2·5	55·1	3·5
9. Western Cotton Region	21·5	33·8	31·7	0·6	1·2	5·9
10. North Deccan	35·5	16·5	32·7	1·0	4·3	4·0
11. South Deccan	26·8	12·9	38·6	11·5	6·1	2·7
12. East Coast	43·7	19·4	25·8	3·6	3·3	4·2
13. West Coast	12·3	12·4	39·3	12·4	8·3	14·5
All India	26·9	13·0	40·9	4·6	4·3	6·8

Source: Reserve Bank of India, *AIRCS*, Vol. I, Pt. 1, p. 309, Bombay, 1956.

proportion of current and capital expenditure was highest (about 63%) in the East Coast (i.e. present Madras state) followed by the Western Cotton region (55·3%) and the North Deccan (52%) and it was low in states like Assam, Orissa, Bengal, Bihar, Rajasthan and some parts of Uttar Pradesh and Madhya Pradesh. In 1961–62 [*RBI, 1965*] the proportion of household expenditure was highest in Jammu and Kashmir (82·2%), followed by Bihar (60·1%) and Kerala (59·7%) whereas it was lowest in Madras (31·2%), followed by Maharashtra (31·5%), Andhra (39·7%) and Mysore (40·4%). In 1961–62 family expenditure was relatively more important than current and capital expenditure in eastern states plus Rajasthan and Jammu and Kashmir in comparison with states like Madras, Maharashtra, Andhra and Mysore. There does not seem to have been a very big change in the pattern of differences in borrowing purposes in the different states in connection with family expenditure. As regards capital and current expenditure, it may be said that their proportion in total borrowing in 1961–62 was highest in Maharashtra (60·9%), followed by Madras (46·2%), Mysore (44%) and Gujarat (41·6%). This proportion was lowest in Jammu and Kashmir (11·3%), followed by Kerala (13·8%), Bihar (18·8%), Orissa (19·5%) and West Bengal (23·7%). Here again, the pattern of differences that emerged, remained broadly the same among the different states between 1951–52 and 1961–62, i.e. the proportion of borrowing for current and capital expenditure remained higher in western and southern states except Kerala in comparison with eastern states and Jammu and Kashmir.

(b) *Evaluation*
Inter-state differences in factors affecting the demand side for rural credit remained broadly the same between 1951–52 and 1961–62. Western and southern states, with the exception of Rajasthan and Kerala, showed a greater tendency to use loans for productive purposes by undertaking current and capital expenditure than eastern states and Jammu and Kashmir, where such productive use of loans has been relatively less. This is also confirmed by the data which are available for family expenditure. Inter-state differences did not narrow down substantially though some shifts may have taken place. It is perhaps plausible, that the level of economic activity, the degree of monetisation, the nature of land tenure as well as differences in the strength of the co-operatives in the supply side might explain some of these variations. In most of the eastern states, land holdings appeared to be smaller than in other states (see Table 4). Operational size holdings were smaller, also, in Jammu and Kashmir in 1961 and in Kerala in both 1961 and 1953–54. States with smaller operational holdings used a greater proportion of borrowings for family expenditure than for current and capital expenditure, whereas the reverse was true in states with larger sized holdings. Again, it is plausible that production of cash crops may lead to an increase in the degree of monetisation and this may lead to greater capital expenditure. Perhaps this may explain the relatively higher proportion of capital and current expenditure in comparison with family expenditure in states like Gujarat and Maharashtra. On the other hand, in states which may be characterised by a low level of monetisation like Bihar and Orissa, a greater proportion of borrowing has been devoted to family rather than to current and capital expenditure. It is interesting to note that the pattern of differences in the nature of use of borrowed funds in the different states followed the pattern of differences with regard to the growth of the organised agencies in the supply side of rural credit. This may not be surprising in view of the fact that the co-operatives generally make advances for productive purposes and moneylenders hardly supervise the utilisation of loans [*RBI, 1957: 499–500*]. Hence the continued dominance of moneylenders may be associated with the unproductive use of loans. It may be added that data on loans outstanding according to purposes and sources generally confirm the same pattern of differences [*RBI, 1956b: 22–23*].

6. BORROWING AND INDEBTEDNESS ACCORDING TO SECURITY: 1951–52 AND 1961–62
(a) *Description*
I turn now to a consideration of differences in the nature of securities against which loans are generally borrowed or outstanding in different states. Table 3 reveals that in 1951–52, in most states, personal security accounted for the greater proportion of loans borrowed or outstanding. However, in the Assam–Bengal region, immovable property accounted

TABLE 3

DEBT OWED TO PROFESSIONAL MONEYLENDERS CLASSIFIED ACCORDING TO SECURITY:
CULTIVATORS: 1951–52

| States | Debt secured by each security as percentage of total debt | | | |
	Personal Security	Bullion & Ornaments	Immovable Property	Guarantee by Third Party
	(1)	(2)	(3)	(4)
1. Assam–Bengal	24·2	0·4	68·8	—
2. Bihar–Bengal	62·1	13·7	18·5	—
3. Eastern Uttar Pradesh	84·7	—	8·1	1·0
4. Western Uttar Pradesh	87·7	10·4	1·9	—
5. Punjab–PEPSU	44·2	0·1	55·7	—
6. Rajasthan	96·7	—	0·7	2·6
7. Central India	93·2	5·3	1·4	—
8. Orissa & East Madhya Pradesh	72·8	6·6	17·2	—
9. Western Cotton Region	72·5	8·4	11·5	—
10. North Deccan	78·7	0·4	19·7	0·4
11. South Deccan	69·9	—	29·3	0·3
12. East Coast	91·4	3·8	4·5	—
13. West Coast	49·3	0·9	49·6	—
All India	77·7	4·3	15·3	0·7

Source: Reserve Bank of India, *AIRCS*, Vol. I, Part 2, p. 587, Bombay, 1957.

for the highest proportion of debt owed to the professional moneylenders (68·8%), followed by Punjab (55·7%), West Coast (49·6%) and South Deccan (29·3%). Bullion and ornaments were partly used for incurring debts in regions like Bihar–Bengal (13·7%), West Uttar Pradesh (10·4%) and Western Cotton region (8·4%).

If we consider the data on borrowing from all sources against different types of securities, it becomes clear that during 1951–52, personal security was once again the most important security in many states. However, in states like Assam, Punjab, Bombay and Madras, immovable property was the other important security against which loans were borrowed. The use of agricultural commodities was of very little significance in most of the states, except Bombay. This may, perhaps, be explained by the introduction of the crop-loan system in Bombay after the Second World War. The predominance of personal security is also observed from the data on loans outstanding against security. However, in states like Punjab, Assam, West Bengal, Bombay, Travancore–Cochin (now included in Kerala) and Madras, immovable property accounted for a substantial proportion of loans outstanding. Indeed, in Punjab and Travancore–Cochin, the proportion of loans outstanding against immovable property was more than 50%, and in Assam it was about 48%.

In 1961–62 [*RBI, 1965*], personal security was again the most important security against which loans were either outstanding or borrowed in many states. In Rajasthan and Jammu and Kashmir it accounted for more than

90% of borrowing, and in states like Andhra, Madya Pradesh, Punjab and West Bengal it accounted for more than 80% of loans borrowed. The lowest proportion of borrowing against personal security took place in Maharashtra (51·7%). First charge on immovable property accounted for 36·1% of total borrowing in Maharashtra, 18·7% in Gujarat, 7·6% in Mysore and 2·9% in Kerala and less than 1% in all other states. Of the total amount of borrowing, mortgage of immovable property accounted for 33·9% in Assam, 19·3% in Bihar, 18·6% in Orissa, 17·7% in Madras, 16·3% in Mysore and 14·3% in West Bengal and less than 10% in the case of other states, while less than 5 per cent was borrowed against bullion and ornaments in almost all the states, except Kerala. Against guarantee by a third party, 17·8% of total borrowing took place in Uttar Pradesh, 13·5% in Punjab, 10·1% in Madhya Pradesh and less than 10% in all other states. Only in Assam and Kerala, where crops accounted for 7·1% and 5·4% respectively of the total borrowing was crop security important. In almost all the other states, borrowing against crop security was negligible.

When loans outstanding are classified according to the different types of securities, we observe similar differences among the different states. In 1961–62 the lowest proportion of loans were outstanding against personal security in Maharashtra (45·4%) followed by Kerala (45·5%) while in Jammu and Kashmir and Rajasthan, the proportion was more than 90%. Against mortgage of immovable property, the proportion of borrowing was 45·7% in Bihar, 35·1% in Kerala, 34·2% in Assam and insignificant in states like Jammu and Kashmir (0·1%), Rajasthan (3·6%) and Uttar Pradesh (8·7%). Loans outstanding against crops were low almost everywhere and bullion and ornaments were of some significance only in Kerala. The other conclusions which are reached in connection with the discussion on borrowing against different types of securities seem to be confirmed by the data on loans outstanding according to security.

(b) *Evaluation*
Personal security formed the major plank for obtaining loans in most of the Indian states. The other important asset (which is generally mortgaged) is immovable property like land and buildings. The use of crops as security was little in almost all the states and this may be due to the inadequate expansion of the crop-loan system. What is similar among the different states is the absence of the use of diversified assets which could be offered as collateral. This may not be surprising in India in view of the paucity of an array of financial assets in many states—paucity which is the result of the low income and low savings of the farmers. There is, thus, a genuine need to increase the cultivator's income and savings which will enable him to build up physical as well as financial assets and this, in its turn, will increase his credit-worthiness, reduce the risk premium on interest rates and lower rural interest rates [*Ghatak, 1975*]. But the growth of financial assets may be hindered, particularly in leading agricultural sectors, if there is a dearth of financial institutions which could offer prospects for savings and investment. In such cases the extension of organised financial institutions (e.g. commercial banks) may be useful in bringing about

greater diversification in the nature of the accumulation of financial assets in the rural sector in most of the states.

7. BORROWINGS AND LOANS OUTSTANDING ACCORDING TO DURATION: 1951–52 AND 1961–62

(a) *Description*

In the absence of suitable data on borrowings according to duration for both 1951–52 and 1961–62, we confine our analysis to the data on loans outstanding according to duration for both 1951–52 and 1961–62.

During 1951–52 it was observed that in most of the states, generally the largest proportion of loans were outstanding for a period of one year or less [*RBI, 1956b: 652–53*]. The proportion was highest in Madhya Pradesh (69·2%), followed by Hyderabad (67%) and Orissa (57·7%)—and lowest in Bihar (33·4%) followed by Mysore (40·3%). In almost all the states the proportion of loans outstanding began to decrease as the period of the loans began to expand. The proportion of indebtedness for 10 years or more was very low in most of the states except Punjab (16·7%). The proportion of loans for five to ten years was also low in many states except Bombay (10·8%), followed by Rajasthan (10%), and Punjab (8·8%) and the proportion of loans for one to three years accounted for about one-half to one-quarter of the total loans outstanding in many states [*RBI, 1956b: 652–53*].

In 1961–62 the proportion of short-term loans for one year or less declined in every state except Maharashtra where it rose slightly. The decline was significant in states like Madhya Pradesh, Orissa, and Assam. In Uttar Pradesh, Maharashtra and West Bengal, the proportion of short-term loans was highest (about 47%). As regards long-term loans for periods exceeding ten years, it is noted that it is once more highest in Punjab (12%). In all other states the proportion of long-term loans tended to rise, although slightly. Regarding loans for other periods, there was little change [*RBI, 1965*].

(b) *Evaluation*

The pattern of loans outstanding on the basis of duration was rather similar for most of the states. Speaking generally, a larger proportion of loans was outstanding against a period of one year or less and indebtedness for three years or less accounted for 75% of the total indebtedness in many states. Excepting Punjab, the proportion of long-term loans was very low in most of the other states. However, it tended to rise slightly in most of the states between 1951–52 and 1961–62. It is noteworthy that short-term loans registered declines everywhere in percentage terms in 1961–62 in comparison with 1951–52, except Maharashtra. The predominance of short-term loans in both the periods of study may partly be explained by the nature of agricultural activity which is largely seasonal in character. Permanent investment in land which calls for long-term loans was not witnessed on a large scale and this may partly account for the low proportion of long-term loans. The other explanation may be the absence of long-term credit facilities from both organised and unorganised sectors at a reasonable price. There would seem to be considerable scope for improving the system of granting long-term facilities in most of the states.

8.   THE COST OF CREDIT: INTER-STATE DIFFERENCES IN INTEREST RATES

For the year 1951–52 data on interest rate differences are given on the basis of different *regions*, and thus a straightforward comparison with the interest rates in different *states* may not be very helpful. Hence, the data given for different districts had to be used for the purpose of our analysis. Here we have mainly compared the average interest rates prevailing in each state by processing the district-wise data and such averages are calculated by multiplying the mid-values of class intervals of the interest rates with their frequencies and dividing their sum by the number of observations.

Attempts have been made to explain rural interest rates in under-developed countries in terms of income and repayments of the farmers, degree of uncertainty in loans advanced and the monopoly power of the moneylenders [*Bottomley, 1963a, 1963b, 1964a, 1964b, 1964c, 1965, 1969, 1971; Chandavarkar, 1965, 1971; Ghatak, 1975; Long, 1968; Nisbet, 1967; Rosen, 1958; Thirumalai, 1956; Wai, 1957*]. To these the relative strength of the co-operatives in the different states may be added where co-operatives are the most important organised agencies. The conventional hypotheses are: (i) the interest rate varies inversely with income and repayment, strength of the organised agencies and the degree of monetisation and (ii) the interest rate varies positively with the degrees of uncertainty and the degree of monopoly power.

Unfortunately, most of these hypotheses are very difficult to test in view of the paucity of data. There are considerable difficulties in measuring the monopoly power of moneylenders in view of limited information. Further, data on time-series either on agricultural income or on repayments and rural interest rates are not available on the basis of different states in the follow-up surveys on rural credit [*RBI, 1960–62*]. Some information is available but it is dangerous to generalise for different states on the basis of the survey of a single district. Again, the construction of an uncertainty index is fairly difficult. An uncertainty index for each state might have been constructed if it were possible to make an estimate of variance of agricultural income on the basis of time-series data. Such data are, however, lacking. Fortunately, the situation is not entirely hopeless since some data are available on agricultural prices for some of the states. Here we have considered price data for 1959–63 for food grains and estimated its variance [*Govt. of India, 1959–63*]. After that, we have ranked the different states according to the variance. Similarly, we have ranked the states on the basis of average interest rates for the year 1961–62 (see Table 4) and Spearman's rank correlation is found to be:

$$\rho = 1 - \frac{6(\Sigma di^2)}{N(N^2 - 1)} = +0.44.$$

The result confirms our hypothesis about a positive correlation between interest rates and the uncertainty index. It is worth observing that the value of ρ is not very high. This may be due to the fact that we have only

TABLE 4

AVERAGE INTEREST RATE, PRICE FLUCTUATION, SIZE HOLDINGS, AND THE GROWTH OF THE CO-OPERATIVES: INTER-STATE DIFFERENCES: 1951–52 AND 1961–62

States	Average interest rate 1961–2	Rank	Variance ($=\sigma^2$) of prices: 1952–53 = 100, 1959–63	Rank	Percentage of loans borrowed from co-operatives to total loans borrowed	Rank	Average interest rate on borrowing 1951–52 all cultivators	Household operational holdings 1961 census 1960–61
	(1)	(2)	(3)	(4)	(5)	(6)	(7)	(8)
1. Andhra Pradesh	11·50	11	21·97	3	12·7	8	20·59	8·04
2. Assam	29·19	1	21·73	2	1·7	14	19·76	4·75
3. Bihar	21·20	3	37·44	4	2·6	13	23·42	4·80
4. Kerala	10·40	12	65·68	5	11·9	9	12·39	1·83
5. Madhya Pradesh	20·42	4	390·13	9	17·4	4	21·42	10·60
6. Madras	11·34	13	133·50	7	16·5	7	11·05	4·58
7. Maharashtra	11·88	9	525·09	10	38·3	1	11·91*	12·87
8. Mysore	11·68	10	190·95	8	20·6	3	12·30	20·48
9. Orissa	19·04	5	1005·92	11	16·6	5	27·81	5·19
10. Punjab	13·81	8	0**	1	10·5	10	19·19	13·78
11. Rajasthan	14·86	7	N.A.	—	3·8	12	16·96	16·01
12. Uttar Pradesh	18·85	6	82·01	6	16·6	6	23·24	5·27
13. West Bengal	24·17	2	1119·31	12	5·9	11	31·25	4·10
14. Gujarat	8·65	14	N.A.	—	25·7	2	N.A.	12·53

Sources: For cols. (1) and (5) *Reserve Bank of India Bulletin,* 1965.

For col. (3) Government of India: Office of the Economic Adviser: *Index Number of Wholesale Prices in India* [Revised series, 1959–63, New Delhi].

For col. (7) Reserve Bank of India: *All India Rural Credit Survey,* Vol. III, pp. 583–84, Bombay, 1957.

* Data available for Bombay only.

 N.A. implies not available.

** The value of variance here is such as to lead one to suspect that prices were administered rather than market determined.

For col. (8) Manilal, B., Nanavati and J. J. Anjaria, *The Indian Rural Problem:* Indian Society of Agricultural Economics, sixth edition: Vora & Co., Publishers Private Ltd., pp. 221–24, Bombay, 1965.

taken the data on price fluctuation and not the data on agricultural income fluctuation.[3]

We have tested the hypothesis regarding the relationship between interest rates and the strength of the organised sector by ranking the states according to the cultivators' interest rate and the proportion of loans borrowed from co-operatives as a percentage of total loans borrowed by the cultivators. The value of the Spearman coefficient is:

$$\rho = -0.52$$

This confirms our hypothesis about the *negative* relationship between interest rates and the growth of the organised sector.

The hypothesis about the negative correlation between interest rates and the degree of monetisation is also substantiated by the empirical test [*Ghatak, 1975*].[4] But unfortunately, here the state-wise division of districts is not given and therefore no conclusion about the states is drawn.

It is, however, possible to give a general description of the levels of interest rates of different states on the basis of our estimates (see Table 4). In 1951–52 the average rural interest rate on borrowing cultivators was highest in West Bengal (30·25%) among all the Indian states, followed by Orissa (27·81%), Bihar (23·42%), Uttar Pradesh (23·24%), Madhya Pradesh (21·42%) and Assam (19·76%). The lowest rate was observed in Madras (11·05%), followed by Bombay (11·91%), Mysore (12·30%), and Travancore-Cochin (12·39%). It is clear that in the eastern states like Assam, West Bengal, Orissa, Bihar, Uttar Pradesh, interest rates were relatively higher than the south and west Indian states. In Madhya Pradesh, however, the interest rate was high. In 1961–62, average interest rates had declined in all Indian states except Assam, where it went up significantly from 19·76% to 29·19% and Madras where it registered a slight rise. The decline was significant in the case of Orissa (19·04% from 27·81%). Assam registered the highest rate (29·19%), followed by West Bengal (24·17%), Bihar (21·20%), Madhya Pradesh (20·42%) and Orissa (19·04%). The lowest rate was observed in Gujarat (8·65%) and rates below 12% were noted in states like Kerala, Madras, Andhra, Mysore and Maharashtra. In other states, rates varied between 12% and 19%.

The pattern of interest rates that we have noted for 1961–62 generally reflects the same pattern as witnessed in 1951–52. Eastern states like Assam, West Bengal, Bihar, Orissa had interest rates which were considerably higher than those in the states of south and west India.

However, although the pattern remained the same, with the decline of rural interest rates in most of the states except Assam, it appears that the differences among the states have slightly diminished. The pattern of interest rate differences lends some weight to the argument that the interest rate may be inversely correlated with the strength of the organised agencies in the supply side[5] as well as with the degree of monetisation in different states. Among other factors which may explain interest rate differences could be the growth of income. But data about agricultural income on a time-series basis are not available between 1951 and 1962. None the less, if we consider the growth rate of agricultural output, then it is noteworthy that both in West Bengal and in Assam the growth rates

on the yearly average are lowest, i.e. 1·2% and 2·1% respectively, whereas
in the case of Maharashtra and Madras such rates had been considerably
higher, i.e. 6·65% and 5·02% respectively. The average interest rates in
West Bengal and Assam were quite high and such rates in Maharashtra
and Madras were quite low. The figures for *per capita* income growth in
these states reinforce this conclusion [*Nat. Council of Applied Econ.
Research, 1967: 58–59*]. Thus, we have some evidence to confirm the
hypothesis about the negative correlation between interest rates and
income. There is, however, room for further investigation on this point.

9. GROWTH OF THE CO-OPERATIVE CREDIT SOCIETIES IN DIFFERENT STATES:
    1957–58 TO 1972–73

We noted in the previous section that the growth of credit co-operatives
in the different Indian states has been associated with the decline in rural
interest rates and here it may be useful to analyse the pattern of growth of
these credit societies in the different Indian states. Here, we shall confine
our analysis to the operation of the agricultural credit societies, because
they are the most important organised rivals of the moneylenders who
still dominate the rural money market.

The growth of the co-operative credit societies in the different Indian
states is marked by unevenness. We shall first look into the changes in the
structure of working capital in different states between 1957–58 and 1972–73
to understand the difference in the financial strength of credit societies
[*RBI, 1948–68, 1969, 1948–73*]. Our analysis starts from the year 1957–58
to take into account the changes in the boundaries of the different states.
For states like Gujarat and Maharashtra, the years of comparison are
1960–61 and 1972–73 because data are available for two separate states
only from 1960–61.

The available data show that in 1957–58 the proportion of deposits to
working capital was highest in the Punjab (18·5%), followed by Kerala
(17%) and Jammu and Kashmir (13·5%). In other states the proportion
was below 10%. It was lowest in Assam (1·1%). In 1972–73, Himachal
Pradesh registered the highest ratio (41·1%), followed by Punjab (22·1%)
and Kerala (14·5%). The proportion was lowest in Jammu and Kashmir
(1·6%). In Assam it moved up to 6·5%. In other states, little significant
change is noted. It follows that, excepting Himachal Pradesh, Punjab
and Kerala, the record of deposit mobilisation was not good.

As regards the borrowing-working capital ratio, borrowing was by far
the most important component if working capital in almost all states.
In eleven out of fifteen states, the proportion was greater than 60%. In
1957–58 it was lowest in Kerala (23%), followed by Punjab (43·4%) and
Uttar Pradesh (54·3%). In 1972–73 it was highest in Assam (78%),
followed by Jammu and Kashmir (69%), Haryana (68%), Madhya Pradesh
(65%) and West Bengal (66%). The increasing proportion was very dis-
quieting for Assam, Jammu and Kashmir, Haryana, Madhya Pradesh
and West Bengal. Himachal Pradesh depended least upon borrowing
(21·3%) followed by Kerala (42·3%) and Punjab (50%), and here the
degree of dependence in Kerala has increased substantially within ten
years. No significant change was noted in the case of Gujarat, Maharashtra,

Mysore, Madhya Pradesh, Rajasthan and Tamil Nadu. The heavy dependence upon borrowing of almost all states, indicates clearly their inability to mobilise internal resources for financing credit requirements. This may also be explained partly by the concessioanl rate (i.e. 2% below the Bank Rate) at which the co-operatives can borrow from the Reserve Bank of India.

The largest proportion of paid-up to working capital in 1957–58 was observed in Uttar Pradesh (31·1%), followed by Kerala (29·1%). It was 24·3% in Gujarat in 1960–61. The lowest proportion was observed in Assam (10·5%) in 1957–58. For a large majority of the states, the proportion varied between 15% and 25%. In 1972–73 Maharashtra occupied the top position (22·2%) and in Kerala, the proportion fell to 14·7%. Some improvement was noted in Assam. The lowest proportion was observed in Jammu and Kashmir (5·5%). When the proportion of reserves to working capital is considered in 1957–58, Kerala topped the list (29·7%), followed by West Bengal (16·1%), Punjab (14·8%) and Tamil Nadu (12%). For many states, the proportion was below 10%. In 1972–73 a sharp decline was noted in this proportion in all states. It was highest in Tamil Nadu (9·0%) and lowest in Rajasthan, Haryana, Jammu and Kashmir (1·0%). The decline was severe in Kerala, i.e. 5·3% from 29·1%, and caused concern in Assam and Bihar.

One important implication of the analysis is that the composition of working capital differed among the states, and in some cases the difference was quite significant. Further, most of the states depended substantially upon borrowing as a source of working capital and the degree of dependence increased in the case of many states between 1957–58 and 1972–73. Excluding Himachal Pradesh, Punjab and Kerala, the record of deposit mobilisation was quite unsatisfactory in most states. While the structure of working capital of Himachal Pradesh, Punjab, Kerala, Maharashtra and Tamil Nadu looked better than many other states, it appeared to be quite weak in states like Jammu and Kashmir, Assam, West Bengal, Bihar and Rajasthan.

TABLE 5

AUDIT CLASSIFICATION OF PRIMARY AGRICULTURAL CREDIT SOCIETIES—
STATEWISE DATA (per cent)

States and years	Per cent of societies audited and classified as				
	A	B	C	D	E
1. *Andhra Pradesh*					
1956–57	—	12·3	82·1	4·8	—
1971–72	—	3·4	70·8	25·1	—
2. *Assam*					
1956–57	—	55·4	21·6	22·7	—
1971–72	—	20·1	49·2	28·6	1·0
3. *Bihar*					
1956–57	—	4·1	80·0	12·6	—
1971–72	—	4·6	65·8	28·5	—

FINANCE IN DEVELOPING COUNTRIES

TABLE 5 (continued)

States and years	Per cent of societies audited and classified as				
	A	B	C	D	E
4. *Gujarat*					
1956–57	10·7	44·2	35·5	9·7	—
1971–72	11·0	39·7	37·4	11·9	—
5. *Haryana*					
1956–57	1·0	11·9	85·9	1·2	—
1971–72	—	7·2	88·4	—	3·2
6. *Jammu & Kashmir*					
1956–57	17·0	12·2	0·3	70·0	—
1971–72	1·3	8·7	81·1	9·0	—
7. *Kerala*					
1956–57	3·6	26·0	50·0	20·4	—
1971–72	3·2	11·1	69·7	15·7	—
8. *Madhya Pradesh*					
1956–57	—	4·9	79·3	13·1	2·5
1971–72	—	3·9	91·5	4·3	—
9. *Maharashtra**					
1956–57	10·6	30·2	49·6	9·5	—
1971–72	5·5	23·9	64·1	6·6	—
10. *Mysore*					
1956–57	6·9	44·5	29·2	19·4	—
1971–72	4·5	29·4	57·2	8·9	—
11. *Orissa*					
1956–57	—	4·5	83·0	11·9	—
1971–72	—	5·8	87·5	6·6	—
12. *Punjab*					
1956–57	4·5	30·4	63·4	1·1	—
1971–72	4·9	15·4	71·1	1·7	6·9
13. *Rajasthan*					
1956–57	1·3	35·6	40·9	21·2	1·0
1971–72	—	3·5	42·2	53·9	—
14. *Uttar Pradesh*					
1956–57	—	0·5	76·0	23·5	—
1971–72	—	—	90·2	9·3	—
15. *West Bengal*					
1956–57	—	—	61·1	19·8	18·7
1971–72	—	—	73·5	17·4	8·3
16. *Himachal Pradesh*					
1965–66	5·2	26·0	64·7	4·1	—
1971–72	4·4	25·1	68·5	1·4	—
17. *Tamil Nadu*					
1956–57	1·4	17·2	75·7	5·7	—
1971–72	—	4·9	72·2	22·0	—

* Bombay in 1956–57.
Source: Reserve Bank of India, *Statistical Statements Relating to the Co-operative Movement in India*, Bombay, 1948–73.
(—) means negligible.

The other important test to consider the relative success of the primary credit societies is audit classification [*RBI, 1948–73*]. In Table 5 it is revealed that in 1956–57 the proportion of 'A' type societies was less than 1% in most of the states. Jammu and Kashmir had the highest proportion of 'A' type societies (17%), followed by Bombay (10·6%), Mysore (6·9%) and Punjab (4·5%). The large proportion of 'A' type societies in Jammu and Kashmir is, indeed, very surprising. Assam had the largest proportion of 'B' type societies (55·4%), followed by Mysore (44·5%), Rajasthan (35·6%), Punjab (30·4%) and Maharashtra (30·2%). Again, the large proportion of 'B' type societies in Assam is surprising. In 1971–72 Gujarat accounted for the highest proportion of both 'A' and 'B' type societies (11% and 39·7%) respectively, followed by Maharashtra with 5·5% 'A' type and 23·8% 'B' type societies. The position of Assam and Rajasthan worsened substantially as the proportion of 'B' type societies fell from 55·4% to 20% in Assam and from 35·6% to 3·5% in Rajasthan. In both these states the percentage of 'A' type societies was negligible. As regards 'A' and 'B' type societies the record of West Bengal, Uttar Pradesh and Bihar appeared to be worst. The proportion of 'C' type societies was very large in almost all states in 1956–57 and the percentage of 'E' type societies was largest in West Bengal (18·7%). Jammu and Kashmir had the highest proportion of 'D' type societies (70%), followed by Uttar Pradesh (23·5%). In 1971–72 Rajasthan had the largest proportion (53·9%) of 'D' type societies. In Jammu and Kashmir the proportion fell from 70% to 9%, and West Bengal managed to reduce the percentage of both 'D' and 'E' types in 1971–72. On the whole, it appears from the audit classification that in West Bengal, Assam, Uttar Pradesh, Bihar, Rajasthan and Orissa, the viability of credit societies has been endangered while better performance has been observed in the case of Gujarat and Maharashtra. For many states the picture was one of stagnation. The present analysis highlights the uneven progress of credit societies.

10. LOANS ADVANCED, OVERDUES AND LOANS OUTSTANDING: INTER-STATE
    VARIATIONS: 1960–61 TO 1972–73

The other important ways of measuring differences in the progress of primary credit societies in different states consist of noting changes in the average loans advanced and changes in the proportions of overdues to loans outstanding [*RBI, 1969d, 1948–73*]. Thus, in terms of average loans advanced per borrowing member in 1960–61, Gujarat topped the list (Rs. 426), followed by Maharashtra (Rs. 330), Madhya Pradesh (Rs. 274), Andhra (Rs. 267) and Madras (Rs. 249); while the lowest amount was noted in the case of Assam (Rs. 45), and Jammu and Kashmir (Rs. 47). In 1972–73 Gujarat still headed the list (Rs. 1762), followed by Maharashtra (Rs. 1004) and Tamil Nadu (Rs. 965), while Jammu and Kashmir advanced least (Rs. 82) though Assam made some improvement (Rs. 504). Hence, in terms of the loans given per borrowing member, the performance of Gujarat, Maharashtra and Madras appeared to be better than that of Assam, Jammu and Kashmir, Bihar, West Bengal and Rajasthan in both 1960–61 and 1972–73.

Taking the proportion of overdues to loans outstanding, we see that in

1960–61 Uttar Pradesh had the lowest proportion (9%) followed by Madras (12%) and Kerala (17%). The record appeared to be worst in Assam (74%), followed by Bihar (45%), Mysore (34%) and West Bengal (33%). In 1972–73 Gujarat and Maharashtra had the best record (19·98%), followed by Himachal Pradesh (27·3%) and Tamil Nadu (27·5%). Once again, Assam staged the worst performance (81%) followed by Orissa (64%), West Bengal (61·5%), Andhra (58%) and Bihar, Jammu and Kashmir (55%). In many states, overdues formed more than one-third of the total loans outstanding. Further, in states like Assam, Jammu and Kashmir and Rajasthan overdues of the last three years as a proportion of total overdues are significantly high.

The above description, once again, highlights the difference in progress of the co-operative credit societies. It also brings to the fore the problem of loan administration and management in different states in view of the rising proportion of overdues. Loan administration apart, the low scale of activity of many credit societies might have stood in the way of promoting viability [RBI, 1969c: 447].

11. COVERAGE OF THE CREDIT SOCIETIES: 1960–61 TO 1972–73
The coverage of the co-operative credit societies is an important way of judging their relative success (or failure) [RBI, 1969d]. In 1960–61 average membership per society was highest in Kerala (345), followed by Madras (191) and Jammu and Kashmir (175). It was lowest in Madhya Pradesh (44) followed by West Bengal (50), Assam (51), Bihar (56), Uttar Pradesh (61) and Orissa and Rajasthan (62). In 1972–73 Kerala, once again, was at the top of the table (924) followed by Tamil Nadu (680). In Orissa an appreciable rise was noted (from 62 to 465) whereas in the case of West Bengal it rose from 50 to only 105.

Turning to the proportion of villages covered by the societies, we see that in 1957–58, in Bihar and Rajasthan only 32·3% of total villages were covered as against more than 90% in both Gujarat and Maharashtra, in 1959–60. In 1972–73 credit societies covered 100% of all villages in Kerala, Haryana, Himachal Pradesh, Madhya Pradesh, Uttar Pradesh and Tamil Nadu, whereas in Assam and West Bengal, about 82% of the total villages were covered. Thus co-operatives *seem* to be covering a greater proportion of the villages in most states. However, this conclusion must be accepted with caution because the percentages of *dormant* societies for more than a year was 67% in Assam, 30% in Rajasthan and 22% in West Bengal.

12. EVALUATION OF THE PROGRESS OF THE CREDIT SOCIETIES IN DIFFERENT STATES
The progress of co-operative credit societies in different states reveals some interesting tendencies. Firstly, it clearly stands out that the progress of these societies in different states has been very uneven. Secondly, the composition of working capital indicates that most states depended heavily upon borrowing and only Punjab and Kerala were relatively successful in mobilising deposits. The overall financial structure of working capital in Punjab, Kerala, Maharashtra and Tamil Nadu looked better than states like Jammu and Kashmir, Assam, West Bengal, Bihar and Rajasthan.

The composite index used in the audit classification also shows weakness in the financial strength of credit societies in states like West Bengal, Assam and Bihar in comparison with states like Gujarat and Maharashtra. Thirdly, the problem of loan administration appeared to be acute in states like Assam and West Bengal, whereas this problem was less severe in states like Punjab, Kerala and Gujarat. Fourthly, the coverage of credit societies seemed reasonably good in states like Kerala and Maharashtra and poor in states like Assam, West Bengal, Bihar, Uttar Pradesh, Orissa and Rajasthan and these are the states which may be reckoned as those where co-operatives developed very little in comparison with states like Gujarat, Maharashtra, Madras, Punjab and Kerala.

It is not realistic to seek a single explanation for all the differences and several reasons may be advanced. Some of them are *a priori* and given the existing state of data, there is little alternative to making some *a priori* judgements. Firstly, it may be argued that the growth of the co-operatives has been more in those states where the system of land-tenure was characterised by the owner–cultivator relationship than in those states where the landlord–cultivator relationship predominated [*RBI, 1969b: 30–31*].[6] This is borne out to some extent by the relative success of co-operatives in west and south Indian states in comparison with east Indian states. Secondly, the scale of transactions of credit societies may partly explain the inability of many societies to attain viability in some states [*RBI, 1969b: 30*]. Thirdly, differences in progress may also be due to differences in the efficiency of loan administration as well as in the management of credit societies [*RBI, 1969b: 29–32*]. Fourthly, greater linkage between credit and marketing, coupled with the introduction of the crop loan system might have enabled some states to stage a better performance [*RBI, 1969b: 16, 29*]. Fifthly, the differential growth rates in agriculture might partly explain the difference in the progress of co-operatives. This was borne out by the examples of states like Maharashtra and West Bengal, or Madras and Assam [*Nat. Council of Applied Econ. Research, 1967: 58–59*]. Further, the nature of the area (dry or wet) might have led to differences in the level of advances of the co-operatives [*Jodha and Bhat, 1968: 36–37*]. Finally, the rate of growth of *per capita* income may also explain, to some extent, the divergent nature of progress of the credit societies. For example, in Maharashtra and Madras (where the progress of co-operatives was much better than states like Assam and West Bengal), *per capita* income changed by 28·4% and 40·5% respectively when such changes were negative for West Bengal (−2·0% per annum) and Assam (−1·8% per annum) between 1951 and 1961 [*Nat. Council of Applied Econ. Research, 1967: 58–59*].

13. CONCLUSIONS

The following conclusions can be reached on the basis of the present study:

(a) Between 1951–52 and 1961–62 the control by moneylenders of the supply side of rural credit has diminished, though not very significantly in almost all states and this decline has been mostly associated with the rise in the share of the co-operatives in almost all states—chiefly in states like Maharashtra and Gujarat in comparison with states like Assam, Bengal and Bihar where progress was very slow. The growth of an unclassified agency called 'Others' in all states creates the suspicion that the money-lenders' hold over the rural money market is still very firm, albeit in a different guise.

(b) Inter-state differences in the extent of the significance of the different variables affecting the demand side did not change substantially during the period under review though some minor shifts might have taken place. The proportions of current and capital expenditure in comparison with that of family expenditure were relatively greater in western and southern states excluding Kerala and Rajasthan while the reverse was true in eastern states plus Jammu and Kashmir. Such differences may, perhaps, be explained in terms of size of land holdings, nature of economic activity and relative growth of organised agencies.

(c) Personal security was the most important asset, in both periods of our survey, against which loans were either borrowed or outstanding in many states, although in some, large proportions of loans had sometimes been granted against immovable property. Loans outstanding against crops formed only a small proportion in all states. There seems to be a paucity of different types of assets and securities in every state because of low income and income and saving. The problem may be tackled by extending the crop loan system, by improving farmers' income and by extending the organised financial institutions in the growing agricultural sectors.

(d) The nature of loans outstanding according to duration was very similar in different states and although the proportion of short-term debt declined in every state between 1951–52 and 1961–62, that of long-term debt still seems to be very low everywhere. The predominance of short-term loans may be largely explained by the nature of agricultural activities and the development of long-term loans may require not only a change in the nature of agricultural activities, but also the growth of the long-term credit agencies.

(e) There are considerable variations in rural interest rates among different states and an explanation was sought in terms of differences in uncertainty, the rate of growth of agriculture, the degree of monetisation and the growth of the organised agencies. There is, however, room for further investigation of these relationships.

(f) Judged by the various criteria of growth, the progress of agricultural credit co-operative societies was very uneven among the different states. This was very much in evidence in the composition of working capital, audit classification, coverage, and loan operation of the credit societies. The problem of loan administration and management seems to be acute in many states. This was partly explained by loan operations and management, partly by the rate of growth of agriculture and partly by the nature of land tenure. The record of progress in this sphere seems to be better in states like Gujarat and Maharashtra in comparison with states like Assam, West Bengal and Bihar.

(g) Last, but not least, paucity of data on some relevant variables, particularly time-series, stood repeatedly in the way of carrying out more rigorous analysis and here there is ample scope for collecting new samples for the purpose of more intensive investigation.

NOTES

1. Defined as those whose main occupation is agriculture but who carry out money-lending business as secondary source of income.

2. See also Table 4. It is seen that co-operatives remained generally underdeveloped in those states where the size of the operational holdings were typically low in comparison with those states where such size was larger.

3. I wish to thank Professor Michael Lipton for kindly pointing out the necessity to test this hypothesis more rigorously. There is surely the need for such testing, but the non-availability of data on time-series is a major obstacle. Further, Lipton pointed out that the price stabilisation scheme may destabilise income. This is, however, only true under some specific assumptions. See, for example, Michael Lipton, 'Farm Price Stabilization', in Streeten, Paul, ed., *Unfashionable Economics: Essays in Honour of Lord Balogh*, London, Weidenfeld and Nicolson, 1970.

4. Using the data from [*RBI, 1954: 194–96*], the rank correlation ($=\rho$) between interest rate and the number of subsistence districts is:

$$\rho = +1 \cdot 0$$

Between the commercialised areas and the rate of interest

$$\rho = -0 \cdot 90$$

See Sengupta [*1957*] for similar conclusions.

5. Let R be the average interest rate in the Indian States in 1961–62 and CP the percentage of loans borrowed from the co-operatives in 1961–62. The *OLS* of the form

$$R = a + \beta \, CP + U \text{ yields the following results:}$$
$$R = 21 \cdot 27 - 0 \cdot 35 \, CP$$
$$t = (8 \cdot 59) \, (-2 \cdot 45)$$
$$R^2 = 0 \cdot 337$$

The result shows that rate of interest is inversely correlated with the growth of the borrowings from the co-operatives and this relationship is significant at 5% level, give the *t*-value of the β coefficient.

6. The cases of Maharashtra and Bihar are cited by the Study Group.

REFERENCES

Bottomley, Anthony, 1963a, 'The Cost of Administering Private Loans in Under-developed Rural Areas', *Oxford Economic Papers*, Vol. 15, No. 2.

Bottomley, Anthony, 1963b, 'The Premium for Risk as a Determinant of Interest Rates in Underdeveloped Rural Areas', *The Quarterly Journal of Economics*, Vol. LXXVII, No. 4.

Bottomley, Anthony, 1964a, 'The Structure of Interest Rates in Underdeveloped Rural Areas', *Journal of Farm Economics*, Vol. 46, No. 2.

Bottomley, Anthony, 1964b, 'The Determination of Pure Rate of Interest in Under-developed Rural Areas', *The Review of Economics and Statistics*, Vol. XLVI, No. 3.

Bottomley, Anthony, 1964c, 'Monopoly Profit as a Determinant of Interest Rates in Underdeveloped Rural Areas', *Oxford Economic Papers*, Vol. 16, No. 3.

Bottomley, Anthony, 1965, 'Reply', *The Quarterly Journal of Economics*, Vol. LXXIX, No. 2.

Bottomley, Anthony and Nudds, Donald, 1969, 'A Widow's Cruse Theory of Capital Supply in Underdeveloped Rural Areas', *The Manchester School of Economic and Social Studies*, No. 2.

Bottomley, Anthony, 1971, *Factor Pricing and Economic Growth in Underdeveloped Rural Areas*, Crosby, Lockwood, London.

Chandavarkar, A. G., 1965, 'The Premium for Risk as a Determinant of Interest Rate in Underdeveloped Rural Areas', *The Quarterly Journal of Economics*, Vol. LXXIX, No. 2.

Chandavarkar, Anand G., 1971, 'Some Aspects of Interest Rate Policies in Less Developed Economies', The Experience in Selected Asian Countries', *IMF Staff Papers*, Vol. XVIII, No. 1.

Ghatak, Subrata, 1975, 'Rural Interest Rates in the Indian Economy', *Journal of Development Studies*, Vol. XI, No. 3, April.

Government of India, 1959–63, *Index Numbers of Wholesale Prices in India*, Office of the Economic Adviser, New Delhi.

Government of India, Ministry of Food and Agriculture, annual, *Indian Agriculture in Brief*, New Delhi.

Government of India, 1972, *Report of the Banking Commission*, Delhi.

Jodha, N. S. and Bhat, M. L., 1968, 'Institutional Finance: Problems and Prospects in Arid Agriculture', *Indian Journal of Agricultural Economics*, Vol. XXIII, No. 4.

Long, Millard, 1968, 'Interest Rates and the Structure of Agricultural Credit Markets', *Oxford Economic Papers*, Vol. 20, No. 2.

National Council of Applied Economic Research, 1967, *Estimates of State Income*, New Delhi.

Nisbet, Charles, 1967, Interest Rates and Imperfect Competition in the Informal Credit Market of Rural Chile, *Economic Development and Cultural Change*, Vol. XVI, Oct.

Reserve Bank of India (RBI), 1956a, *All India Rural Credit Survey* [AIRCS], Vol. I, Part I, Bombay.

RBI, 1957, *AIRCS*, Vol. I, Part II, Bombay.

RBI, 1954, *AIRCS*, Vol. II, Bombay.

RBI, 1956b, *AIRCS*, Vol. III, Bombay.

RBI, 1965, *Bulletin*, September.

RBI, 1969a, *Financing of Agriculture by Commercial Banks*, Bombay.

RBI, 1969b, *Organizational Framework for the Implementation of Social Objectives*, Report of a Study Group of the National Credit Council, Bombay.

RBI, 1969c, *Report of the All India Rural Credit Review Committee, Bombay*.

RBI, 1969d, *Selected Statistics on Co-operative Credit in India*, Bombay.

RBI, 1948–68, *Review of the Co-operative Movement in India, Bombay*.

RBI, 1960–62, *Rural Credit Follow-up Surveys*, 1956–1960, 4 Vols., Bombay.

RBI, 1948–73, *Statistical Statements Relating to the Co-operative Movement in India*, Bombay.

Rosen, George, 1958, 'Capital Market and the Industrialization of Under-developed Economies', *The Indian Economic Journal*, Vol. VI, No. 2.

Sengupta, J. K., 1957, 'Role of Monetization in Agriculture', *Indian Journal of Agricultural Economics*, Vol. XII, No. 4.

Thirumalai, S., 1956, 'Rate of Interest in Reorganization of Rural Credit', *Indian Journal of Agricultural Economics*, Vol. XI, No. 2.

Wai, U Tun, 1957, 'Interest Rates Outside the Organized Money Markets in Underdeveloped Countries', *IMF Staff Papers*, Vol. VI, No. 1.

Exchange Rate Policies for Developing Countries

*by Andrew D. Crockett and Saleh M. Nsouli**

Developing countries have generally favoured adjustable par values as the
basis for the world exchange rate system. This has been apparent both in
their attitude in negotiations on reform of the international monetary
system and in their reactions to the exchange rate developments of recent
years. For example, following the move to general floating in March 1973,
a group of ministers representing developing countries stated 'that a system
of stable exchange rates based on adjustable par values . . . constitutes an
essential element of a satisfactory international monetary order'.[1] As a
reflection of this view, most developing countries have, in the management
of their own exchange rates, maintained a fixed peg against a single
intervention currency, though a significant minority have moved to floating
exchange rates or have pegged their rates to a basket of currencies.

The case for flexible or floating exchange rates versus a system of
adjustable par values has usually been made abstracting from the level of
development of countries. But the economic characteristics and institutional
realities that differentiate developing from developed countries have an
important bearing on the argument. Whereas there may be persuasive
theoretical reasons for exchange rate flexibility among large diversified
economies, the differentiating characteristics of developing countries may
play an important role in their conviction that a system of adjustable par
values can better serve their interests. This paper does not consider the
question of which exchange rate system, if adopted on a world-wide basis,
would most suit the interests of developing countries. Rather, it indicates
some of the considerations that these countries, given their policy objectives
and in the light of their particular economic circumstances, should take
into account in deciding what exchange rate strategy to follow when the
currencies of the major industrial countries are floating.

The paper is divided into three parts. In the first part, we discuss the
differentiating characteristics of developing countries that may affect
their preference for a particular exchange rate system. In the second part,
we consider the various possible policy reactions of developing countries
to the current situation, where the industrial nations' currencies are floating,
while the third part provides a summary of the main results of this study.

1. CHARACTERISTICS OF DEVELOPING COUNTRIES

Various characteristics of developing countries have an important bearing
upon the costs of alternative exchange rate regimes for this group of
countries. In this section we shall indicate what these characteristics are
and what bearing they have on the adjustment process.

The main differentiating characteristics of developing countries (LDCs)

---

* International Monetary Fund, Washington, D.C.

of relevance to this paper relate to their high specialisation pattern in production, to their inability to affect export or import prices in foreign currency through their own exchange rate policies, to the inelastic nature of their demand for imports and, in the short run, of their supply of exports, to the rather rudimentary nature of their financial sector, and to the fact that capital flows are probably less responsive to conventional yield considerations.

Most less developed countries have the large majority of their labour force in the primary sector. Production is mainly agricultural, with a high dependence on a few major crops. Some developing countries may, in addition, have a mining sector that contributes a large proportion of total production. Relatively few have a highly developed manufacturing sector, or have more than a trivial volume of exports of manufactures. This contrasts dramatically with more developed countries, where the labour force is concentrated more in the secondary and tertiary sectors and where there is a large diversity of industrial products produced and traded.[2]

Reflecting the highly specialised production structure of developing countries, their foreign sector differs in nature and importance from that of more developed economies. First, since there is very little substitutability between locally produced goods and imported goods, the price elasticity of demand for imported goods is likely to be low. Second, since the production of primary products typically involves long gestation periods and since the proportion of most of the major export crops absorbed domestically is limited, the price elasticity of the supply of exports is also likely to be rather low in the short run. Third, since primary products are fairly homogeneous and the export share of each less developed country in the international market for its particular export good is in most cases small, most less developed countries are 'price-takers'. By comparison, in the industrial countries there is usually a greater degree of substitutability between imported and locally produced goods (because of their diversified production pattern); there is greater resource mobility[3] between sectors, and there is less homogeneity in the nature of the export product.

Economic growth in developing countries, as contrasted with that in industrial countries, is significantly more dependent upon the foreign sector for two basic reasons. First, foreign aid and long-term private capital flows into less developed countries play a greater role in supplementing domestic savings and increasing the rate of growth; domestic savings being in many cases not sufficient to enable the country to attain the desired growth target. Second, the fact that capital equipment is mostly manufactured abroad renders developing countries heavily dependent upon imports of capital equipment from developed countries. Thus, domestic savings are insufficient in themselves as a means of capital formation and the availability of foreign exchange plays an important role in channelling domestic savings into productive investment.

In addition, the financial markets in most less-developed countries are rudimentary. The process of financial intermediation is still at an early level of development and, hence, very limited; there are only a few banks that provide short-term credit, rationing mainly on the basis of credit-worthy and established customers rather than through an interest rate mechanism; the foreign exchange market functions mainly through the central bank with very few, if any, foreign exchange dealers; a forward market for the country's currency is virtually non-existent.[4]

Related to the level of development of the financial market, capital flows to and from less developed countries are often governed by factors other than interest rate differentials. Official development aid and long-term private capital flows are influenced more by political considerations and expectations of political stability than by pure yield factors. Short-term capital flows, which in the industrial nations respond quickly to changes in interest rate differentials and to expected changes in the exchange rate, may also be less responsive in less-developed countries given the greater uncertainty generated by lack of sufficient information and by the greater probability of change in the political climate.

Although less-developed countries may share many of the economic policy objectives of the more developed countries, such as full employment, growth and price stability, adjustment and financing mechanisms will work differently in the developing countries as a result of their differentiating characteristics.[5] The relative changes in the magnitudes of such instruments as the exchange rate, monetary and fiscal policies, and controls may have to be considerably greater than in the more developed countries to attain the same objective for the balance of payments. For example, the balance of trade may be less responsive, at least in the short run, to a change in the exchange rate, given the inelastic demand for imports, and the inelastic supply of exports. Similarly, a contractionary monetary policy leading to an increase in interest rates may have very little effect on capital flows into the country.

2. THE OPTIONS UNDER MANAGED FLOATING

Prior to the breakdown of the Bretton Woods system, nearly all the developing countries maintained a par value by official intervention by prescribing margins against their intervention currencies. The most commonly used intervention currencies were the US dollar, the French franc and the pound sterling, though a few other currencies were used in territories which had close links with countries other than the U.S.A., France and Britain. The most significant exceptions to the established pattern were Lebanon and the Philippines. Lebanon had allowed its currency to float independently since 1947. The Philippines started floating in February 1970.[6] Some countries, although pegging to a particular intervention currency, changed the par value by relatively small amounts at relatively frequent intervals. Even though this practice involved considerable exchange rate flexibility, it probably reflected less a deliberate preference for flexibility, than a necessary response to a situation of high domestic inflation, since this practice was followed by such high inflation countries as Brazil, Uruguay, Chile, and Colombia.

Most industrialised nations began to float in August 1971. During the initial floating period, which lasted from August to December 1971, other countries mostly continued to peg to their pre-existing intervention currency and, therefore, allowed the market value of their currencies to move in a manner determined by the movement of the intervention currencies. There was no move to free rates from intervention obligations or to set rates in terms of a group of currencies rather than a single currency. This apparent unwillingness to reappraise exchange rate policy can probably be explained in terms of the temporary nature of the floating system in the months after August 1971. It was known that efforts were under way to re-establish a new pattern of par values; this was in fact achieved after a period of a little over four months, by the Smithsonian agreement of December 1971.

The situation was different when floating was next introduced. Sterling was allowed to float in June 1972, and the Smithsonian pattern of rates finally broke down in February–March 1973, when a system of managed floating between most major countries appeared likely to persist for the foreseeable future. Furthermore, early experience with floating indicated that wide swings in the relative value of major currencies (of the order of 20 per cent within a few months) was possible and even likely. In these circumstances, the developing countries clearly had a greater need to reappraise their exchange rate policy than in the initial floating period, when floating appeared to be a temporary expedient. The three main options available to less developed countries in these circumstances were: (1) to continue to peg to a single intervention currency, (2) to peg to a basket of currencies, or (3) to float independently (with or without official management of the exchange rate).

Most less developed countries chose to remain pegged to a single intervention currency, although a number of countries which had previously been in the sterling area elected to switch to a dollar peg. However, a few appear to have subsequently felt that their interests would be better served by some other exchange rate system. For instance, Malaysia and Singapore have allowed their currencies to float independently since June 1973. Nigeria has followed a policy of allowing its currency to move midway between its trading partners. Several countries have adopted a policy of valuing their currencies in terms of a weighted basket of the currencies of their major trade partners. Morocco started pegging to a basket of currencies in May 1973, Malawi in November 1973, Algeria in January 1974, Fiji in April 1975, and Kuwait in March 1975. In the early part of 1975 several countries decided to peg to the SDR basket; these included Burma, in January, Iran, in February, Qatar and Saudi Arabia, in March, and Malawi in June.[7]

This section examines the advantages and disadvantages of the three alternative courses of action open to less-developed countries in the present circumstances and the practical problems involved in adopting any one option. First, we consider the implications of continuing to peg to a single intervention currency. Next, we discuss the arguments for pegging to a basket of currencies, and the relative merits of the two most favoured baskets, the SDR and an import-weighted basket. Finally, we note briefly the implications and problems involved in the option of independent floating.

(a) *Pegging to a Single Currency*
Pegging to a single major currency seems to have been the option most

favoured by less-developed countries. From a practical standpoint, it is perhaps the simplest; it appears to involve no more than continuing the exchange market policy which prevailed prior to the abandonment of the system of adjustable par values. However, under present arrangements, the consequences for the country may be different from those under adjustable par values, since the value of the country's currency is no longer held within narrow margins around a common world numeraire. Rather, the value of the currency will change vis-à-vis the rest of the world with changes in the value of the currency to which it is pegged.

Various advantages may be attributed to pegging the value of a developing country's currency to that of its major trading partner. First, pegging to a particular currency may reduce, relative to other alternatives, the fluctuations of the exchange rate between the less-developed country and the developed country. This facilitates trade between the two countries by reducing the uncertainties associated with changes in relative currency values. For the same reason, capital flows for investment purposes from the developed country may increase. Second, to the extent that the exchange rate of the industrial nation is more stable vis-à-vis the rest of the world than the exchange rate of the less-developed country would have been without pegging, trade with and investment from the rest of the world may also be stimulated. Third, a developing country that chooses to peg its currency to an external standard, such as the currency of a major country, gives expression to its intention to align its policies broadly with those of the partner country. If the policies of the partner country are regarded as adequate to the promotion of relatively stable prices, there might be increased *confidence* in the currency of the less-developed country. Consequently, foreign investment may be stimulated. Furthermore, pegging provides a clear criterion for intervention in the foreign exchange market. Lastly, the disciplinary aspects of pegging can sometimes be viewed as an advantage if a fixed rate acts, in the words of 1970 Report of the Fund's Executive Directors,[8] as 'a fulcrum for domestic stability'. This report put the argument as follows: '. . . the need to defend a fixed exchange rate against depreciation may promote political willingness to impose unpopular domestic restraints; and where the attempt to defend the parity is ultimately unsuccessful, the psychological shock of a devaluation may promote broad support for the adoption of the necessary associated measures to curtail domestic demand . . .'.

As noted earlier, however, single currency pegging in a world where major currencies are floating does not have the same consequences as adopting a fixed exchange rate in a world of stable parities. Such a policy involves at least four potential disadvantages over a system in which all countries adhere to par values. First, the need for reserves may increase. Movements in the pegged exchange rate of the less-developed country will not reflect actual developments in its balance of payments; rather, they will reflect the developments in the balance of payments of the industrial country to which the developing country is pegging. Whether this will result in a greater or lesser need for reserves than under adjustable par values depends on the nature of the relationship between the equilibrium exchange rates of the two countries. If the relationship is close and positive, induced changes in the developing country's exchange rate vis-à-vis the rest of the world will usually be in the right direction, with the result that there may be a lower need for reserves by the less-developed country than under adjustable par values. However, if, as is perhaps more likely, the factors affecting the equilibrium exchange rates of the two countries are not closely related, the need for reserves may be greater than under adjustable par values.[9]

A second drawback to a single currency peg is that fluctuations of the exchange rate, since they are exogenous and independent of government policy, may interfere with the pursuit of internal policy objectives. Consider, for instance, the case of a developing country attempting to stimulate local production and employment. An increase in the value of the intervention currency will lower the local price of imports and exports, stimulating imports and reducing the incentives to export. The overall effect may be a reduction in local production and employment. In the opposite case, where a country is concerned about inflation, a rise in the cost of imports caused by depreciation in the exchange rate of the intervention currency, may give an unwelcome stimulus to price increases. To some extent, of course, ups and downs in the country's exchange rate will cancel out over time. But in the meantime, the country may have been subjected to undesired and largely unpredictable inflationary and deflationary impulses transmitted through the foreign sector. There may even be unwelcome permanent effects. To the extent that the production and consumption of tradable goods becomes subject to greater uncertainty, there may be a diversion of activity towards non-traded sectors. And if there is a 'ratchet' effect in the inflationary process (i.e. if prices go up more readily when the exchange rate depreciates than they come down when it appreciates) then pegging to a floating currency may exacerbate inflation.

A third disadvantage with single currency pegging, as compared with a world of par values, is that exchange rates between the currencies of developing countries will be subject to variation, since not all these countries peg to the same major currency. This will be particularly disadvantageous when many of these countries, being small economic units, are trying to attain some of the advantages of market size by promoting intra-regional trade.

A fourth disadvantage is the possibility of a tendency towards higher import prices. For suppliers in countries whose currencies are fluctuating against that of a developing country, some increase in product prices may be needed to compensate for the increased uncertainties involved in trade with the developing country. For suppliers in the industrial country to whose currency the developing country is pegged, their stronger market position, as a result of the diversion of trade patterns in their favour, will increase their ability to claim higher profit margins.

Pegging to a particular currency in a system of managed floating therefore is *not* a continuation of the exchange market policy under adjustable par values since the world conditions are not the same. The single currency peg does have some clearly identifiable disadvantages, which we have noted. It is, in fact, in an attempt to limit these problems that some countries have decided to peg to a weighted basket of currencies that takes into account the trade shares relationships.

(b) *Pegging to a Basket*

Pegging to a particular major currency entails, as noted above, movements in the exchange rate of the developing country that are independent of factors affecting its own balance of payments. An alternative approach, which attempts to retain the advantages of pegging while minimising the disadvantages, advocates stabilising the *effective* exchange rate of a currency, where the effective exchange rate is a suitable average of market rates vis-à-vis the currencies of trading partners.

Changes in the effective exchange rate are intended to measure the hypothetical uniform change in the exchange rate of a currency against all other currencies, that would be equivalent, in its impact on the balance of payments of the country concerned, to the pattern of exchange rate changes that actually occurred. The most comprehensive measure of a country's effective exchange rate would take into account its trade and payments structure, including the price effects generated by exchange rate changes, the price elasticities for different products, the competitive relationships of a country's exports in foreign markets, the pattern of bilateral trade, and the effects on capital flows. Such a comprehensive index has yet to be constructed. Perhaps the closest approximation, which takes into account most of the effects mentioned above except the effects on the service, transfer, and capital accounts, is the index constructed for the industrialised nations based on the Fund's Multilateral Exchange Rate Model.[10] Given the amount of data required for the construction of the Multilateral Exchange Rate Model index, and given that such data are not available for most developing countries, it is necessary to consider simpler indices, which can be computed from available data, and which will take into account some of the conditions in the foreign exchange market.

There are essentially three such indices based on the pattern of merchandise trade:[11] (1) the export-weighted index, (2) the import-weighted index, and (3) the bilateral trade index. The export-weighted index of a country's currency is the arithmetic average of its exchange rate against other currencies, relative to a base period, weighted by the share of each trading partner in the exports of the country concerned. The import-weighted index is the arithmetic average of its exchange rate against other currencies, relative to a base period, weighted by the share of each country in the imports of the country concerned. The bilateral trade index is the arithmetic average of the export-weighted index and the import-weighted index, weighted by the shares of exports and imports, respectively, in the sum total of imports and exports. Although these three indices all allow in some way for the pattern of bilateral trade, they do not take into account repercussions on prices, substitution effects, changes in competitive relations in foreign markets, and effects on the service, transfer, and on capital accounts.

It can be argued that for less-developed countries, the import-weighted index provides the closest approximation among the three described, to the effective exchange rate index. The argument for an import-weighted index as a peg for a developing country's currency runs as follows: since primary commodities are relatively homogeneous, their prices will be set in world markets independently of the precise geographic pattern of trade. Thus, with a given volume of exports, a developing country's foreign exchange receipts will not be affected by changes in the exchange rates of the countries to which it exports, unless advance commitments to prices in a particular foreign currency have been made. However, since industrial products are not homogeneous, no uniform international price prevails. Accordingly, changes in the exchange rates of industrial countries vis-à-vis a developing country will affect the price which the developing country pays for particular industrial products. Thus, its import price index denominated in local currency will be affected by changes in the source of supply of its imports or by changes in exchange rates among supplying countries. Accordingly, the purchasing power of the foreign exchange earned by a given volume of exports will vary with the geographical distribution of imports. By weighting the changes in the exchange rates of the major industrial countries by their shares in the imports of the less-developed country, the effect on the average level of local prices of variations in foreign exchange rates is offset. This enables some unnecessary fluctuations in the relative prices of domestic and foreign prices to be avoided, and thus reduces distortions in the goods market.

The import-weighted basket peg has the advantage of reducing the price instability engendered by foreign exchange rate changes. For countries which wish to retain a system of pegging, but are concerned at the instability which a single currency peg causes in import prices, some such composite peg may be an appealing compromise. However, such a policy retains a number of disadvantages, some of which are common to any pegging system. Besides the familiar difficulties of pegging (deriving mainly from the fact that the foreign exchange market is not continuously in equilibrium) there is the problem that, since each developing country would use a different basket, there would be varying cross rates between *all* developing countries using such baskets, while under single-currency pegs, there is at least stability amongst those currencies which utilise the same peg. Furthermore, the use of an unfamiliar peg for each developing country's currency might render the countries less attractive outlets for foreign investment. This would be because investors would feel less able to predict the value of each developing country's currency, and might feel that this value was more likely to be manipulated (e.g. through changes in the composition of the basket) than under some alternative regime.

It is to overcome some of these rather intangible drawbacks to the construction of separate baskets for each country, that certain countries have elected to peg on a common numeraire with an already-existing international status—namely the SDR. A case can be made that if developing countries are going to peg, reducing cross-rates variability between LDCs would be a desirable objective in stimulating their intra-regional trade. Furthermore, pegging to the SDR is 'convenient 'from a practical point of view; it has an established value that is determined and published daily on the basis of the exchange rates in major financial markets and is based on trade shares of sixteen major industrial countries.

Pegging to the SDR has the drawback that it probably does not reflect movements in the effective exchange rate quite as closely as an import-weighted basket. However, if the divergence between the SDR rate and the import-weighted basket is not large, developing countries could probably benefit from pegging to the SDR.[12] Since there is clearly a trade-off in this case—somewhat greater variability in the effective exchange rate against greater convenience and the promotion of intra-regional trade—each country will have to determine whether the benefits outweigh the costs. In general, one can say that the case for pegging to the SDR will be stronger, the smaller the deviations of the SDR basket from the import-weighted basket and the greater the level of intra-regional trade that will occur.

Table 1 shows the divergence of the SDR basket peg and of a single currency peg from the import-weighted basket peg for several less-developed countries.[13] This table provides some indication as to the relative desirability of pegging to the SDR vis-à-vis a single currency peg *on the basis of deviations from the import-weighted basket peg*. The period covered runs from January 1970 to March 1975. Computations were made using monthly data.

The table was prepared as follows: the import-weighted index was computed for the countries listed using January 1970 as the base period.[14] Next, the relation of the exchange value of the SDR and the appropriate intervention currency to the import-weighted index was calculated. This relation will be referred to as a deviation-index, where a value of one implies a coincidence of the particular peg index with the import-weighted basket peg. Then the square root of the mean square deviations of the deviation-index from one was computed to obtain the standard percentage deviation of the SDR and the appropriate intervention currency from the import-weighted basket peg.[15]

A few interesting results emerge from the table. First, for most countries the SDR peg deviates very little from the import-weighted basket peg.

TABLE 1

STANDARD PERCENTAGE DEVIATION OF THE SDR, U.S. DOLLAR, U.K. POUND, AND FRENCH FRANC PEG FROM THE IMPORT WEIGHTED BASKET PEG, JANUARY 1970– MARCH 1975 (MONTHLY DATA)

	SDR Peg	US $ Peg	UK £ Peg	FF Peg	Current Exchange Rate Policy*
Europe					
Greece	04·5	12·8			US $ Peg
Malta	06·4	03·9	03·5		Floating
Turkey	03·3	11·6			US $ Peg
Latin America					
Argentina	00·8	09·5			US $ Peg
Brazil	01·4	10·0			US $ Peg[b]
Chile	02·4	09·3			US $ Peg[b]
Colombia	01·8	07·3			US $ Peg[b]

TABLE 1 (*continued*)

	SDR Peg	US $ Peg	UK £ Peg	FF Peg	Current Exchange Rate Policy[a]
Costa Rica	00·6	08·4			US $ Peg
Dom. Republic	02·0	07·2			US $ Peg
Ecuador	01·5	07·5			US $ Peg
El Salvador	01·2	09·8			US $ Peg
Guatemala	00·4	09·0			US $ Peg
Haiti	02·5	06·7			US $ Peg
Honduras	03·3	06·0			US $ Peg
Mexico	03·3	06·0			US $ Peg
Nicaragua	02·8	06·4			US $ Peg
Panama	01·6	10·1			US $ Peg
Paraguay	03·5	11·8			US $ Peg
Peru	00·7	09·4			US $ Peg
Uruguay	02·6	11·0			US $ Peg[b]
Venezuela	01·4	07·6			US $ Peg
Caribbean					
Bahamas	04·2	05·1	05·3		US $ Peg
Barbados	06·9	03·4	02·9		UK £ Peg
Guyana	05·1	04·8	04·3		UK £ Peg
Jamaica	05·9	03·8	04·0		US $ Peg
Trinidad	04·6	05·1	04·7		UK £ Peg
Middle East					
Bahrain	03·1	06·9	06·2		US $ Peg
Cyprus	01·1	08·5	08·1		Floating
Egypt	03·5	11·7			US $ Peg
Iran	03·5	11·9			SDR Peg
Iraq	01·2	09·7			US $ Peg
Israel	00·8	09·3			US $ Peg
Jordan	02·0	10·5	10·2		US $ Peg
Kuwait	02·5	10·9	10·6		Basket Peg
Lebanon	02·3	10·8		02·9	Floating
Oman	07·1	04·5	02·8		US $ Peg
Qatar	01·8	07·9			SDR Peg
Saudi Arabia	02·1	10·7			SDR Peg
Syria	04·2	12·5			US $ Peg
United Arab Emirates	01·0	9·4			US $ Peg
Yemen Arab Republic	04·4	12·4			Floating
Yemen	03·0	11·3	10·8		US $ Peg
Asia					
Afghanistan	05·4	13·5			Floating
Bangladesh	00·5	08·8	08·5		UK £ Peg
Burma	03·9	12·2	11·8		SDR Peg
Khmer Republic	04·5	11·6			Floating
Sri Lanka	02·0	10·4	09·9		UK £ Peg
Republic of China	05·3	13·2			US $ Peg
India	00·9	08·0	08·0		UK £ Peg
Indonesia	04·6	12·8			US $ Peg
Korea	05·1	13·0			US $ Peg
Laos	02·5	10·8			US $ Peg
Malaysia	02·4	10·6	10·2		Floating
Nepal	02·6	10·7	10·1		US $ Peg
Pakistan	00·5	08·8	08·5		US $ Peg

TABLE 1 (*continued*)

	SDR Peg	US $ Peg	UK £ Peg	FF Peg	Current Exchange Rate Policy*
Philippines	03·1	11·2			Floating
Singapore	02·8	11·0	10·6		Floating
Thailand	04·9	13·0			US $ Peg
Viet-Nam	01·6	08·3			US $ Peg^b
Africa					
Algeria	03·8	11·9		01·3	Basket Peg
Burundi	05·9	14·0	13·5		US $ Peg
Cameroon	03·4	11·5		01·5	FF Peg
Central Af. Rep.	04·7	12·7		00·9	FF Peg
Chad	04·9	12·9		01·0	FF Peg
Congo Republic	04·2	12·3		01·0	FF Peg
Zaire	04·0	12·4			US $ Peg
Dahomey	05·6	13·6		01·9	FF Peg
Eq. Guinea	02·0	10·3			Spanish Peseta Peg
Ethiopia	02·5	10·8			US $ Peg
Gabon	04·1	12·2		01·1	FF Peg
Gambia	02·0	10·0	09·5		UK £ Peg
Ghana	00·7	09·0	08·7		US $ Peg
Guinea	01·4	09·0		04·4	US $ Peg
Ivory Coast	03·5	11·7		01·5	FF Peg
Kenya	01·3	08·5	08·0		US $ Peg
Liberia	06·7	14·6			US $ Peg
Libya	02·1	07·3	07·0		US $ Peg
Malagasy Rep.	04·6	12·7		01·0	FF Peg
Malawi	02·2	07·6	07·0		SDR Peg
Mali	02·2	09·3		04·3	FF Peg
Mauritania	02·3	10·4		02·7	FF Peg
Mauritius	01·2	09·5	09·0		UK £ Peg
Morocco	03·8	12·0		01·5	Basket Peg
Niger	05·5	13·4		01·5	FF Peg
Nigeria	00·8	08·8	08·4		Basket Peg
Rwanda	07·6	15·5			US $ Peg
Senegal	04·4	12·4		01·0	FF Peg
Sierra Leone	01·4	08·8	08·3		UK £ Peg
Somalia	02·2	09·8			US $ Peg
South Africa	01·3	09·9	09·6		US $ Peg
Sudan	01·0	09·4	09·1		US $ Peg
Tanzania	01·9	10·3	09·9		US $ Peg
Togo	04·6	12·8		01·8	FF Peg
Tunisia	03·6	11·8		01·4	Basket Peg
Uganda	01·5	09·7	09·2		US $ Peg
Upper Volta	05·1	13·0		00·9	FF Peg
Zambia	01·2	08·5			US $ Peg
Oceania					
Fiji	02·8	10·7	10·5		Basket Peg
Western Samoa	01·8	09·3			US $ Peg

* In some cases the classification is not clear-cut. The current exchange rate policy indicated is the closest approximation. A cut-off date of 30 June 1975 was applied.
  ^b With frequent changes.

In most cases, the standard deviation does not exceed three per cent.[16] In some cases the results are rather striking. For such diverse countries as Argentina, Costa Rica, Guatemala, Peru, Israel, India, and Ghana, for instance, the SDR index coincides almost exactly with the import-weighted index peg, the standard deviation in each case being less than one per cent.

Second, the SDR basket peg shows, for most countries, a smaller standard percentage deviation than a single currency peg. For countries pegging to the US dollar, the differences are dramatic. Some examples suffice to highlight this point. For instance, the ratio of the standard percentage deviation of the US dollar peg from the import-weighted basket to the standard percentage deviation of the SDR peg from the import-weighted basket is approximately 12 for Argentina, 8 for Bolivia, 16 for Brazil, 4 for Chile, 3 for Syria, 4 for Yemen (PDR), 3 for Thailand. A notable exception is Jamaica, where the standard percentage deviation of an SDR peg is larger than that of the US $ peg. For countries pegging to sterling, the results are mixed. In the case of Guyana and Barbados, the standard percentage deviation of the sterling peg is less than of an SDR peg, though the difference in the case of Guyana is not very significant. In the case of Trinidad the SDR peg and the UK pound peg have almost the same standard percentage deviation from the import-weighted basket peg. For Zambia and Sierra Leone, the results are reversed. Zambia's standard percentage deviation in the case of an SDR peg is 3·0 while it is 9·5 for the UK pound peg. For Sierra Leone, the difference is equally significant; the mean percentage deviation of an SDR peg is 1·3 as contrasted with 8·3 for a UK pound peg. With regard to the countries pegging to the French franc, the table shows that a French franc peg for this group of countries is significantly better than the SDR peg. For instance, the standard percentage deviation of the SDR peg as compared with the French franc peg is two times more for Cameroon, four times more for the Central African Republic, five times more for Chad, four times more for the Congo, five times more for Dahomey, four times more for Gabon, and so on. The only exception is Mali.

Examining the pattern of trade of these nations, we can arrive at the following conclusion. In general, the more diversified the import structure of a country, the closer will be the movements of the SDR basket index to the import-weighted index. Only in the case of countries that maintain very close trading ties with one major industrial country, in particular the francophone African countries, will a particular currency peg be closer than the SDR peg to the import-weighted basket peg.[17]

Third, all the countries that have recently moved to the SDR peg show a smaller standard percentage deviation for the SDR peg than for a single currency peg. These include Burma, Iran, Malawi, Qatar, and Saudi Arabia. For both Qatar and Saudi Arabia, the standard percentage deviation of the SDR peg is, respectively, one-fourth and one-fifth the size of a US dollar or UK pound peg. For Burma and Iran, it is one-third the size of a US dollar or UK pound peg. For Malawi, the SDR peg also shows a standard percentage deviation a third the size of a peg to any of the three major currencies considered. If past movements are any indication, the actual exchange rate for all these countries pegged to the SDR should approximate more closely their effective exchange rate than any other single-currency peg considered.

This discussion leads us to two conclusions with regard to pegging to a basket of currencies. First, if it were possible to arrive at an effective exchange rate accurately and stabilise the value of a currency in terms of it, developing countries would be able to offset the impact of exchange rate changes abroad on their underlying balance of payments position. Since this hypothetically ideal effective exchange rate cannot be computed, it is argued that an import-weighted index is the best approximation for developing countries. In so far as the country attempts to maintain the movements of its exchange rate to this 'average' change, it retains some of the advantages of pegging. Namely, the country benefits from the 'discipline' imposed by this rigidity and, at the same time, gives an indication that it is maintaining its exchange rate in line with those of its trading partners. If this results in greater exchange rate stability vis-à-vis its trading partners than an alternative strategy, the country can benefit from greater trade and more capital flows. However, the disadvantages of 'pegging'—need for reserves, rigidities in adjustment, and distortions introduced by the fact that the peg does not totally reflect the conditions in the foreign market—remain.

The second conclusion relates to the use of the SDR as a peg. It was shown that for most countries the divergences of the SDR basket from the import-weighted basket over the period January 1970–March 1975, were small with, in most cases, a standard deviation of under 3 per cent. It was also demonstrated that a single currency peg usually shows a standard percentage deviation 3 to 4 times greater than the SDR basket peg. Hence, most countries could reduce the divergences of their actual exchange rate from their import-weighted exchange rate by moving from a single currency peg to the SDR basket peg, provided they do not do most of their trade with one major industrial country.

(c) *Independent Floating*

Although pegging to some composite of currencies can help to offset the effect of exchange rate fluctuations among major currencies on the effective exchange rate of developing countries, it does not, of course, do anything to counter other influences on these countries' payments positions. In other words, it does not promote adjustment to exogenous shocks, or ensure an equilibrium in the foreign exchange market.

The question therefore arises whether it might be advisable for developing countries to consider permitting greater flexibility in their exchange rates (i.e. by abandoning any peg) in order to achieve more continuous adjustment to external equilibrium. Here, too, a trade-off operates: the benefits of pegging, noted above, on the one hand, against the advantages of a more continuous adjustment of the external position, on the other. In considering this question it must be noted that flexible exchange rates for developing countries have different implications than for industrial countries, mainly because of their different institutional characteristics. Our discussion will centre around the costs and benefits involved in floating, with particular emphasis upon the issues of exchange rate stability, on the use of the exchange rate as a policy instrument and on the freedom of internal policy making.

Relatively stable exchange rates for less developed countries vis-à-vis the developed countries have several beneficial effects: the greater the stability of the exchange rate, the greater the level of trade (i.e. the greater the demand for the exports of the less-developed countries), the greater the production of the export good, the greater the capital inflows from developed countries, and the greater the level of capital formation.[18] If floating were to lead to relatively unstable exchange rates between these two country groups, this strategy would clearly be undesirable for less-developed countries.

For flexible exchange rates to be stable without government intervention, a well-functioning foreign exchange market with arbitrageurs is needed. Since such a market is virtually non-existent in most less-developed countries, there is certainly a danger that, if less-developed countries were to float, the private institutional structure would be unable at least initially to dampen satisfactorily exchange rate fluctuations.

For such a private market to emerge, the government would have to bow out of the foreign exchange market and accept the initial fluctuations. Arbitrageurs, becoming aware of the potential gains that could be made in the foreign exchange market, would then be attracted and start operating, reducing thereby the impact of transient and reversible movements in the exchange rate. If the government were, however, to undertake the stabilising function, the incentives for arbitrageurs, stemming from the initial wide movements, would be considerably reduced, and the foreign exchange market would develop very slowly, if at all.

Another point to be taken into consideration is the possibility of divergence between the long-term equilibrium exchange rate for a country's currency, and the *short-term* market-clearing rate—a point of considerable importance for less-developed countries. The short-term equilibrium rate can be defined as the one that would be established at a point in time by the interplay of market forces. The long-term equilibrium rate can be conceptually defined as the long-term exchange rate of the country when the 'appropriate' structural changes have taken place. For instance, a less-developed country may view its balance of payments in a long-term perspective, involving a period of sustained deficits while heavy investment is occurring within the country in the context of a development programme. The government may regard the deficit-incurring exchange rate as the appropriate 'long-term' exchange rate that would promote structural changes through sectoral investment that would result in a more diversified production structure. This would, in time, increase and stabilise exports leading eventually to a more balanced position in the external account. The short-term equilibrium exchange rate, which would be established under free floating, would then be regarded as an impediment toward the attainment of long-term policy objectives.[19]

The above argument highlights the fact that allowing the exchange rate to float freely implies a renunciation on the part of the authorities of use of the exchange rate as a policy instrument. In developing economies, where large structural changes are occurring and are desired, the loss of the exchange rate as a policy instrument may limit the ability of the government to bring about the desired structural changes. In particular, certain sectors may be implicitly encouraged and others discouraged by maintaining a specific exchange rate, a policy that would amount to actual subsidisation of some sectors at the cost of others. It may be argued that the same objective could be attained by direct taxes or subsidies. However, political realities may make it difficult to use direct instruments as compared with the indirect instrument of the exchange rate.

It is sometimes argued that the costs of the loss of the exchange rate instrument are outweighed by the gain of the ability of the authorities under flexible rates to pursue monetary and fiscal policies in accordance with their internal policy objectives while the exchange rate movements ensure balance of payments equilibrium. There are two major problems with this argument. First, the exchange rate may move in such a way as to offset the intended impact of fiscal and monetary policies, thus interfering with the attainment of internal policy objectives. For instance, a government attempting to increase the use of productive resources, while keeping to a minimum the inflationary tendencies of its expansionary monetary and fiscal policies, will find that the resulting decline in the exchange rate makes the task of controlling domestic inflation much more difficult. Second, it is not really true that under flexible exchange rates the government can follow monetary and fiscal policies very different from those of other countries. For instance, an expansionary monetary and fiscal policy, relative to the rest of the world, would result in a continually declining exchange rate, reinforcing the inflationary impact of the internal policies. Since this is immediately felt by the public, there will be a quick public reaction to any such policies. By contrast, under any of the two previous options, the maintenance of a peg would help to limit the inflationary forces. Hence, independent floating cannot be construed as freeing the country from 'discipline' in the pursuit of monetary and fiscal policy.

Another point of considerable consequence for less-developed countries is whether or not the exchange rate is effective as an equilibrating factor for the balance of payments, given the characteristics of less-developed countries. On the one hand, it can be argued that the exchange rate is the instrument which acts most directly on trade and capital flows, and to equilibrate the balance of payments through a flexible exchange rate avoids the need for distorting controls on trade and capital flows. It also obviates the additional adjustment costs associated with step changes in the exchange rate. On the other hand, there may be costs in allowing the exchange rate to play the major role in equilibrating the balance of payments on a more or less continuous basis. In the first place, since the responsiveness of trade flows to exchange rate fluctuations is probably less in developing countries than in industrialised ones, greater movements in rates will be necessary to adjust to external shocks. Given the uncertainties in the adjustment process (relating both to the timing and magnitude of price effects) there is a clear danger that private markets may overshoot the required exchange rate change in order to minimise risks. Furthermore, in so far as foreign investors see exchange rate flexibility as reducing the willingness of a country to follow restrained domestic monetary policies, there may be a harmful effect on capital inflows—at least until the country has established a 'track record' of responsible monetary and fiscal management.

An advantage that is sometimes claimed for floating for developing countries, is the economy in reserve holding that such a policy is thought to permit. Given the greater priority accorded to economic growth in developing countries, and the usefulness of foreign exchange in providing funds for the purchase of capital equipment from abroad, any reduction in reserve holdings would be a positive factor in increasing economic growth. Too much should not be made of this argument, however. In so far as official reserves are held for the purposes of financing reversible factors affecting the balance of payments, floating would simply transfer the rate-smoothing function from the authorities to the private sector, without effecting economies in foreign exchange holding to the country as a whole. Furthermore, many developing countries hold reserves also for the purpose of enhancing their credit-worthiness in international capital markets, and the savings in foreign exchange stemming from a reduction in reserves may be offset for them by higher cost, or greater difficulties, in borrowing abroad.

To recapitulate: independent floating for less-developed countries involves various costs that the country has to consider relative to the benefits. On the cost side, there are the institutional costs of developing a well-functioning foreign exchange market and renouncing the use of the exchange rate as a policy instrument. On the benefit side, there is the possibility of more continuous adjustment in the balance of payments; a reduction in distortions that may occur as a result of an artificially high or low exchange rate or as a result of direct controls on trade and capital flows; some additional freedom in the pursuit of internal policy objectives, and some reduction in the costs of reserve holdings. As is apparent from the above analysis, however, there are qualifications to the various arguments and it is not possible to weigh in a clear-cut manner the benefits against the costs. Much will depend upon the particular conditions of the country in question. Where trade flows are responsive to price factors (as, for example, for developing countries which have a substantial manufacturing sector) there is more likely to be a balance of advantage in rate flexibility. The same will apply to countries (like Singapore and Lebanon) where there is a developed capital market with substantial capital flows. In these cases, there is more likely to be a self-correcting tendency in the balance of payments which will tend to prevent exchange rate changes from moving too far in response to external shocks. In other cases, however, where trade flows are not very responsive to exchange rate changes (because export prices are determined in world markets and there are no close domestic substitutes for imports), the exchange rate changes needed to secure equilibrium in the balance of payments will be large. For these countries, the repercussions of exchange rate variability on domestic objectives, such as investment promotion and income distribution, may be a more potent factor on the negative side.

3. CONCLUSION

This study has examined the considerations to be taken into account by developing countries in determining their policy response to the current situation of floating among industrial nations. Three major categories of policy reactions were considered: (1) continuing to peg to the currency of a single industrial country, (2) pegging (a) to an import-weighted basket and (b) to the SDR basket, and (3) independent floating. While the characteristics of each particular country will undoubtedly have a bearing upon the appropriate policy response, the analysis in this paper leads us to the following conclusions.

First, pegging to a single currency will usually be sub-optimal in purely economic terms mainly because movements in the exchange rate of the industrial country will, in most cases, not reflect the conditions in the foreign exchange market of the developing country.

Second, pegging to an import-weighted basket takes into account some of the conditions affecting trade of the less-developed country and will, therefore, reduce distortions and costs arising from movements in exchange rates among other currencies. One of the drawbacks of this option, however, is that there will be varying cross-rates among developing countries' currencies, since each will be pegged to a different basket. In addition such a basket does not take account of other possible objectives of exchange rate policy, such as minimising fluctuations in the local currency price of exports, or recognising the particular importance of a few major currencies in capital transactions. It would consequently be beneficial if a common peg, which was a reasonable approximation of the import-weighted basket, but also took some of these other considerations into account, could be adopted. Computations show that during the five year period 1970–75, movements in the SDR basket closely approximated the import-weighted basket peg for most developing countries, except for those with very close trading ties with one major industrial nation.

Third, with regard to independent floating, it was indicated that problems may arise, stemming mainly from the particular economic characteristics and institutional structure of developing countries; the benefits and costs of such a policy depend in part on the level of development which a country has reached. For those relatively few that have either developed industrial sectors or efficient and open capital markets, exchange rate flexibility may facilitate the problem of external adjustment, while not interfering with domestic objectives very much. These countries can generally rely on the working of private institutions in the exchange market to achieve external equilibrium with relatively minor changes in the exchange rate. For the majority of developing countries, however, the costs of floating could initially be large, since at their existing stage of development, foreign exchange markets would probably not be able to efficiently stabilise exchange rate fluctuations. While foreign exchange markets might eventually develop in response to the wide fluctuations that would initially result from floating, the costs resulting from these fluctuations may be unacceptable to the authorities, in particular when they impede economic growth objectives.

NOTES

1. Intergovernmental Group of Twenty-four on International Monetary Affairs, Third Meeting of Ministers, Communiqué, 24 March 1973. This view was reiterated in a more recent meeting of the Group held in Paris in June 1975. The Communiqué of the meeting stated: 'On exchange rates, Ministers reaffirmed the stand that they had taken at the previous meeting against the legalization of floating other than in particular circumstances subject to conditions which should take account of the characteristics of countries and in a manner designed to prevent undue instability in the value of major trading currencies. Ministers expressed support for amendments envisaging a return at the appropriate time to a system of par values, containing provisions for the establishment of central rates, and empowering the Fund to authorize individual countries to continue the float thereafter in particular circumstances.'

2. See Kuznets [1966] and Hagen [1968].

3. See Kindleberger [1956].

4. For an excellent theoretical analysis of the implications of the rudimentary financial markets in developing countries, see Black [1975]. A detailed discussion of these markets in developing countries can be found in McKinnon [1973].

5. For instance, the Mundellian framework which, with reservations, can be useful in the analysis of adjustment in more developed countries, cannot be used even as a close approximation in the case of developing countries, given that one of its basic assumptions—the responsiveness of capital flows to interest rate differentials—is not applicable to less developed countries. For a useful alternative framework, see Black [1975].

6. In addition, a number of countries had multiple exchange rate practices. By redesignating certain categories of transactions from one rate to another, these countries could influence the overall value of their currency. This, however, cannot really be considered as a conscious step toward exchange rate flexibility, but rather a manipulation of an exchange rate restriction for balance of payments reasons.

7. Changes in exchange practices since June 1975 are not recorded here. A more complete record may be found in *Annual Reports* of the International Monetary Fund.

8. IMF, *The Role of Exchange Rates in the Adjustment of International Payments* [1970].

9. For a more extended treatment of this, see Ripley [1974]. Note, however, that her analysis is static and relates only to random shocks.

10. See Artus and Rhomberg [1973].

11. For a detailed discussion of effective exchange rate indices, see Rhomberg [1975]; Hirsch and Higgins [1970].

12. It should be noted that, although the SDR is inferior to the import-weighted basket in reducing fluctuations in import-prices, it may be somewhat better than the import-weighted basket in other respects. For example, world prices of raw materials may be affected by exchange rate movements among major currencies (e.g. a depreciation in the rate of a country which is a major importer of a particular commodity will tend to push the price of that commodity downwards). In general, the SDR may be expected to reflect the world pattern of absorption of primary products better than a particular country's import-weighted basket. To this extent, it may perform somewhat better in stabilising export receipts in local currency. Furthermore, the fact that the dollar has a heavier weight in the SDR than its share of world trade may be considered an appropriate reflection of that currency's relative importance in capital transactions.

13. This table is a development of an earlier unpublished study by J. Artus, whose assistance the authors gratefully acknowledge.

14. The formula utilised for computing the index of import-weighted exchange rates, relative to a numeraire currency, k, is:

$$E_{ik} = \sum_j (M_{ji}/\sum_j M_{ji}) R_{jk}$$

where M_{ji} is the imports of country i from country j in 1970 and R_{jk} is the value of currency j in terms of currency k, where $R_{jk} = 1$ at Jan. 1970.

15. Figures for the deviation of the SDR and the US dollar from the import-weighted basket peg are given for each country. Where the French franc or pound sterling was

used as the intervention currency (or was thought to be under consideration) these figures are also given.

16. To the extent that a particular peg diverges from the import-weighted basket peg by an increasing amount over time, the standard deviations will be an underestimate of deviations in the latter part of the period.

17. Though the superior performance of the French franc (as compared with the US dollar and UK pound) probably also owes something to the fact that the French franc followed a middle course during this period between currencies which depreciated on balance (US dollar and UK pound) and those which appreciated (Deutschemark and the Japanese yen).

18. See Nsouli [1975] for a rigorous proof of three of these results—greater level of exports, greater production of export goods, and a greater level of capital formation— in a formal mathematical model developed with respect to the stability of the terms of trade.

19. In theory, private speculators should be able to foresee the long-term improvement in the balance of payments, and thus be willing to finance current deficits through inflows of short-term capital. In practice, this is unlikely to occur where uncertainties are considerable and speculators are risk-averse. Nsouli [1974] provides an analytical model which shows rigorously the need for government interference when private and social risk perception differ.

REFERENCES

Artus, Jacques R. and Rudolf R. Rhomberg, 1973, 'A Multilateral Exchange Rate Model', *International Monetary Fund Staff Papers*, November.
Black, Stanley W., 1975, 'Exchange Policies for Less Developed Countries in a World of Floating Rates', manuscript, Nashville: Vanderbilt University.
Hagen, Everett E., 1968, *The Economics of Development*, Homewood: Irwin.
Hirsch, Fred and Ilse Higgins, 1970, 'An Indicator of Effective Exchange Rates', *International Monetary Fund Staff Papers*.
Intergovernmental Group of Twenty-four on International Monetary Affairs, Third Meeting of Ministers, Communiqué, 1973.
Intergovernmental Group of Twenty-four on International Monetary Affairs, Tenth Meeting of Ministers, Communiqé, 1975.
International Monetary Fund, 1970, *The Role of Exchange Rates in the Adjustment of International Payments*, SM/70/98, SM/70/132 (Revision 1), SM/70/132 (Revision 2), Washington D.C.: IMF.
Kindleberger, Charles P., 1956, *The Terms of Trade: A European Case Study*, New York: MIT-Wiley.
Kuznets, Simon, 1966, *Modern Economic Growth: Rate Structure and Spread*, New Haven: Yale University Press.
McKinnon, Ronald I., 1973, *Money and Capital in Economic Development*, Washington D.C.: Brookings.
Nsouli, Saleh M., 1974, *Stabilization of Export Proceeds and Economic Growth*, DM/74/90, Washington D.C.: International Monetary Fund.
Nsouli, Saleh M., 1975, 'Theoretical Aspects of Trade, Risk and Growth', *Journal of International Economics*, August.
Rhomberg, R. R., 1976, 'Indices of Effective Exchange Rates', *International Monetary Fund Staff Papers*, March.
Ripley, Duncan M., 1974, *Some Factors Affecting Reserve Needs in Developing Countries*, DM/74/110, Washington D.C.: International Monetary Fund.

Payroll Taxation in Developing Countries:
The Philippine Case

by Richard E. Rosenberg*

Recognising the need for increased tax revenues, especially direct tax revenues, and the inadequacy of their own revenues [*UNCTAD, 1967*], governments of many developing countries have been seeking to increase the proportion of national income collected in taxes. This study evaluates the possibility of using the payroll tax as a means of increasing tax revenues in developing countries. Payroll taxes have never been seriously considered as a major source of *general* tax revenue by development economists or in developing countries such as the Philippines[1] even though in some cases they have yielded significant revenues for financing Social Security expenditures.[2] There seem to be two major reasons for this state of affairs. First, payroll taxation in developing countries has not received the attention it deserves because it is believed that this is inherently a regressive form of taxation.[3] Thus, economists who have been urging progressivity in developing countries have generally ignored payroll taxation. This conclusion results from the incorrect generalisations about the experience of developed countries where the payroll tax is predominantly a regressive tax, considerably more so than even a flat rate tax on income [*Pechman et al., 1968: 180–81*]. Secondly, there is a widespread, but mistaken, view that payroll taxation is likely to increase the cost of labour to the employer thus increasing unemployment by encouraging the substitution of capital for labour.

This study involves an examination of the payroll tax in the context of developing countries such as the Philippines which indicates that payroll taxation is progressive in the Philippines (under a wide range of incidence assumptions) and is likely to be progressive in other developing countries as well. This study also concludes that it is unlikely that the payroll tax will increase the cost of labour to the employer and thus is unlikely to increase unemployment or stifle growth. In addition, it is argued that payroll taxation is relatively easy to administer and politically feasible thereby suggesting a reconsideration of the payroll tax as an additional source of general tax revenue for developing countries.

THE PHILIPPINE SOCIAL SECURITY SYSTEM
The Philippine Social Security System (SSS) uses a payroll tax to raise all its revenue. It was authorised in 1954 and began operation in 1957 with

* Assistant Professor at the University of Wisconsin-Parkside. The issues considered here grew out of a more general study entitled *The Effects of the Philippine Social Security System on Income Redistribution*, and was undertaken as a doctoral dissertation at the University of Wisconsin. Research for the dissertation in the Philippines was financed by a grant from the Midwest Universities Consortium for International Activities, Inc. (MUCIA).

1,768,222 employees registered as of 1967. The SSS legally covers all wage and salary workers excluding government workers covered by their own social insurance system and domestic workers in private homes. The bulk of Philippine SSS coverage consists of non-governmental wage and salary earners between the ages of 15 and 65. The Bureau of Census and Statistics (BCS) estimates there are approximately 2·1 million wage earners in this group [Bureau of Census and Statistics, 1963]. Comparing the Social Security registration figures of 1·7 million workers with BCS figures indicates that the Philippines has registered 80% of its wage and salary workers. Actual compliance differs considerably from legal coverage and registration, however. In 1967 the social security administration reported, after an extensive compliance drive, that only 39% of the registered employers and 53% of the employees were actually complying.[4] By the first quarter of 1968 these figures seem to have fallen even lower. From a complete enumeration of social security employer records [Rosenberg, 1970, Ch. I: 33] it was found that only 16,066 employers had made their full quarterly payments out of 60,974 registered employers (net of terminations). Thus, only 26% of social security employers were not delinquent.

This compliance structure has, however, been found to be biased towards the non-agricultural, highly modernised large-scale firms in the capitalist sector. In fact, only 1·6% of Philippine agricultural wage and salary workers comply [Rosenberg, 1970, Ch. I: 38]. Not surprisingly, the compliance, as opposed to the legal structure, reflects the basic 'dualism' between the 'subsistence' agricultural and 'capitalist' non-agricultural sectors, and within the industrial sector there exists an additional dichotomy between the large-scale firms with advanced technology and the small-scale firms backward in technology and modern business procedures. Thus, compliance is biased in favour of higher wage, wealthier members and against lower wage, poorer members of the Philippine wage force [Rosenberg, 1970, Ch. IV: 43-44]. This structural bias is not unique to the Philippines. For example, Davis [1964] has described similar findings for Chile.

The payroll tax amounts to 6% of wages and salaries up to 500 pesos a month and is distributed between employer and employee depending upon the employee's salary bracket. As one moves up the wage and salary scale, the employer pays a percentage that decreases from 5% for the lowest wage worker to 3·5% of the 500 pesos maximum while the employee pays a correspondingly increasing amount from 1 to 2½%. In 1967 the payroll tax yielded 124 million pesos. This added approximately 6·4% to the 1967 Philippines Government National Revenue of 1·9 billion pesos while other direct taxes accounted for only 417·8 million pesos of national revenue. The payroll tax is approximately 29% of this figure [Joint Legislative-Executive Tax Commission, 1970]

PAYROLL TAX INCIDENCE

A longtime popular assumption in public finance literature has been that both the employees and the employers share of[5] the payroll tax is borne entirely by labour, even when employees do not consider the tax payment as a quid pro quo for later benefits.[6] Support for this view has centred around the marginal productivity theory.[7] It is argued that, in the long run, a payroll tax will not make labour more productive, so profit-maximising employers will therefore have no reason to pay higher total compensation after the imposition of the tax. The validity of this view rests largely upon the reaction of wage earners to reduced wages. Wage earners may react by partially withdrawing from the work force (i.e. choosing more leisure) or where the tax is not universal, as is the case in the Philippines, by moving into uncovered employment. The first reaction is unlikely since it has never been demonstrated that the substitution effect of lower wages outweighs the income effect.[8] The second reaction, that workers may try to move into uncovered employment, is here considered to be more likely. This reaction is possible, however, only if there are comparable employment opportunities generally available in a sector not subject to the tax. While there are many areas in the Philippine economy which are not covered by or do not comply with the tax, it seems highly unlikely that employees will withdraw from covered employment due to the superiority of covered in comparison to uncovered employment. Covered employment is overwhelmingly centred in the large scale firms in the 'capitalist sector' where high wages are paid whereas uncovered firms are low wage firms in the subsistence sector. Another factor which would prevent a general movement of employees from the covered to the uncovered areas are the high levels of unemployment, both disguised and visible, in the Philippines.

In the absence of employment effects, the full payroll tax is borne by the employee because he is unable to shift his portion of the tax and because he cannot prevent the employer from shifting his portion of the tax back onto him. While employment effects are unlikely, especially in developing countries where coverage and compliance are likely to mirror the basic dualism which characterises these countries, the possibility of an employment effect cannot be completely ruled out. In addition and in actual practice, the shifting mechanism, especially in the short run, would probably be a combination of backward and forward patterns since it would be difficult for firms to cut the basic wage after the imposition of the tax. Instead, backward shifting is likely to take place by restraining the pace of wage increases below productivity increases. The balance of the shifting can be accomplished by cuts in real wages through price increases. Even in the case where some forward shifting occurs, it has been convincingly argued that you cannot rule out the possibility that labour bears the full burden of the tax.[9] Full shifting simply requires a combination of the two actions sufficient to maintain the real pre-tax share of capital. The final answer should, however, be sought in empirical analysis. For example, using cross-sectional data for over forty countries and later intra-industry comparisons in the US, Brittain [1971 and 1972, Ch. III] finds that at any given level of productivity, countries and industries with relatively high payroll taxes pay a basic wage that is relatively lower by the same amount.

It is important to discuss the possibility that these conclusions could be modified by any of the institutional or economic conditions that are unique to developing countries. Primary among such institutional possibilities in developing countries such as the Philippines are: (1) Union resistance to wage decreases and (2) minimum wage legislation.

Brittain's work suggests that unions generally have not been successful in preventing backward shifting in developed countries although they are relatively powerful and well established in these countries. It is therefore unlikely that they could prevent full backward shifting in developing countries where, by and large, they are generally immature and weaker. This is certainly true for the Philippines where economists' analyses of unions have found little or no evidence that they have had significant effects on wages [*Wurfel, 1959*]. Minimum wage legislation appears to have had a greater effect on wages than union action in the Philippines [*Wurfel, 1959: 600*]. While minimum wage legislation in the US has more often than not institutionalised existing minimum wage levels, in the Philippines the minimum wage has often been set at rates well above minimum wages at levels closer to average wages.[10] There exist two other factors in the Philippines that make it likely that minimum wages may prevent a full backward shifting of the employer tax. First, those firms complying with the Social Security System are those most likely to comply with minimum wage legislation.[11] Secondly, it should be remembered that a greater proportion of the tax is being initially levied on the employee in low wage brackets. Other developing countries, especially in Latin America, have similar forms of minimum wage legislation so this factor may be significant in preventing full backward shifting, in the long run, in other developing countries as well as the Philippines.

Some authors believe that factor proportions in developing countries are often 'fixed'.[12] If production does require fixed factor proportions, the payroll tax becomes, in effect, a general excise tax assessed on the general cost of production. Under these conditions, the full cost of the tax will not be shifted back onto labour. This proposition has received no substantial empirical support in the developmental literature. In fact, Williamson [*1971*] has shown that entrepreneurs in Philippine manufacturing do change factor proportions quite readily in response to changes in factor prices. Thus, for the Philippines, the available evidence seems to indicate that factor proportions are not fixed and thus are not obstacles to a backward shifting of the tax.

If full backward shifting of the tax does not occur, to what extent is the employer tax shifted forward? Forward shifting is generally believed to be positively related to industry concentration because such concentration implies some control over product price. Not only has it been observed that industry concentration is high in developing countries but recent unpublished evidence compiled by Sicat on concentration in Philippine manufacturing in 1960, seems to add support to this hypothesis.[13] If high concentration is typical of other sectors of the economy, then forward shifting should be relatively easy for firms throughout the Philippine economy.

Other factors may present obstacles to forward shifting in developing countries. According to Reviglio [*1967a: 516–17*] the forward shifting of the payroll tax in developing countries is limited because prices in export industries and import competing industries are determined by the world market. Although world market prices may constrain forward shifting in some developing countries, it does not seem to prevent forward shifting in the Philippines, for two reasons. First, those areas where social security compliance and coverage are significant are not those areas significantly engaged in export activity. Philippine exports stem primarily from agricultural, mining, and crude materials such as lumber [*Power, 1969: 13*] where social security compliance and coverage is virtually non-existent [*Rosenberg, 1970: 38*]. Secondly, in those sectors where compliance and coverage are high, all, except manufacturing, were in non-import competing industries such as construction, commerce and services. In the Philippines, average effective rates of protection in manufacturing have been computed to be 68% (Balassa method) and 65% (Corden method) [*Power, 1969: 52*]. These rates are high enough to allow Philippine manufacturers room to shift the payroll forward if necessary. This conclusion is likely to hold for many other developing countries where similar circumstances are likely to exist.

It is clear from the above discussion that while there is no one correct assumption about the incidence of the payroll tax, it is most likely to be borne entirely by labour. It is not entirely clear whether labour will be made to bear the tax though forward shifting which, due to price increases, will reduce his real wages or directly through wage restraint. Therefore, to get a measure of the whole range of possibilities, this study will analyse the incidence of the payroll tax under the following assumptions:

Assumption A: The employer tax is borne $\frac{1}{3}$ by the employer, $\frac{1}{3}$ is shifted forward to consumers, and $\frac{1}{3}$ is shifted backward onto the worker. This assumption applies most realistically in the very short run.

Assumption B: One-half of the employer tax is shifted backward and $\frac{1}{2}$ forward. This applies to the short run situation.

Assumption C: The full employer tax will be shifted backward on the workers. This assumption is most likely to apply, especially in the long run.

Although other assumptions could be made, the effect on the results would be similar to one of the above assumptions since these three assumptions cover the full range of possible effects.

THE PROGRESSIVITY OF PAYROLL TAXATION IN THE PHILIPPINES
The Progressivity of a Hypothetical Flat Rate Payroll Tax
The most realistic assumption about the incidence of payroll tax in a developing country is that, in the long run, it will be shifted backwards onto the worker. Let us initially assume this to be the case for the Philippines while considering only the effects of a flat rate payroll tax of 6%. This is comparable to the actual tax that exists in the Philippines under the assumption of full backward shifting. Furthermore, assume that this tax is levied and collected on all wage and salary income in the Philippines with coverage and compliance complete. These assumptions will be relaxed as we proceed.

To determine whether a flat rate payroll tax of 6% of all wage and salary incomes would be progressive, regressive, or proportional, we need to know how the distribution of wage and salary income is related to the distribution of all family income. These data are not readily available in most developing countries but, by using the unpublished records of the 1965 Household Survey of the Philippine Bureau of Census

TABLE I
PAYROLL TAX INCIDENCE IN THE PHILIPPINES

Family income class[a]	(1) % of family income[f]	(2) % of families	(3) Hypothetical 6% payroll tax on all wage & salary income	(4) Hypothetical 6% payroll tax on all non-agricultural wage & salary income	(5) Actual payroll tax incidence.[b] Assumption A	(6) Actual payroll tax.[c] Assumption B	(7) Actual payroll tax.[c] Assumption C	(8) Hypothetical tax. Assume revenue raised by 6% actual payroll tax.[d] Assumption A
500—below	1·4	11·6	1·40	0·49	0·04	0·66	0·44	0·56
500—999	5·3	17·7	1·29	0·44	0·03	0·46	0·26	0·52
1,000—1,499	8·1	16·7	1·42	0·72	0·16	0·42	0·29	0·58
1,500—1,999	9·2	13·5	1·52	0·78	0·44	0·58	0·44	0·61
2,000—2,499	8·8	9·9	2·32	1·94	0·71	0·76	0·60	0·94
Low	32·3	69·4	1·67	1·01	0·37	0·57	0·42	0·68
2,500—2,999	8·1	7·6	2·60	2·08	0·81	0·84	0·66	1·06
3,000—3,999	12·1	8·9	2·57	2·11	0·89	0·91	0·72	1·04
4,000—4,999	8·0	4·6	2·98	2·64	1·12	1·05	0·84	1·21
Middle	28·2	21·1	2·71	2·26	0·93	0·93	0·74	1·10
5,000—5,999	6·0	2·8	3·13	2·96	1·66	1·33	1·18	1·27
6,000—7,999	6·8	2·5	2·99	2·88	1·63	1·39	1·63	1·21
8,000—9,999	5·4	1·5	3·20	3·15	1·89	1·59	1·90	1·30
10,000—above	20·8	2·6	2·28	2·26	1·23	1·14	1·50	0·92
High	39·0	9·4	3·14	3·07	1·46	1·27	1·53	1·28

[a] Data on the Philippine family income distribution comes from Bureau of Census and Statistics of the Philippines *Family Income Distribution in the Philippines 1965.* Special release No. 62 series of March 1968.
[b] Assumes full backward shifting of the employers share of the payroll tax.
[c] Assumes ⅓ employer portion of the tax shifted forward, ⅓ shifted backward.
[d] Assumes ⅔ employer portion of the tax shifted forward, ⅓ shifted backward, ⅓ borne by the employer.

and Statistics[14] and going through the over 6,000 sampled households, it was possible to determine the distribution of wage and salary income for the Philippines.[15] The incidence of this hypothetical 6% payroll tax was then determined simply by multiplying wage and salary income in each income bracket by 6% and by dividing the tax by the total family income gross of all tax in each income bracket. The results appear in column 3 of Table I.

As one moves up the income distribution, the tax, as a proportion of income, generally increases (except for one or two minor exceptions), from 1·4% of the families in the lowest income bracket to 3·20% of those in the highest income bracket indicating that the tax is progressive. The tax averages out to be 1·67% for low income families (below 2,449 P a year), 2·71% for middle income families (between 2,500 P and 4,999 P per year) and 3·14% for high income families (those with incomes above 5,000 P a year). The income distribution here has been classified into low, middle and high incomes according to the Philippine Bureau of Census and Statistics official classification scheme. According to this definition, 69·6% of the families are considered low income, 21·10% middle income and 9·40% high income (see column 1 and 2 of Table I).

While the above data showed the payroll tax to be generally progressive, in order to measure the overall change in the family income distribution a statistic is needed which summarises the effects of the tax on the whole income distribution. The most widely used among a variety of measures of income distribution is the Gini coefficient or concentration ratio R. The concentration ratio R measures the extent to which a given tax structure causes a shift in distribution of income toward equality by measuring the area between the Lorentz curve and the line of absloute equality; the larger R is the greater the inequality of income distribution. This measure depends on three variables: the steepness of the rate structure, the overall level of taxation, and the equality of the initial income distribution.[16]

The Philippine family income distribution data was taken from the 1965 Bureau of Census and Statistics survey of households. Income is gross of all taxes. The concentration ratio R for the Philippines in 1965 was $R = 0·5111$. Subtracting the payroll tax estimated under the above assumption, the after tax ratio was $R = 0·5049$. A decline in R indicates a move toward greater equality. This increased equality moves the income distribution 1·26% (62/4899) of the way toward zero inequality.[17] This result is interesting and somewhat surprising since a flat rate payroll tax in the context of most developed countries is largely regressive. The difference in the results can be explained by the fact that wage and salary employment tends to be concentrated among higher income workers in the Philippines. In fact, these results indicate that in a developing country where most of the poorest people belong to the subsistence sector, in either agricultural or petty trading, and large proportions of the work force are unemployed, or under-employed, wage and salary employment appears to represent something of an 'élite' position.

This conclusion is reinforced if we estimate the incidence of this hypothetical payroll tax on non-agricultural wage and salary employment instead of all wage and salary employment. Column 4 of Table I shows the incidence of this payroll tax on all non-agricultural wage and salary income which is clearly more progressive than a payroll tax on all wage and salary income. In fact, the concentration ratio for the Philippines personal income distribution after this tax is netted out is $R = 0.4821$. Comparing the value of this concentration ratio with that of flat rate payroll tax on *all* wage and salary income which was $R = 0.5045$, it can be seen that this tax would move the income distribution considerably closer to zero inequality. In fact, a 6% flat rate tax on all non-agricultural wage and salary income moves the income distribution 5.9% towards zero inequality. This increase in progressivity occurs because a disproportionately large number of low wage and salary workers are in agriculture.

It has been demonstrated that a hypothetical flat rate payroll tax of 6% on all wage and salary income and on all non-agricultural wage and salary income are progressive in the Philippines. It has not yet been determined whether the actual payroll tax levied in the Philippines is progressive. Everyone is all too familiar with tax structures that appear to be progressive but whose progressivity is nullified or seriously reduced by biased coverage and compliance. Therefore, it is necessary to determine what the progressivity of the actual Philippine payroll tax is.

The Progressivity of the Philippine Payroll Tax
Because adequate survey data does not exist, the determination of the progressivity of the payroll tax requires a two-step process. First, the wage and salary distribution of the payroll tax must be determined. Secondly, wage and salary distribution of the tax must be allocated to the proper family income brackets.

A random sample of 2,318 complying Social Security System employees was used to determine the wage and salary distribution of the Philippine SSS.[18] Using this distribution and the schedule of payroll taxation, the wage and salary distributions of the portion of the payroll tax borne by the employees was determined. The problem now is to allocate this portion of the tax to its appropriate family income class.

To allocate data distributed by salary brackets to family income brackets, one has to know the income distribution of wages and salaries in each salary bracket. These distributions vary primarily with variations in: (1) percentages of wage income to other types of income by family income class, (2) the number of wage earners in each family by income class. Previously, both factors were analysed and allocation made by subjective assumptions based on these data.[19] This was, at best, a very imprecise procedure. What is needed is a wage and salary family income distribution matrix, that is, the percentage of wage and salary workers in each total family income class for each wage and salary bracket (see Table II). Then, by multiplying the amount of payroll taxes in the salary bracket by the percentage of wage and salary workers in each family income bracket, one can allocate the wage and salary distribution of the payroll tax to the appropriate family income bracket.

A wage and salary/family income distribution matrix was constructed by going through the over 6,000 sampled households of the 1965 Household Survey of the Philippines Bureau of Census and Statistics and placing each

TABLE II

PHILIPPINE EMPLOYEE WAGE AND SALARY/FAMILY INCOME DISTRIBUTION MATRIX, 1965*

Wage and Salary \ Family Income	500 below	500–999	1,000–1,499	1,500–1,999	2,000–2,499	2,500–2,999	3,000–3,999	4,000–4,999	5,000–5,999	6,000–7,999	8,000–9,999	10,000–above	Total Per cent
500-below	10·45**	18·38	19·69	17·68	11·55	4·83	8·34	4·03	2·12	2·12	0·41	0·50	100%
500–999		10·18	18·45	14·82	13·98	9·66	14·13	7·24	2·59	5·17	2·08	1·72	100%
1,000–1,499			14·12	25·62	11·12	8·06	13·32	7·40	5·75	6·41	1·98	3·29	100%
1,500–1,999				18·69	19·60	13·95	11·49	11·70	8·79	4·96	4·73	6·08	100%
2,000–2,499					18·19	15·99	16·40	10·74	9·78	9·93	7·17	11·85	100%
2,500–2,999						14·90	24·81	10·18	16·72	10·45	10·95	12·00	100%
3,000–3,999							17·60	12·96	15·04	18·43	7·85	28·00	100%
4,000–4,999								20·27	13·95	21·43	13·95	30·40	100%
5,000–5,999									17·79	15·55	17·79	48·91	100%
6,000–7,999										13·72	35·29	50·99	100%
8,000–9,999											30·78	69·24	100%
10,000–above												100	100%
Total	2·41	5·67	9·13	11·73	11·73	9·09	13·20	8·19	7·21	7·25	4·93	9·57	100%

* For all non-agricultural workers including government workers.

** Read as: 10-45% of the wage and salary workers whose wages and salaries fall below 500 pesos have family incomes below 500 pesos a year.

wage and salary worker in each family in his or her appropriate wage and salary/family income bracket. Since the compliance data revealed that agricultural wage workers are almost totally excluded from coverage by the Social Security System, agricultural wage and salary workers were excluded from the matrix.[20] (The results appear in Table II.)

It is now a simple matter to allocate each salary bracket tax borne by the employee to the appropriate family income class by multiplying the payroll taxes in each salary bracket by the percentage of wage and salary workers in each family income bracket.[21] The incidence of the tax, under the assumption of full backward shifting, appears in column 5 of Table I. The total employee payroll tax shifted back on the employees was allocated in the same manner.

The portion of the employer tax shifted forward (assumptions B and C) was allocated according to the nonfood-consumed-at-home-expenditures for each income bracket.[22] Forward shifting of the tax, in this manner, is regressive since nonfood-consumed-at-home-expenditures decline as a proportion of income as one moves up the income distribution in the Philippines. Nonfood-consumed-at-home-expenditures by income class were chosen instead of total expenditures because it was believed that the overwhelming share of price increases caused by the forward shifting of the employer tax would be in nonfood expenditures. Analysis of compliance has shown that agriculture and fishing are for all practical purposes not covered by the Philippine Social Security System and only a small percentage of payroll taxes for the Social Security System comes from small scale establishments where the great majority of Filipinos buy their food. Furthermore, many Filipinos are subsistence farmers who grow their own food. Allocation of the portion of the tax shifted forward according to total expenditures by income class, would have made forward shifting slightly more regressive than it is under the above assumption.

The employer tax, borne by the employer, was allocated to the 6,000 pesos a year class and above. Since most (if not all employers) fall into this class, the total tax borne by employers was divided proportionately according to the relative amount of income in each family income bracket above 6,000 pesos. This assumption, *ceteris paribus*, reduces the progressivity of the incidence of the payroll tax estimated here, since it is likely that most employers' incomes substantially exceed 6,000 pesos. For example, the study *Tax Burden by Income Class in the Philippines* assumed that the employer tax is borne by the income class 10,000 pesos and over.

Table I shows payroll taxes as a proportion of income for each of the family income brackets in the Philippines. This table reveals that under the three alternative incidence assumptions (A, B, and C) payroll taxes are *progressive*—that is, the tax as a fraction of income increases from low to high income brackets. This is a somewhat surprising conclusion since the Philippine payroll tax (under assumption A for example) takes a constant proportion (6%) of wages and salaries up to 500 pesos a month. That is, the tax schedule is proportional up to 500 pesos a month and thereafter it is regressive taking a lower and lower proportion of higher and higher wages and salaries. The explanation lies in the fact that wage and salary income generally increases as a proportion of all family income as total family income increases[23] and compliance and coverage is biased towards high wage workers. These two forces overcome the regressivity of the rate structure.

To measure precisely the change in the overall income redistribution brought about through the Philippines payroll tax, concentration ratios (or Gini coefficients) must again be estimated. Our previous estimate of the concentration ratio (R) for the Philippines in 1965 was $R = 0.5111$. Payroll taxes for each income bracket estimated for 1967 under assumptions A, B, and C were then subtracted from the distribution of family income in the Philippines producing the following results: $R = 0.5061$ for incidence assumption A, and 0.5069 and 0.5054 for assumptions B and C respectively. Since R has decreased under all incidence assumptions the income distribution has become more equal. This increase in equality moves the income distribution 1·08 per cent (53/4899) of the way toward zero inequality under assumption A, and 0·85% and 1·16% of the way toward zero inequality under assumptions B and C respectively. This increase in equality is small, but it substantiates the previous conclusion that the overall impact of the payroll tax is progressive.

Since concentration ratios (or Gini coefficients) provide an overall measure of the effects of the payroll tax on the income distribution, they can be used to compare the degree of progressivity of the tax under these three alternative incidence assumptions. The differences in progressivity of the tax under the three alternative incidence assumptions is slight. There are differences, however. The payroll tax is most progressive under assumption C; the concentration ratio is closest to zero $(R = 0.5054)$. Assumption A is slightly less progressive than C $(R = 0.5061)$, since the regressive effect of shifting ½ of the employer tax forward is offset by the progressive effects of the employer bearing ½ of his tax. B is the least progressive of the three assumptions $(R = 0.5069)$ since under this incidence assumption ½ of the employer tax is shifted forward, and forward shifting is the most regressive of all possible incidence assumptions.

The progressivity of the hypothetical payroll taxes (estimated in columns 3 and 4 of Table I) was caused solely by the fact that wage and salary income increased as a proportion of family income as family income increased. The estimates of the incidence of the actual Philippine payroll tax, which is also progressive, additionally takes into account the biased coverage and compliance in the Philippine Social Security System. Comparing the results of such a hypothetical payroll tax with full compliance and coverage whose rate is set to yield the same total revenue as the actual Philippine payroll tax (the estimated incidence of this tax appears in column 8 of Table I) with the estimated incidence of the actual tax under assumption A (column 5 of Table I) will make it possible to determine to what extent the biased coverage and compliance alone effects progressivity. Both the actual and potential payroll tax are compared only under the incidence assumption of full backward shifting.[24]

Comparing these two taxes (column 5 and column 8 of Table I) reveals that the hypothetical tax is more regressive than the actual Philippine payroll tax. For example, it taxes low income workers 0·68% of income as compared to 0·37% of income for the actual tax and 1·10% of middle income, and 1·28% of high income members as compared to 0·93% and 1·46% respectively for the actual tax. The differences between these two tax incidences measures the extent that the biased compliance increases the progressivity of the Philippine payroll tax.

ADDITIONAL CONSIDERATIONS
This analysis has shown that a hypothetical flat-rate payroll tax on all wage and salary income in the Philippines is progressive. It has also shown that the actual Philippines payroll tax of 6% on all wage and salary income up to 500 pesos a month is progressive. These estimates were made for a range of realistic incidence assumptions.[25] The two reasons for this progressivity, the increasing proportion of wage and salary income moving up the income scale and the biased compliance which reflect the 'dualistic' structure of the Philippine economy, are conditions which are likely to be present in many other developing countries. This inference removes what is here believed to be one of the major stumbling-blocks prevalent in developing countries against serious consideration of the payroll tax as either a means for financing social security programmes or as a source for much needed general tax revenues.

It is interesting to inquire whether any other considerations would inhibit the use of the payroll tax for general revenue purposes. The effects of a flat rate payroll tax under the most realistic assumption of full backward shifting is examined to simplify the following analysis.

A major issue raised in the literature focusing on labour taxes is the possibility that if payroll taxation is borne in part by the employer, thus increasing the cost of labour, it will increase unemployment by promoting the substitution of capital for labour. This fear appears to be largely groundless in the light of recent theoretical and empirical discussions in the professional literature. Since the opposite view has often been mistakenly assumed, these findings need to be summarised. Professor Shoup has shown that in a two-factor, closed economy, a general payroll tax would be equivalent to a value added tax (consumption type) on the prospective stream of incomes excluding gross profits and thus, by definition, reduces to a tax on labour incomes only.[26] It has been shown that this conclusion will hold, even in the case of a selective payroll tax [Brittain, 1972: 33–36]. If this were not the case, and if the tax increased the cost to the employer, Samuelson has shown that, in the long run, under certain assumptions, the cost of capital will tend to rise with the cost of labour and the tax will, therefore, have no effect on the relative price of capital and labour.[27] In addition to these theoretical arguments, there is the previously cited empirical support for the proposition that labour bears the full burden of the payroll tax [Brittain 1971 and 1972, Ch. III]. While there are important qualifications to these studies[28] the most likely conclusion that can be drawn from them is that the payroll tax is generally unlikely to lead to significant unemployment or re-allocation of labour. In fact, if the relative prices of capital and labour are unaffected, the issue of overall substitution of capital for labour does not even arise and we are left with only the minor rate differentials within the payroll tax itself as a potential source of allocative effects. While these microeconomic effects cannot be ignored, they are likely to be small because labour mobility between diverse sectors is likely to be low within the covered 'capitalist' sectors and virtually nonexistent for reasons already discussed between 'capitalist' and 'subsistence' sectors of developing countries.

Some commentators, W. A. Lewis being the most notable,[29] have taken the view that in developing countries the present trends in rural–urban migration which have turned rural disguised unemployment and underemployment into open urban unemployment are unacceptable. This view is valid because the former, unlike the latter, carries with it the attendant risks of crime and political unrest as well as causing the explosion of cities and towns demanding higher investment in social overhead capital.[30] This migration is attributable, at least in part, to what is considered to be excessively high wages in the 'capitalist sectors' of developing countries.[31]

If the picture of the developing world described by Lewis is accurate (there is still considerable controversy on this point) then some instrument must be developed for lowering the take-home wages of labourers in the modern 'capitalist' sector, thereby reducing the attractiveness of employment in this sector. Payroll taxation would seem to be an ideal instrument for this purpose because it is most likely borne entirely by the worker, in the long run, no matter how it is levied. And, if the structure of coverage and compliance described here for the Philippines is typical, this tax would almost exclusively reduce the real *take-home wage* of those workers in the capitalist, high wage sector.

The payroll tax would not reduce the wage bill to the employer, i.e. the take-home wage plus payroll tax bill is unchanged. Thus, employment in the capitalist sector would be unchanged. But by reducing the real take-home pay of workers in this sector, it may reduce the migration of workers from the subsistence to the capitalist sector. Thus, payroll taxation could be used to restore the 'normal' balance in the relative wage structure between the 'subsistence' and 'capitalist' sectors and the growth process may proceed more rapidly.

A further advantage of payroll taxation is that it is not likely to reduce saving and investment. If, in the long run, labour bears the whole tax, as our analysis has shown that it is likely to, capitalist saving and investment out of profits would not be affected. It is possible, however, that the payroll tax would reduce the savings of workers. This is a likely result of any tax on workers' income. However, the adverse effect of payroll taxation on these savings from this source is likely to be slight. Williamson [1967], using a model which introduces explicitly the effects of functional income distribution into the aggregate savings function, presented evidence that Asian savings are mainly a function of non-labour income (the coefficient attached to non-labour income, in the aggregate saving function, far exceeds that of labour income). In fact, Williamson found that non-labour income, by itself, is an excellent predictor of total personal savings in Asia [*Williamson, 1967: 19*]. Furthermore, if a part of the payroll tax is earmarked for social security purposes, there is evidence from developed countries[32] and some limited evidence from the Philippines,[33] that taxation for Social Security System purposes actually increases other savings, particularly institutionalised savings which are a main concern for developing countries.

The payroll tax is likely to have other advantages when compared to other forms of direct taxation such as personal income tax. It does not require dealing with as great a number of individual returns nor as high standards of literacy or accounting, and would not depend as heavily on voluntary compliance as does personal income tax. Thus, the payroll tax would appear to be significantly easier to administer than personal income taxation since the conditions necessary for its successful implementation are less demanding. Another important advantage of payroll taxation is that it usually encounters less political resistance than other forms of direct taxation. This is due to employers' expectations of being able to shift the tax either forward or backward enabling them to view the tax more favourably, than a tax which directly and progressively taxes the income of the enterprise. Employees are not violently opposed to the tax, because they are often under the illusion that the employers are paying their fair share of the tax.[34] Furthermore, the payroll tax is likely to have a higher income elasticity of yield than other forms of taxation because of the rapid expansion of wage and salary employment at early stages of development.[35]

To summarise, therefore, the payroll tax is a progressive tax which is relatively easy to administer. It is politically feasible, and it is unlikely to reduce savings, investment or incentives and may even improve the regional allocation of labour if Lewis's analysis is valid. It is also less likely to interfere with resource allocation and savings than the other leading forms of direct taxation (e.g. corporate income and personal income taxation).

NOTES

1. A few countries already levy payroll taxes for general revenue purposes. However, few if any developing countries outside of Africa use the payroll tax for other than the financing of social security.

2. See [Reviglio, 1967] for a survey of revenues raised by payroll taxation in developing countries for social insurance purposes.

3. The fact that the progressivity of taxes is a major concern to developing countries has been expressed most recently by Richard Bird, 'Taxation in developing countries is not only a means of providing public savings and of correcting imperfections in the market system it is also usually conceived of as a major means of effecting any income redistribution thought desirable. The role of taxes in achieving economic equality is sometimes considered even in the poorest country to be as important as their role in economic growth.' [Bird, 1970: 519.]

4. See section on coverage in [Social Security Administration, 1967].

5. The general theorem in public finance that it makes no difference, as to incidence, which side of the market a tax is collected from, is valid here. If, in fact, the tax is viewed as a quid pro quo for later benefits, it strengthens the conclusion that labour will bear the full burden of the tax because in these circumstances workers will not try to avoid paying the tax by moving into uncovered employment. This statement is valid, irrespective of the form that these later benefits will take (e.g. bonuses, dividends, or direct payments for contingencies). For substantiation of this view see Pechman, Aaron and Taussig [1968: 176].

6. The earlier literature on the incidence of the employer tax was summed up in 1941 by S. Harris, 'The economists who, in the years preceding the introduction of the Social Security Act, had given the problem of incidence careful consideration, seem to have been in general agreement that a payroll tax, whether levied on the worker or the employer, would be paid ultimately by the workers. . . . In the years that have passed

since the Social Security Act became law, the weight of informed opinion seems to be that the payroll tax is borne largely by the workers.' [*Harris, 1941: 285–86.*]

7. A more recent view states that, 'the marginal productivity theory has led most economists to believe that in the long run both the employer and employee share of the tax are borne by the employee' [*Pechman et al., 1968: 175–83*]. For another more complete review of thoughts on this subject which confirms this proposition, see Brittain [*1972*].

8. See Shoup [*1969: 410*], and for a more complete analysis, Musgrave [*1959: 232–40*].

9. Brittain reaches this conclusion after an exhaustive discussion of the issues. This result rests on two simplifying, but not unrealistic assumptions. (1) the tax is considered in the context of an assumed balanced budget implying spending changes corresponding to each tax that are distributionally neutral in their impact on money incomes available for private use, (2) with respect to capitalists and labourers the product price changes due to the tax do not affect the relative costs of the bundles of goods consumed by each group. See Brittain [*1972, Ch. 11*].

10. L. O. Stifel reports that in 1959 when the minimum wage in the Philippines was set at 4 pesos a day the median wage in the textile industry was 4·47 pesos.

11. L. O. Stifel suggests this is the case for the textile industry.

12. See Ekhaus [*1955*] for the initial statement of this view.

13. Using concentration ratios (per cent shares of three largest establishments in fixed assets) for Philippine manufacturing, based on two digit ISIC classification, Sicat showed that the three largest establishments have over 45% of the fixed assets of manufacturing firms in 7 out of the 18 sectors for which data were available. In none of the 18 sectors did the largest three establishments have less than 20% of fixed assets. Although concentration ratios based on two digit classifications are rather crude, these estimates reveal that concentration is high in Philippine manufacturing.

14. The Philippine Statistical Survey of Households was initiated in 1956. The 1965 survey sample comprised 6,500 households selected by a random two-stage sample design. At the aggregate level, with the exception of the figures for unemployment, the standard errors attributable to sample design and size do not appear to be excessive. (See Bureau of Census and Statistics *Survey of Households Bulletin*, Series No. 19 for estimates of standard errors.) Apart from the sampling error, some response error may be implicit in the information obtained from households. In this study we are concerned primarily with the accuracy of the estimates of family income. Family income is most likely inaccurate because estimates of non-monetary or subsistence income are likely to be underestimated. It should be noted that the survey questionnaire was designed to minimise this source of error. The survey questionnaire estimates, for example, wages paid not in cash, income from petty trading, production of articles for own use, income from livestock poultry, crops, fruit, etc., consumed, bartered and paid for debts. The survey also imputes the income from owner occupied houses and farm land (see Bureau of Census and Statistics Survey Part II, Income from 2 January to 31 December 1965, Box No. 1–10). Whatever errors are present in this survey are likely to relate to absolute rather than relative figures. For a more detailed discussion of the validity of this survey see Rosenberg [*1970: 215–19*].

15. Wage and salary income for each income bracket was estimated by putting the wage and salary workers in each household in their appropriate cell of a wage and salary family income distribution matrix similar to Table II. Then the number of workers in each cell was multiplied by the median salary of the corresponding wage and salary bracket to get the wage and salary income for each cell. The total wage and salary income for each income bracket was determined by adding together all the wage and salary income in the appropriate column of the matrix. It should be noted that this method underestimates slightly the amount of wage and salary income, and thus the amount of payroll taxes, allocated to the higher income brackets because it assumes that within each wage and salary bracket (i.e. row of the matrix) the median salary is the same in all family income brackets while, in fact, it is likely that the median salary within each wage and salary bracket (row of the matrix) increases with increasing total family income. Thus this method of estimation, if anything, slightly *underestimates* the progressivity of payroll taxation.

16. The major weakness of this measure is that it is relatively insensitive to small

changes in the income distribution (i.e. the value of the Gini coefficient changes relatively little with small changes in the equality of the distribution of income). Thus, it often underestimates the impact of tax or expenditure policies on the distribution of income. It is still considered, however, to be the most reliable of all the measures of overall changes in the distribution of income. For a discussion of the various measures of progressivity, their strengths and weaknesses, see Musgrave and Tun Thin [1948].

17. Okner uses this method of comparing concentration ratios [Okner, 1966: 283].

18. See Rosenberg [1970, Appendix I & V] for discussion of reliability of these data.

19. This approach, for example, is adopted by Carroll [1960].

20. The non-agricultural rural–urban matrix includes all wage and salary workers including government wage and salary workers. However, the Social Security System systematically excludes all government wage earners who are covered by the Government Social Insurance System (GSIS). It was not possible to exclude the government workers from the matrix since it would have been very difficult to identify these workers in the Bureau of Census and Statistics sample. A random sampling of 1,140 government wage and salary workers, undertaken by the author, has shown that the wage and salary distribution of government workers is quite similar to the wage and salary distribution of SSS workers. Therefore, it is unlikely that the inclusion of government workers in the matrix biased the results.

21. To simplify the calculations, our analysis assumes that the median wage and salary for each row is the same for each income column of the matrix. When this assumption is made, the proportion of wage and salary workers in each income bracket would be identical to the proportion of wage and salary income in each bracket. Multiplying the payroll tax associated with each wage and salary bracket by the percentage of wage and salary workers in each income bracket, thus gives us a very close approximation of the payroll tax paid in each income bracket. If anything, this method understates the progressivity of the payroll tax. See footnote 15, op. cit.

22. Data were taken from [Bureau of Census and Statistics, 1968].

23. The income/salary matrix (Table II) shows the proportion of wages and salary workers in each salary bracket that fall in each income bracket. The income/salary matrix, shown in Table II, does not directly show that wage and salary income increases as a proportion of total family income as total family income increases. This tendency is present, however, and can be observed by looking at column 3 of Table I which was derived from an income/salary matrix, comparable to that shown in Table II, and shows the effect of a flat rate payroll tax (6%) on all wage and salary income. The fact that this hypothetical flat rate tax (6%) on all wage and salary income generally increases as a proportion of total family income, as total family income increases, indicates that wage and salary income must be increasing as a proportion of total family income as total family income increases. See footnote 15, op. cit., for a detailed description of how the incidence of this hypothetical flat rate tax is estimated from the income/salary matrix.

24. This hypothetical tax is only estimated on wage and salary income up to 500 pesos a month since this is the maximum taxable wage and salary income in the Philippines SSS.

25. Two qualifications are in order. First, the present study is one which is primarily concerned with vertical equity. That is, it studies the relative treatment of families in different income brackets. Studies of vertical equity almost always assume that horizontal equity exists, i.e. that families with the same income are treated equally. This assumption is obviously violated here. In fact, it has been shown that to some extent the vertical equity (the progressivity) of the payroll tax is at the expense of horizontal equity since it is due in part to the incomplete and biased compliance. All wage and salary workers with equal wages and salaries within identical groups are not necessarily being treated equally, let alone all families with identical incomes. This situation nullifies to some extent the equitability of the payroll tax and makes this form of progressive taxation less desirable, everything else being equal, than progressive taxation which would be less at the expense of vertical equity; e.g. progressive income taxation. It should be remembered that progressive income taxation as actually implemented, with exemptions and loopholes, does not insure horizontal equity either. This is especially true in the context of today's developing countries where inefficient and dishonest tax administration is more often the rule than the exception. Secondly, it should be noted that the

survey data used here do not provide a clear picture of the progressivity of the tax beyond
the cut-off point of the open ended class (i.e. 10,000 pesos and above bracket). Table I
reveals, however, that this is not a serious problem since this class includes only 2·5%
of the highest income Philippine families.

26. C. Shoup states, 'But the labour-income tax cannot, as is so often mistakenly
assumed, drive producers to more capital intensive methods or induce them, generally,
to modernize their methods of production any more than can its virtual twin, the value-
added tax, consumption type.' [Shoup, 1969: 412.]

27. The basic reason for this conclusion is that labour makes machinery (machinery
does not make labour) and an increase in labour costs forces an equal percentage increase
in the cost of machinery. For discussion of this point see P. Samuelson [1965]. For a
similar conclusion see also E. J. Mishan [1961].

28. See Brittain [1972], Prest [1971]. Prest generally tends to think the qualifications
are more significant than does Brittain.

29. The following idea appears often in Lewis' writings.

30. Prest [1971: 317–18], states a similar view, '. . . there is a need in the short run for
countering artificially induced capital intensive methods of production and for increasing
the relative attractiveness of rural work (i.e. in developing countries)'.

31. In the Philippines the large-scale modern 'capitalist' firms in manufacturing are
paying a yearly wage (2,853 pesos) more than 2½ times that of small-scale 'traditional'
enterprises (1,156 pesos). Wage differentials between 'subsistence' agriculture and
'capitalist' industry are of even greater magnitude. See Rosenberg [1970: 61].

32. For the United States, Cagan [1965] has shown total savings are greater for those
workers covered by pensions.

33. Insurance savings are the closest substitute for Social Security savings. Interviews
with officials of the two largest insurance companies in the Philippines supported the
hypothesis that insurance savings are increased by SSS savings. Thus it is possible that
the payroll tax used to finance SSS in the Philippines did not reduce other savings.

34. F. Reviglio [1976b: 324], has expressed a similar view.

35. A cross-country analysis of 115 countries showing the Pearsonian Correlation
Coefficient between GNP per capita and wage and salary earners as per cent of working
age population is 0·76. See G. D. Ness [1970: 8]. F. Reviglio [1976b: 346] also suggests
that this is an advantage of Social Security taxation.

REFERENCES

Bird, R. M., 1970, 'Income Distribution and Tax Policy in Columbia', Economic
    Development and Cultural Change, July.
Brittain, J. A., 1971, 'The Incidence of Social Security Payroll Taxes', American Economic
    Review, March.
Brittain, J. A., 1972, The Payroll Tax for Social Security, Washington, D.C.: Studies
    of Government Finance, The Brookings Institution.
Bureau of Census and Statistics, 1963, Survey of Households Bulletin, Series 19, October,
    Manila.
Bureau of Census and Statistics, 1968a, Family Income Distribution in the Philippines,
    Special Release No. 62, March.
Bureau of Census and Statistics, 1968b, Family Living and Expenditures in the Philippines
    1965, April.
Cagan, P., 1965, The Effect of Pension Plans on Aggregate Savings: Evidence from a
    Sample Survey, Occasional paper 95, National Bureau of Economic Research,
    University of Columbia Press.
Carroll, J., 1960, 'Alternative Method of Financing OASDI', The University of Michigan,
    Michigan Government Studies No. 38. Institute of Public Administration, The Uni-
    versity of Michigan, Ann Arbor.
Davis, T. E., 1964, 'Dualism, Stagnation and Inequality; the Impact of Pension
    Legislation in the Chilean Labor Market', Industrial and Labor Relations Review,
    April.
Eckhaus, R. S., 1955, 'The Factor Proportions Problem in Underdeveloped Areas',
    American Economic Review, September.
Harris, S. E., 1941, The Economics of Social Security, New York.

Joint Legislative-Executive Tax Commission, 1970, *The Tax Monthly*, Vol. XI, No. 6, December.

Lewis, W. A., 1954, 'Economic Development with Unlimited Supplies of Labor', *The Manchester School of Economics and Social Studies*, Vol. XII.

Lewis, W. A., 1964, 'Unemployment in Developing Countries', *Lecture to Midwest Research Conference*, October.

Mishan, E. J., 1961, 'The Emperor's New Clothes: The Payroll Tax Stripped Bare', *Bankers Magazine*, July.

Musgrave, R. A., 1959, *The Theory of Public Finance*, New York: McGraw-Hill.

Musgrave, R. A. and Tun Thin, 1948, 'Income Tax Progression 1928–48', *The Journal of Political Economy*, Vol. 56, December.

Ness, G. D., 1970, *The Sociology of Economic Development*, a Reader. New York: Harper & Row.

Okner, B., 1966, *Income Distribution and the Federal Income Tax*, Ann Arbor.

Pechman, J., H. Aaron and M. Taussig, 1968, *Social Security: Perspectives for Reform*, Washington D.C.: The Brookings Institution.

Power, J., 1969, 'The Structure of Protection in the Philippines', *I.E.D.R.*, *Discussion Paper No. 69–8*, University of the Philippines.

Prest, A. R., 1971, 'The Role of Labour Taxes and Subsidies in Promoting Employment in Developing Countries', *International Labour Review*.

Reviglio, F., 1967a, 'The Social Security Sector and its Financing in Developing Countries', *International Monetary Fund: Staff Papers*, Vol. 14, November.

Reviglio, F., 1967b, 'Social Security: A Means of Savings Mobilization for Economic Development', *International Monetary Fund: Staff Papers*, Vol. 14, July.

Rosenberg, R. E., 1970, 'The Effects of the Social Security System on Income Re-distribution in the Philippines', unpublished dissertation, Madison.

Samuelson, P. A., 1965, 'A New Theorem on Non-substitution', in his *The Collected Scientific Papers of Paul A. Samuelson*, Cambridge, Mass.: The MIT Press, Vol. 1.

Social Security Administration, 1967, *Annual Report of the Social Security System*, Manila.

Stifel, L. O., 1963, 'The Textile Industry: A Case Study of Development in the Philippines', *Data Paper No. 249, Southeast Asia Program*, Cornell University, November.

Shoup, C. S., 1969, *Public Finance*, Chicago: Aldine Publishing Company.

UNCTAD, 1967, 'Mobilization of Internal resources by the Developing Countries', *UNCTAD, secretariat, T.D. 171, sup. 2*, September 15.

Williamson, J. G., 1967, 'Determinants of Personal Savings in Asia: Long Run and Short Run Effects', *IEDR Discussion Paper No. 67–11*, University of the Philippines, September 15.

Williamson, J. G., 1971, 'Relative Price Changes, Adjustment Dynamics and Productivity Growth: The Case of Philippine Manufacturing', *Economic Development and Cultural Change*, Vol. 19, No. 4, July.

Wurfel, D., 1959, 'Trade Union Development and Labor Relations Policy in the Philippines', *Industrial and Labour Relations Review*, XII, No. 4, July.

Land Taxation and Economic Development: The Model of Meiji Japan

by Richard M. Bird*

One of the few concessions to political realities made by some of those who urge land tax reforms as one way of resolving some of the major problems of developing countries is to point to some other country as exemplifying their solution and its hoped-for outcome. Since most writers on this subject are apparently not willing to propose the imitation of the totalitarian regimes which are the only recent practitioners of the heavy land tax path to development, the inevitable result of this custom is a reverential mention of the case of late nineteenth-century Japan, with or without qualifications as to its applicability to the case in hand.[1]

The Japanese experience with land taxation is important not only because it is so often suggested as a model for presently developing countries but also because the conventional interpretation of this experience has shaped many 'general' models of agricultural and economic development. The usual presentation of the dual-sector development model, with agriculture serving essentially as a source of savings and labour for the non-agricultural sector, has, for example, been heavily shaped by nineteenth-century Japanese experience. The argument that the non-agricultural sector is the engine of growth and tax revenues from agriculture the necessary fuel rests as much on a particular interpretation of Japanese economic history as on general development theory. This paper summarises Japan's experience with land taxation, suggests that the apparently conventional interpretation of this experience is misleading, and comments briefly on its implications for presently less-developed countries.

THE CONVENTIONAL INTERPRETATION

The usual interpretation of the role of agriculture and agricultural taxation in Japan in the Meiji period (1868–1911) has been well summarised as follows:

> Agricultural production and real income are said to have risen at more than 2 per cent per year which is somewhat more than twice the 0·9 per cent growth rate of population. Since the agricultural labor force declined somewhat during this period, it is claimed that the speed of growth is attributable to agricultural developments which caused labor productivity to increase at about 2·6 per cent per year. A proposition of major importance is therefore advanced that this remarkable increase in agricultural labor productivity released a cheap and 'unlimited' supply of labor to other sectors since most of the population growth was taking place in farm families. Meanwhile, it is said, a large part of agricultural income was appropriated by the government through various taxes that weighed heavily

---

* Professor of Economics, Institute for Policy Analysis, University of Toronto.

on the agricultural sector. It is also said that agricultural saving mounted, inasmuch as consumption in the agricultural sector rose slowly if at all, and the tax burden is believed to have declined owing to inflation. During this period net agricultural investment is believed to have remained at low levels. This led to a second important proposition; namely, that the speed of growth of agricultural production was responsible for a large transfer of savings to other sectors. Landlords are believed to be responsible for most of these savings, and they invested a large part of their savings in the non-agricultural sector as entrepreneurs in their own right [*Nakamura, 1966: 140–41*].[2]

The general view is thus clearly that Meiji fiscal policy was a great success from a developmental point of view: 'Meiji fiscal policy was able to raise

TABLE 1

LAND TAXES IN JAPAN, 1868–1911

Year	Land tax as per cent of Central Government taxes[a]	Direct taxes on agriculture as per cent of net agricultural income[e]
1868–72	87[b]	—
1873–78	88	—
1879–83	64	17 (8)
1884–88	62[c]	22 (12)
1889–93	56	16 (9)
1894–98	40	12 (8)
1899–1903	32	12 (8)
1909–11	27[d]	13 (9)

Sources and notes:

[a] Calculated from data in Kee Il Choi, 'The Evolution of the Tax System of Meiji Japan', in R. M. Bird and O. Oldman, eds., *Readings on Taxation in Developing Countries* (3rd ed.; Baltimore: Johns Hopkins Press, 1975), p. 413. The percentages for the periods after 1878 refer to data for only part of the period, as follows: 1882, 1884–86, 1892, 1897, 1902. One estimate is that in 1880–89, 90 per cent of land tax receipts derived from farmland (Harry T. Oshima, 'Meiji Fiscal Policy and Agricultural Progress', in William W. Lockwood, ed., *The State and Economic Enterprise in Japan* (Princeton, N.J.: Princeton University Press, 1965), p. 360).

[b] Motokazu Kimura, 'Fiscal Policy and Industrialization in Japan, 1863–1895', in International Economic Association, *Economic Development with Special Reference to East Asia* (New York: Macmillan, 1964), p. 277, gives a lower estimate of 80 per cent for 1868–72 but a similar one for 1873–78—although Oshima, 'Meiji Fiscal Policy', p. 358, gives a lower estimate of 80 per cent for the latter period also.

[c] This figure is the average of an 1887 figure given in Choi, 'The Evolution of the Tax System', and apparently comparable 1886 and 1888 figures in Harley H. Hinrichs, *A General Theory of Tax Structure Change during Economic Development* (Cambridge, Mass.: Harvard Law School International Tax Program, 1966), p. 52.

[d] Figure for 1907 only.

[e] Gustav Ranis, 'The Financing of Japanese Economic Development', *Economic History Review*, XI (April 1959), 448. The figures in parentheses represent Nakamura's correction for the undervaluation of agricultural production in the official statistics (James I. Nakamura, *Agricultural Production and the Economic Development of Japan 1873–1922* (Princeton, N.J.: Princeton University Press, 1966), p. 161). As noted elsewhere, other scholars think this correction is too large, though most would probably now agree that some downward revision of the conventionally accepted figures is desirable.

large amounts of funds internally to finance the enormous expenditures required for the development and modernisation of the economy. It did this mainly by taxing heavily the agricultural sector, without interfering with the healthy growth of the sector.' [*Oshima, 1965.*] This basic thesis is thus that a rapid growth in agricultural productivity, with very little capital investment in agriculture, provided a surplus that could be used for capital formation elsewhere and that through the land tax—which in the 1870s provided over three-quarters of central government taxes and took probably ten per cent or more of agricultural income (see Table 1)—the state was able to rechannel much of this 'surplus' to industrial activities without hurting the growth of agricultural productivity, while landlords themselves did the rest of the job.[3]

THE TOKUGAWA BACKGROUND
Japan undoubtedly used the land tax extensively in the Meiji period, but this practice signified no change from the well-developed system of land taxation in pre-Meiji Japan. In general, by the 1860s, as one author has put it: 'Because of efficient and productive taxation systems and its tradition of economic activity and control, government was well placed to play an important role in the process of economic modernization' [*Crawcour, 1965: 44*].

At the end of the sixteenth century, for example, early in the Tokugawa era, a comprehensive survey was carried out to identify, measure, and classify land for tax purposes. Although it was later revised only partially and irregularly, this very early cadastre provided the basis for the establishment of the well-entrenched land tax which formed the essential starting point for the Meiji reforms almost three centuries later.

The main Tokugawa land tax was based on the estimated gross yield (in rice or rice equivalents) per unit area of land in normal years.[4] Taxes were levied on villages as a whole rather than on individual plots and were then allocated by a consultative process within the village. The mechanics of this process are not known in detail, but it may well have resembled in its virtues and defects the process used to this day in some African countries for personal tax assessments.[5] Originally, taxes were paid in kind but by the nineteenth century commutation to cash payment was increasingly accepted.

In principle, the land tax was levied on gross produce, as estimated either on the basis of sample harvests or by regular or irregular resurveys. In practice, wide differences in tax rates, land and harvest measurement practices, and tax administration resulted in a very diverse system with substantial differences in tax burdens among individuals, villages and provinces. By the end of the Tokugawa period land taxes took over 55 per cent of estimated crop yields in some parts of the country, and less than 25 per cent in others, with the modal burden apparently around 40 per cent.[6] In fact, owing to the obsolete nature of assessments—many of which were 100 to 150 years old by the middle of the nineteenth century—the real burden of the tax in many areas was almost certainly much less than this. Both increased productivity and the inevitable initial assessment errors point in this direction. In other areas, however, tax policies appear to have been considerably harsher, as suggested by various stories of tax revolts and peasant impoverishment.[7] The height of the taxes levied on agriculture may in part be explained by the fact that in Japan, unlike most countries, the ruling class did not itself own much land by the end of the Tokugawa period: the uniqueness of this situation deserves more attention than it has generally received [*Choi, 1975: 411*].[8]

THE MEIJI REFORM

For the first few years of the Meiji era the Tokugawa land tax system was simply carried on by the new leadership, which attempted to centralise the system and to halt the inevitable erosion of revenues which occurred in the first uncertain years of the new order. The first major reform legislation was the 'Land Tax Revision Act of 1873'. This law and subsequent revisions ensured that the cadastral survey would remain the basis for land tax assessment and collection. The tax rate was initially set at 3 per cent of assessed value.

As Table 1 suggests, the yield of land tax was probably not much changed by this reform, the main purpose of which was to complete the process of centralising the feudal revenues and to make the tax more uniform throughout the country.[9] Other aspects of the old system were altered considerably, however. For example, all tax payments were henceforth to be made in money rather than in kind, both in order to alleviate problems of storage and handling and in the expectation that more economic use would be made of land. (The preference for rice payments in the Tokugawa period had allegedly encouraged the uneconomic use of land for rice [*Nakamura, 1966: 184*].) More important, the tax base was changed to land value instead of the estimated annual harvest. Further, the 1873 law stipulated the land tax rate would be reduced to 1 per cent as soon as revenues from other sources exceeded two million yen. In response to pressures from landowners following a fall in rice prices in 1876 the rate was in fact lowered to 2·5 per cent in 1877—where it remained for the next 60 years.

As with all land taxes, the most difficult aspect of the Meiji reform concerned the valuation of the land. Legally, land value was to be derived by applying the following formula:

> First, the money value of the average yield (over a five-year period) from one tanbu (0·245 acres) of land was calculated on the basis of the price of rice prevailing in that area. From this was deducted the cost of fertilizer and seed rice (legally fixed at 15 per cent), the land tax, and the local tax which was usually one third of the land tax. What was left was called the 'net profit' despite the fact that no deduction had been made for the cost of labor. Then the 'net profit' was capitalised at a rate ranging from 6 to 7 per cent, giving the 'legal value' of the land. The land tax was to be 3 per cent of this. . . . [*Ike, 1947: 164*][10]

The Meiji land tax was thus usually based on the capitalised value of 'normal' net farm income rather than market value. The interest rates and prices used in the application of this formula were reportedly chosen so that revenues from the land tax system would not be less than they were prior to 1874.[11]

The necessary information for these calculations was gathered by an elaborate new cadastral survey, which was begun in 1875 and completed around 1881. The procedures followed in this survey were similar to those in any cadastre, except that—despite the shift of responsibility for tax payment to the individual himself—primary reliance continued to be placed on the village to report area and production.

As is common in other countries also, no other general revaluation was ever carried out in Japan. Indeed, in a move reminiscent of some British legislation in India at an earlier date, a new Land Tax Law in 1884 abolished the previous stipulation for periodic reassessment (which had never been carried out in practice) and fixed assessments at the 1875 levels, except when land was reclassified.[12] There were only minor revisions in the tax assessments thereafter (notably in 1898–99, when total assessed land values were reduced) until the 1930s.

Dissatisfaction with the Meiji reform, and especially with the requirement that the tax should be paid in cash—and in an amount not correlated with harvest conditions—resulted in several immediate amendments to the 1873 legislation. In 1875, for example, a rice deposit system was instituted permitting peasants to pay up to one-third of their taxes in kind. In 1877 it was further determined that paddy field taxes could be paid one-half in kind on the basis of the prices used in calculating the 'legal value' in 1873. In addition, as noted above, the tax rate was lowered in the same year from 3 to 2·5 per cent in response to a rash of peasant revolts.

Some of these problems were more significantly alleviated by an inflation in rice prices as a result of the Meiji government's general political and fiscal plight. The immediate beneficiaries of the inflation were the landowners, who could increase the rent in kind received from the peasant and convert it into cash profits, while at the same time their tax liability was fixed in money terms. One estimate is that the landowners' share of the proceeds from the land rose from 18 per cent before 1868 to 56 per cent in the inflationary period of 1878–87, while the state's share fell correspondingly from 50 per cent to 11 per cent [Kimura, 1964: 281]. A substantial reduction in land tax burdens was thus the result of inflation in nineteenth-century Japan, as in many other countries since.

In an attempt to reform the chaotic currency and fiscal situation, a severe deflationary policy was instituted from 1881 through 1885. Rice prices, which had doubled from 1877 to 1880, fell back almost to their previous levels, so that the fixed land tax in effect doubled. The result was that substantial numbers of peasants were forced to sell their lands to meet tax arrears, thus clearing the way for a conisderable concentration of land (and an increase in the already high level of tenancy). After the late 1880s, however, prices rose again and agriculture appears to have generally prospered, while tax burdens fell.

EVALUATION OF THE MEIJI REFORM

The account to this point of the nature and workings of the Meiji tax reforms should contain few surprises to those familiar with land taxes elsewhere. Before 1873 the principal tax on Japanese agriculture was a tithe or gross product tax levied at different effective rates and to some extent on different bases, in various parts of the country. The basic Meiji tax legislation, enacted in that year, completed the centralisation of this traditional levy and converted it into a land value tax by capitalising the gross value of production (less certain arbitrarily defined costs, notably the land tax and the costs of seeds and fertilisers) at the prevailing interest rate. This value of production was, in turn, determined by the area of cultivated land, the yield per unit area, and the price level. The first two of these elements were, in accordance with Japanese tradition, based primarily on reports by the landowners and villages and were thus almost certainly subject to some understatement (also by tradition) although these estimates were supervised and reviewed by tax officials.[13] Initially, the general level of tax burden was probably not much affected by this change in nature of the tax, although its distribution may have been. Thereafter, however, owing to the fixed nature of the assessments, the impact of the land tax on Japanese agriculture became dependent primarily on movements in the general price level and in particular on the level of rice prices. Its real yield first fell sharply in inflation, then rose equally sharply in deflation, and thereafter declined gradually as prices again rose. All this is very conventional, indeed, and leaves one wondering just what the Japanese 'land tax miracle' was.

Controversy arises only when we consider, first, the impact of the land tax on agricultural production and, second, the role which the land tax played in transferring resources out of agriculture during the 1868–1911 period. There are opposing views on each of these crucial matters. What has come to be the conventional view in the literature on development taxation has already been stated: agricultural productivity grew moderately rapidly from the 1870s onwards, complementing the rise of modern industry in Japan through the resources provided from the increased surplus created in agriculture. Most of those who hold this view, point to the land tax as the main transfer mechanism utilised.

Recent literature suggests, however, that there are several contentious and important points in this conventional interpretation. First there may not really have been much of a *net* outflow of resources from the farm sector in Meiji Japan anyway [*Ishikawa, 1967: 318–20*]. Second, while the tax system clearly transferred a significant amount (gross) from agriculture to the *public* sector, much of this appears to have been wasted from the point of view of development (largely in military expenditures) [*Oshima, 1965: 372–80*]. Third, recorded agricultural productivity was based largely on land tax records, and there is evidence of substantial initial underestimation of agricultural production for tax purposes, so that the rate of subsequent productivity growth was probably much lower than was at one time thought [*Nakamura, 1966, Chs. 5–6*]. Finally, there appears to be growing sympathy for the view that '... the extraction of large sums of money from the farm population was generally detrimental to the healthy development of agriculture, especially as so much was used relatively unproductively for military purposes [*Oshima, 1965: 354*]. While the fixed nature of the land tax presumably exerted favourable (if unmeasurable) incentive effects, the sheer size of the payment and its regres-

sivity may well have offset these effects in the initial years by draining
liquidity from the countryside and forcing smaller peasants under. On
the other hand, the decreasing land tax burden as prices rose has led some
to suggest that the key to resource transfer in Japan lay in the hands of the
private landlords, who in a very non-Ricardian way became the vanguard
of the capitalist class.[14]

It is not possible for a non-specialist to arbitrate in the battle of the
giants as to just how fast agricultural production rose in the early Meiji
era [*Rosovsky, 1968*]. Nor, in a sense, is it necessary to do so. It is clear
that the contention that savings were transferred from agriculture to the
government by the land tax is correct. But it seems equally likely that
Nakamura's arguments on the existence of considerable evasion of the
land tax have much merit, as do Oshima's arguments on the extent to
which these savings were 'wasted' from a developmental point of view.

The real question that must be answered is the extent to which this
heavy tax burden penalised agricultural growth (and perhaps, as Oshima
has suggested, even social stability?).[15] As Ishikawa has argued, even if
there was a net resource flow out of agriculture, and agriculture continued
to grow under its heavy tax load, this result at least in part probably
reflected the exceptionally favourable initial conditions in Meiji Japan.[16]
Either there was a pre-existing surplus at the beginning of this period, or
else partly fortuitous technological progress may have served to generate
an agricultural surplus simultaneously with industrialisation as, for
example, the removal of the feudal restraints of the Tokugawa period
permitted the wider diffusion of already known agricultural techniques.[17]
While public expenditures on agriculture were apparently very small in
the early Meiji era, a substantial infrastructure of land development,
market access, and knowledge had been built up over the previous
centuries and was on hand when the opportunity came to utilise it as a
result of the political upheaval marking the end of the feudal era. The
basic capital-intensive investments in land—flood control, irrigation, and
drainage—undertaken in the Tokugawa period were thus a necessary
prerequisite for the widespread introduction of fertiliser, better seeds, and
better farming techniques in the Meiji period. The side effects of the land
tax change on productivity, while perhaps not insignificant, would probably
not have amounted to much, without this prior foundation—and were
in any case clearly unintended. The land tax reform was motivated primarily
by the desire of the new central government to stabilise and unify its
pre-existing major revenue source and was not intended either to *increase*
revenues from this source or to achieve any non-fiscal purpose other than
greater central control.

WAS JAPAN ATYPICAL?

On closer examination, then, while many key aspects of late nineteenth-
century Japanese economic history are still in dispute, the Japanese 'land
tax miracle' appears less miraculous—and considerably less different
from experience elsewhere—than many accounts would lead one to
believe.

The common view is clearly that Japanese experience is atypical:

Landes, for example, has noted that, 'in general, then, the land did not perform in Western Europe the function of generator of savings for industrial development to the same extent as in Japan. On the contrary, not only did it compete for funds with the modern sector on purely rational grounds, but it drew more than its share of capital resources' [*Landes, 1965: 169*]. In Germany, for example, during the same nineteenth-century period the land tax provided a far smaller proportion of government revenue than in Japan, and it appears the intersectoral flow of capital favoured agriculture, largely because of the capital-intensive nature of the land clearing and drainage operations which made possible the increase in agricultural output. But, as already noted, these expenditures had largely been made in Japan prior to the Meiji period.

Similarly, 'in the years of Britain's industrial revolution, agriculture was taking as much capital as it was giving; indeed, in the period from 1790 to 1814, when food prices rose to record levels, the net flow of resources was probably toward the land' [*Landes, 1965: 167*]. The Japanese response to similar pressures may not, however, have been much different: '. . . we may conclude that the final judgment as to whether or not the net result of resource flows between the farm and the nonfarm sectors was an outflow from the former sector, must wait for further investigations. Even if it was, as usually thought, an outflow, its magnitude does not seem to be so large as to be the major source of financing Japan's early industrialization' [*Ishikawa, 1967: 322*].

Rather than heavy land taxes financing industrialisation, the real economic key to Japanese success, as to that of the United States, may have been '. . . the ability to generate a continuous technology biased toward saving the limiting factors' [*Hayami and Ruttan, 1970a: 1115*], just as it has been argued by some that a crucial aspect of India's relative failure to date has been its difficulty in successfully adapting foreign models to its own needs, customs, and capabilities. It is easy in these circumstances for the economist to draw the lesson from this that presently developing countries should, as did Japan, direct their efforts to exploiting the opportunities afforded by their peculiar factor endowment.

But this recommendation plays down too much the crucial significance of history: Japan's history had not only well equipped her agricultural sector with capital, it had also, and probably more importantly, provided her with a well-ordered and disciplined population that was capable of implementing, adapting, and diffusing new technologies at a rapid pace. The role of such minor instruments as the land tax in this process, while not wholly clear, was certainly not nearly as significant a determinant of whatever actually happened as was Japanese history of the previous six centuries. The same could be said of Western Europe in the nineteenth century and is to some extent probably true of China today. India, on the other hand, like many other poor countries in Asia and elsewhere, appears to have a long way to go before its institutional development in most of the relevant respects comes close to that of Japan a century ago.[18] In addition, the much greater disparities in traditional and modern technologies that now exist, the greater openness (and vulnerability) of most developing countries to outside influences in general, and the much greater differences in the scale of institutional adaptation which are therefore required, make the task of development increasingly harder in some important respects than it was 100 years ago.

THE LESSONS OF HISTORY

One interpretation of ancient history is that the vast empires of China, the Middle East, and Meso-America did not progress, despite their highly successful agricultural systems, because they were too good at what some economists today consider a primary task of a development-oriented government: transferring capital and labour out of agriculture. Of course, the crushing tax burdens (and labour obligations) imposed on the peasantry in ancient times were largely wasted from a strictly developmental point of view on defence (the Great Wall of China) and monuments (the Pyramids)—which properly points up the vital importance of how the resources are used, since such employment of public funds is not unknown even in this enlightened age. More important, however, 'the chances that the peasantry might raise their own standard of living significantly and thus provide a broadly based market were severely circumscribed. Tax burdens were so onerous and collection was (all-considered) so efficient that local consumption was kept at low, often a subsistence level, and might be further depressed in times of stress.'[19] As we have seen, some have suggested that in and of itself heavy land taxation may have had similar effects even in Japan.

In a similar vein, it has been argued that nineteenth-century Italy too provides an example of the successful use of the fiscal mechanism to transfer resources out of agriculture, though not without the usual cost:

> [The state finances] . . . constituted a powerful mobilizer of capital in Italy, transferring it from agriculture to the infrastructure, both through taxation and through the public debt. But agriculture, which was flourishing in no region and was in a very poor condition in some regions, suffered heavily from this haemorrhage . . . it is easy to understand the economic result of this primitive fiscal policy: contraction of internal demand, a serious obstacle to the formation of a national market. . . . What it [Italian agriculture] gave, in financial terms, was torn from it more or less coercively; one should remember that entire regions lived in a virtual state of siege for some decades after Unity. In consequence, as already stated, agricultural demand for industrial products was restricted, creating an obstacle to a balanced and continuous industrial expansion which was not overcome for half a century. [*Zangheri, 1969: 28–29*.]

The similarity of parts of this historical interpretation to the effects of heavy export taxes in some agricultural regions in Nigeria and certain other presently developing countries is striking.[20]

When economies, whether in Europe and Japan, underwent the transition from basically agricultural to non-agricultural, they were enabled to do so, it appears, by a constellation of non-capital-intensive biological and organisational improvements and agricultural innovations which substantially increased productivity and produced a food surplus.[21] These changes were, on the whole, adopted on a widespread basis only in societies prepared by centuries of commercialisation of large sections of their agriculture, which had produced many 'deviant' individuals.[22]

One result of this process almost everywhere appears to have been the creation of that rural inequality now widely noted in connection with the Green Revolution—though perhaps less socially destructive than is the case in countries like Mexico or Pakistan today, because of the relative size of the adaptive population in Europe and, in Japan, by the marked strength of tradition and social discipline. Everywhere and always, it appears to be true that new technology has first been adopted by the better-off farmers and that the net incomes of the less efficient are likely to be hurt by innovation: in North America today, this is the 'farm problem'. So was it, in a very different context, in Japan in the nineteenth century. The same is true today in India, Mexico, and elsewhere. The major notable difference appears to be that some countries—those, including Japan, we call 'developed'—appear to have been much more successful at enlisting within a relatively few decades the bulk of their active population in the innovative ranks than have others—the 'less developed'.

Today, the developing countries face higher rates of population growth and more difficulties in taxing agriculture in ways that do not damage production incentives because of the responsiveness of most governments in one way or another to the mass of the people.[23] Furthermore, as a result of the great backlog of innovations now available and the availability of foreign loans, developing countries are pressed—a pressure sometimes greatly accentuated by their own policies—to adopt more capital-intensive technology in both industry and agriculture, regardless of their own factor endowments. The availability of this technological backlog (on a world-wide basis) may make social and institutional reforms a less necessary prerequisite to innovation in any particular country, but the extra leeway thus provided as a result of being backward may eventually accentuate rather than alleviate the development problem by leading most countries to follow an extreme version of what has been called the 'Mexican model' (of increasing yields by mechanisation and improved seed varieties) to agricultural development, without even the initial primary redistribution that took place in Mexico.[24]

'The pitfalls of the historical perspective as a guide to policy are many', a noted historian has said [*Black, 1966: 159*]. The conventional facile interpretation of the Japanese experience as providing a classic exemplar of the case for heavy land taxes provides a good illustration of these pitfalls; yet, without a sound conception of the overwhelming importance in any given situation of the historical development of ideas and institutions, one may go equally wrong. The real 'lesson' of history is that there is not any one guide to policy, whether derived from Japan or elsewhere, which is readily applicable either to developing countries in general or to any one country in particular. Each historical instance appears on close examination to be a complex and unique special case in many important respects. This, perhaps, is the real lesson of historical experience for present-day policy-makers.

For these reasons, the main lessons for presently developing countries on the role of land taxation in economic development suggested by history are, first, that no one policy instrument such as a land tax can do much in and of itself and, second, that tax structure, and desirable and possible changes in it, can only be analysed sensibly in the context of a close analysis of the circumstances of each particular nation. The experience of other countries may be suggestive, but it can never be conclusive—especially since, as this paper has argued, it is seldom well understood.

NOTES

1. A few examples of this practice may be cited: Fei and Ranis [*1966: 38–39*]. Johnston and Mellor [*1961: 470–71*], Gandhi [*1966: 171*].

2. This account is a fair summary of the views put forward in such well-known and frequently cited papers as Ohkawa and Rosovsky [*1960: 43–67*]; Ranis [*1959: 440–54*]; Johnston [*1951*].

3. Fei and Ranis [*1966: 39*] stress the latter transfer mechanism: 'the Japanese government's role, using the famous land tax, was undoubtedly of considerable importance in financing social and economic overheads in the early Meiji period. But it was really the flow of private voluntary savings through a large number of small hands which was responsible—increasingly throughout the nineteenth century—for financing of the prodigious Japanese industrialization effort. It was, in fact, mainly the medium-sized landlords, with one foot in the agricultural and one in the industrial sector, reacting to the intersectoral terms of trade and the changing relative returns to investments of this time and ingenuity, who propelled the dualistic system forward.' In contrast, Ohkawa and Rosovsky [*1965: 70*] emphasise the role of the land tax, as do Johnston and Mellor [*1961: 578*], and a well-known FAO study reprinted in Bird and O. Oldman, eds. [*1967: 485*].

4. The main sources for this account are Beasley [*1960*] and Smith [*1958*].

5. Smith [*1959: 181–82*] suggests some of the probable difficulties with this assessment process in feudal Japan.

6. Nakamura [*1966: 178–81*], outlines the complex nature of the system at the time of the Meiji reform of 1873.

7. Tokugawa Iyeyasu, founder of the Shogun line, when asked how much should be left to the peasants for their own support, reportedly replied that they should be left with an amount such that 'they can neither live nor die' [*Levy 1966: 801*].

8. By 1872, for example, '. . . there were no remaining feudal estates', according to Fairbank, Reischauer and Craig [*1973: 509*].

9. 'High as the rate of tax on land was, however, it did not represent an increase over the Tokugawa period. Already at the end of that period the take from agriculture by the warrior class was immense, and the Meiji government merely redirected it into new channels' [*Smith 1959: 211*].

10. Nakamura [*1966: 188*] summarises the formula as:
$V = (R - C)/(i + t + t^1)$, where V = capitalised value, R = value of gross output, C = cost of seeds and fertiliser, t = rate of national land tax, t^1 = local surtax rate, and i = prevailing interest rate. Nakamura's Appendix A (pp. 182–96), describes the valuation procedure in the Meiji period in detail.

11. Choi [*1975*] suggests that land tax revenues from wet fields under the new system may have initially amounted to over 25 per cent of rice output.

12. The British experiments in India in the eighteenth and nineteenth centuries are described and commented on in R. M. Bird [*1974 chapter 6*], which also contains an earlier version of this paper.

13. On the question of understatement, see the persuasive account in Nakamura [*1966 chapters 2–4*]. His estimates of the degree of evasion may be questioned, but to anyone with experience of land tax administration in any country, his general argument has the ring of truth.

14. See note 3 above; also Nakamura [*1966: 155–69*]. This conclusion is disputed, however, by Kee Il Choi in a forthcoming study of Meiji economic policy.

15. '. . . The frequency of disputes, uprisings and riots, the rise in unpaid taxes and

land confiscated in lieu of tax payments, the increase in debts and mortgage foreclosures, and the rapid rise in the amount of tenanted land . . . were clear signs of the difficulties experienced by the majority of agriculturalists in the period' [*Oshima 1965: 364*].

16. Ishikawa [*1967: 347*]. Nakamura shares this view; Rosovsky and Ohkawa do not. The list on both sides could be extended.

17. Some evidence along these lines is presented by Smith [*1959*], and by Hayami and Yamada [*1960: 135-57*].

18. An exhaustive discussion of India's failure in this regard on many counts may be found in Gunnar Myrdal's monumental *Asian Drama*, although his emphasis on the 'soft state' probably overstresses the ability of *any* leadership, no matter how 'hard' and modernising in intent, to impose Japanese (or Chinese?) habits on Indian (or Latin American?) institutions.

19. Jones and Woolf [*1969: 2*]. Compare the quotation in note 7 above.

20. See, for example, some of the research summarised in Eicher [*1970: 19-29*].

21. Jones and Woolf [*1969b: 4-12*]. For a cross-sectional analysis pointing in the same direction, see Hayami and V. W. Ruttan [*1970*].

22. Dore, IX [*1960*], documents this for Japan.

23. This point is stressed by Johnston [*1969*]

24. For a discussion of the Mexican case, see Bird [*1974 chapter 6*].

REFERENCES

Beasley, W. G., 1960, 'Feudal Revenue in Japan at the Time of the Meiji Restoration', *Journal of Asian Studies*, May.

Bird, R. M., 1974, *Taxing Agricultural Land in Developing Countries*, Cambridge, Mass.: Harvard University Press.

Bird, R. M., and O. Oldman, eds., 1967, *Readings on Taxation in Developing Countries* (revised edition), Baltimore.

Black, C. E., 1966, *The Dynamics of Modernization*, New York: Harper & Row.

Choi, Kee Il, 1975, 'The Evolution of the Tax System of Meiji Japan', in Bird, R. M. and O. Oldman, eds., *Readings on Taxation in Developing Countries*, 3rd edition.

Crawcour, E. Sydney, 1965, 'The Tokugawa Heritage', in Lockwood, W., ed., *The State and Economic Enterprise in Japan*, Princeton, N.J.

Dore, R. P., 1960, 'Agricultural Improvement in Japan 1870-1900', *Economic Development and Cultural Change*, October.

Eicher, Carl K., 1970, *Research in Agricultural Development in Five English-Speaking Countries in West Africa*, New York: Agricultural Development Council, Inc.

Fairbank, J. K., E. O. Reischauer and A. M. Craig, 1973, *East Asia: Tradition and Transformation*, Boston: Houghton Mifflin.

Fei, J. C. H., and G. Ranis, 1966, 'Agrarianism, Dualism and Economic Development', in Adelman, I., and E. Thorbecke, eds., *The Theory and Design of Economic Development*, Baltimore.

Gandhi, Ved P., 1966, *Tax Burden on Indian Agriculture*, Cambridge, Mass.: Harvard Law School International Tax Program.

Hayami, Y., and V. W. Ruttan, 1970a, 'Factor Prices and Technical Change in Agricultural Development: The United States and Japan, 1880-1960', *Journal of Political Economy*, September-October.

Hayami, Y. and V. W. Ruttan, 1970b, 'Agricultural Productivity Differences Among Countries', *American Economic Review*, December.

Hayami, Y. and Saburo Yamada, 1960, 'Technological Progress in Agriculture', in Klein, L., and K. Ohkawa, *Economic Growth: The Japanese Experience since the Meiji Era*, Homewood, Ill.: Richard D. Irwin, Inc.

Ike, Nobutaka, 1947, 'Taxation and Landownership in the Westernization of Japan', *Journal of Economic History*, November.

Ishikawa, Shigeru, 1967, *Economic Development in Asian Perspective*, Tokyo: Kinokuniya Bookstore Co. Ltd.

Johnson, Bruce F., 1951, 'Agricultural Productivity and Economic Development in Japan', *Journal of Political Economy*, December.

Johnson, Bruce F., 1969, 'The Japanese "model" of agricultural development; its relevance to developing nations', in Ohkawa, K., Bruce F. Johnson and Hiromitsu

Kareda, eds., *Agriculture and Economic Growth: Japan's Experience*, Tokyo: University of Tokyo Press.

Johnson, Bruce F. and John W. Mellor, 1961, 'The Role of Agriculture in Economic Development', *American Economic Review*, September.

Jones, E. L., and S. J. Woolf, eds., 1969, *Agrarian Change and Economic Development*, London: Methuen & Co. Ltd.

Jones, E. L., and S. J. Woolf, 1969b, 'The Historical role of agrarian change in economic development' in Jones, and Woolf, eds., 1969a.

Kimura, Motokazu, 1964, 'Fiscal Policy and Industrialisation in Japan, 1868–1895', in International Economic Association, *Economic Development with Special Reference to East Asia*, New York: Macmillan.

Landes, David S., 1965, 'Japan and Europe: Contrasts in Industrialisation', in Lockwood, W., ed., 1965.

Levy, Marion J., 1966, *Modernization and the Structure of Societies*, Princeton, N.J.: Princeton University Press.

Lockwood, W., ed., 1965, *The State and Economic Enterprise in Japan*, Princeton, N.J.: Princeton University Press.

Myrdal, G., 1969, *Asian Drama*, New York: Pantheon Books.

Nakamura, James I., 1966, *Agricultural Production and the Economic Development of Japan 1873–1922*, Princeton, N.J.

Ohkawa, K. and H. Rosovsky, 1960, 'The Role of Agriculture in Modern Japanese Development', *Economic Development and Cultural Change*, October.

Ohkawa, K. and H. Rosovsky, 1965, 'A Century of Japanese Economic Growth', in Lockwood, W., ed., 1965.

Oshima, Harry T., 1965, 'Meiji Fiscal Policy and Agricultural Progress', in Lockwood, W., ed., 1965.

Ranis, Gustav, 1959, 'The Financing of Japanese Economic Development', *Economic History Review*, April.

Rosovsky, H., 1968, 'Rumbles in the Ricefields: Professor Nakamura versus the Official Statistics', *Journal of Asian Studies*, February.

Smith, T. C., 1958, 'The Land Tax in the Takugawa Period', *Journal of Asian Studies*, November.

Smith, T. C., 1959, *The Agrarian Origins of Modern Japan*, Stanford: Stanford University Press.

Zangheri, R., 1969, 'The Historical Relationship between agricultural and economic development in Italy', in Jones, E. L., and S. J. Woolf, eds., 1969.

Printed in the United States
by Baker & Taylor Publisher Services